G000060263

Annual Perspectives in Mathematics

Rehumanizing Mathematics for Black, Indigenous, and Latinx Students

2018

Imani Goffney
Volume Editor
University of Maryland
College Park, Maryland

Rochelle Gutiérrez
Volume Editor
University of Illinois at Urbana-Champaign
Champaign, Illinois

Melissa Boston
Series Editor
Duquesne University
Pittsburgh, Pennsylvania

NATIONAL COUNCIL OF
TEACHERS OF MATHEMATICS

www.nctm.org/more4u
Access code: REH15626

Copyright © 2018 by
The National Council of Teachers of Mathematics, Inc.
1906 Association Drive, Reston, VA 20191-1502
(703) 620-9840; (800) 235-7566; www.nctm.org
All rights reserved
Fifth printing 2022

ISSN 2332-6336

ISBN 978-1-68054-009-3

The National Council of Teachers of Mathematics advocates for high-quality mathematics teaching and learning for each and every student.

When forms, problems, and sample documents are included or are made available on NCTM's website, their use is authorized for educational purposes by educators and noncommercial or nonprofit entities that have purchased this book. Except for that use, permission to photocopy or use material electronically from *Annual Perspectives in Mathematics Education 2018: Rehumanizing Mathematics for Black, Indigenous, and Latinx Students* must be obtained from www.copyright.com, or contact Copyright Clearance Center, Inc. (CCC), 222 Rosewood Drive, Danvers, MA 01923, 978-750-8400. CCC is a not-for-profit organization that provides licenses and registration for a variety of users. Permission does not automatically extend to any items identified as reprinted by permission of other publishers and copyright holders. Such items must be excluded unless separated permissions are obtained. It will be the responsibility of the user to identify such materials and obtain the permissions.

The publications of the National Council of Teachers of Mathematics present a variety of viewpoints. The views expressed or implied in this publication, unless otherwise noted, should not be interpreted as official positions of the Council.

Printed in the United States of America

CONTENTS

Preface

This 2018 volume of the National Council of Teachers of Mathematics' (NCTM) *Annual Perspectives in Mathematics Education* (*APME*) series showcases the efforts of classroom teachers, school counselors and administrators, teacher educators, mathematicians, and education researchers to ensure mathematics teaching and learning is a humane, positive, and powerful experience for students who are Black, Indigenous, and/or Latinx. The eleven chapters in this volume provide images of mathematics instruction that honor the perspectives and experiences of learners and teachers, respect cultural and indigenous contributions to mathematics, and recognize the value of engaging students in ways of knowing and doing mathematics that arise from a variety of cultures. The authors of chapter 6 (Caswell, Jones, LaPointe, and Kabatay) capture well the intention of this volume to celebrate efforts in "creating spaces for voices that have previously been silenced and marginalized, building meaningful and mutually beneficial relationships, and finding ways to relearn and observe mathematics as a human endeavor" (p. 79).

The volume is subdivided into three sections. The first section, **Attending to Students' Identities through Learning,** opens the book by showcasing mathematics learning environments that place relationships and connections with students at the core of teaching and learning mathematics through attending to students' backgrounds, lived experiences, interests, and aspirations. The second section, **Professional Development That Embraces Community,** features efforts to rethink professional development experiences for mathematics teachers in ways that support teachers in improving the mathematical experiences they provide to students. The chapters in the final section, **Principles for Teaching and Teacher Identity,** illustrate how the effort to rehumanize mathematics can lead teachers to reconsider their teaching practice and their own place within the mathematics education community. Together, the collection of chapters in this volume illustrate pathways for rehumanizing mathematics for Black, Indigenous, and Latinx students.

Acknowledgments

Along with Rochelle Gutiérrez and Imani Goffney, the 2018 *APME* volume editors, I would like to express our thanks to the many individuals who contributed to the development and success of this volume. First, we extend our respect and admiration to the chapter authors for the work they do to provide or promote rehumanizing experiences in teaching and learning mathematics for students who are Black, Indigenous, and Latinx. We are very grateful for their decision to share their work with NCTM's membership and with all the readers of this book. We extend deep appreciation to the Editorial Panel, who generously read and reviewed the manuscripts submitted to this volume:

- Julia Aguirre, *University of Washington, Tacoma*
- Robert Q. Berry III, *University of Virginia*
- Kyndall Brown, *University of California, Los Angeles*
- Erika Bullock, *University of Wisconsin–Madison*

- Sylvia Celedón-Pattichis, *University of New Mexico*
- Maisie Gholson, *University of Michigan*
- Marrielle Myers, *Kennesaw State University*
- Cynthia Oropesa Anhalt, *University of Arizona*
- Esther Song, *Lindblom Math & Science Academy, Chicago Public Schools*

We also thank Larry Shea, Glenn Fink, and all of the NCTM staff who contributed to *APME* for their direction and guidance with the production of this volume, and Kathleen Richardson for her support in arranging the Editorial Panel meeting. Finally, we would like to thank NCTM's 2016 Educational Materials Committee, chaired by Kevin Dykema, for their support of this *APME* volume.

Melissa Boston
Series Editor, APME
Associate Professor, School of Education
Duquesne University

The Need to Rehumanize Mathematics

Rochelle Gutiérrez, *University of Illinois at Urbana-Champaign*

Our field has experienced a heightened focus on equity-based school reforms that seek to help students "play the game" of mathematics (e.g., addressing access and achievement). Yet we have not sufficiently interrogated how such reforms can ignore the need to "change the game" of mathematics (e.g., address students' identities and power dynamics inside and outside of schools) (Gutiérrez 2009, 2012). Beyond being seen as a legitimate participant (a "doer" of mathematics), a student should be able to feel whole as a person—to draw upon all of their cultural and linguistic resources—while participating in school mathematics. That is, every student should be provided with windows and mirrors (Style 1996) onto the world through mathematics (Gutiérrez 2007); they should see aspects of themselves reflected back (mirror) as well as obtain views of new worlds outside of their own (windows). Unfortunately, for many students, mathematics classrooms are experienced almost exclusively as windows. We are in need of research-based illustrations of teachers' and researchers' initiatives that promote forms of what I refer to as *rehumanizing mathematics*.

■ Why a Focus on Indigenous, Latinx, and Black?

Teaching and learning are not universal or neutral endeavors; the identities of teachers and students, as well as the contexts in which they work, all matter (Aguirre, Mayfield-Ingram, and Martin 2013; Anhalt et al. 2018; Berry 2008; Brown 2009; Celedón-Pattichis and Ramirez 2012; Gutiérrez and Irving 2012; Larnell, Bullock, and Jett 2016; Turner et al. 2013). Not only do teachers need to develop specific knowledge of the mathematics they will teach, they also need to connect that knowledge with an understanding of their own privileges (Goffney 2016), the students they seek to serve (Aguirre, Mayfield-Ingram, and Martin 2013; Berry and Thunder 2015; Goffney 2010; Myers 2014; Myers et al. 2015), and the social justice goals they hold (Anhalt, Cortez, and Smith 2017; Brown 2016, 2017). In fact, standards documents and reform initiatives that emphasize "mathematics for all" or that implicitly perpetuate a universal view of teaching and learning miss the point that many of the structures that exist in mathematics education are the very things that have created the inequities for historically marginalized students in the first place (Berry, Ellis, and Hughes 2014; Bullock 2017b; Martin 2013, 2015; National Council of Supervisors of Mathematics and TODOS Mathematics for ALL [NCSM and TODOS] 2016). As I have noted elsewhere:

... knowledge and power are inextricably linked. That is, because the production of knowledge reflects the society in which it is created, it brings with it the power relations that are part of society. What counts as knowledge, how we come to "know" things, and who is privileged in the process are all part and parcel of issues of power ... Without an explicit focus on issues of identity and power, we are unlikely to do more than tinker with the arrangements in school that contribute to the production of inequities in the lived experiences of learners and educators. We must be willing and able to embrace the socio-political turn. Such embracing will help us better understand the current situation in its moment in history as it has been constructed so we can open the door for other possible arrangements. (Gutiérrez 2010/2013, p. 8, pp. 26–27)

In fact, mathematics education cannot truly improve until it adequately addresses the very students who the system has most failed. As such, merely tinkering or basically repeating the same approaches is not likely to produce different results (Gutiérrez 2017c). Instead, we need a central focus on students who are Latinx, Black, and Indigenous in ways that build upon their strengths (Aguirre and del Rosario Zavala 2013; Celedón-Pattichis, Musanti, and Marshall 2010; Turner et al. 2012) and consider intersectionality (Bullock 2017a; Gholson 2016; Gholson, Bullock, and Alexander 2012; Morton and Smith-Mutegi [chapter 2, this volume]). This central focus does not mean simply supporting students who are Indigenous, Black, and Latinx to do well by Whitestream standards. It means developing practices and measures that feel humane to those specific communities as a means to guide the field.

Throughout this introduction, I change the order of the terms Black, Indigenous, and Latinx so as to maintain the importance of each. Moreover, changing the order discourages the reader from thinking this group of three can be reduced to a single acronym (e.g., BIL) and thought of as a homogenous entity. Varying the order also encourages the reader to consider what is highlighted when one begins with a different group first, as well as how the groups relate to and intersect with one another, even while recognizing there is often more variation within a given group than between groups. For similar reasons, the sections of this volume are not divided by racial/cultural identities but by conceptual focus.

This volume begins with the assumption that people throughout the world already do mathematics in everyday ways that are humane (Carraher, Carraher, and Schliemann 1985; Lave 1988; Masingila 1994, 2002; Nuñes, Schliemann, and Carraher 1993; Saxe 1998). Yet schooling often creates structures, policies, and rituals that can convince people they are no longer mathematical. In this way, those structures, policies, and practices can be experienced as dehumanizing. Take the notion of students' misconceptions. Many teachers have been trained to anticipate the misconceptions that students have so that they can address them in their lessons. Yet, students don't have misconceptions. They have conceptions. And those conceptions make sense for them, until they encounter something that no longer works. They are only "misconceptions" when we begin with the expectation that others need to come to *our* way of thinking or viewing the world. For too long, that expectation has meant that the teaching and learning of mathematics continues to support an agenda of White supremacist capitalist patriarchy and settler colonialism (Leyva 2017; Martin 2008; Stinson 2013; Tuck and Yang 2012; Warburton 2015, 2017). Not until we seek to stand in the shoes of our students, to understand their conceptions, will we be on the path toward recognizing and embracing their humanity. When I have asked students and teachers across the nation what kinds of practices can feel dehumanizing in mathematics education, among other things, they report—

- measuring categorizing bodies (e.g., tracking, mathematics as a filter);

- evaluation that does not honor complexity, context, or individuals' own goals (e.g., high-stakes and standardized testing, value-added modeling);

- being asked to leave one's identity at the door (e.g., color-blind teaching, strict pacing guides, being unable to use "foreign" algorithms from one's home country, being unable to use one's native language);

- rule following as opposed to rule breaking or creation (e.g., following what seem to be arbitrary rules developed by others);

- speed valued over reflection (e.g., get the answer quickly, cover the curriculum regardless of whether students understand); and

- separation of mathematical practice from politics/values/ethics (e.g., perpetuating the myth that mathematics is objective and culture free, being expected to teach/learn without bringing in politics).

It is striking how many of the aforementioned practices that feel dehumanizing for students are experienced similarly by teachers. I use the term *dehumanizing* to highlight the fact that although each of these individual practices might only be felt as a microaggression or frustration in the moment, there is a kind of slow violence (Nixon 2011) that occurs when one is subjected to such practices over twelve to thirteen years of compulsory mathematics education (K–12) or a career of teaching. Moreover, when students and teachers are treated as if they are interchangeable with others—with little or no attention to their identities—it can feel dehumanizing. As such, we should ask ourselves why are we complicit with a set of practices that fail to serve our needs. Instead, we need to seek ways to rehumanize mathematics teaching and learning.

This volume features evidence-based examples of theorizing and practicing what I refer to as *rehumanizing mathematics* with students and teachers who are Indigenous, Black, and/or Latinx. As a whole, the volume is built upon a set of guiding principles that include not just identifying dehumanizing practices but offering rehumanizing ones; privileging the voices of teachers, students, and communities; attending to intersectionality where possible; and positioning the authors as humans.

■ Why Rehumanizing?

Given that there is a long history of conceptualizing and seeking to address equity, one might ask why the field needs a new term. Elsewhere (Gutiérrez 2017a), I have argued that equity might not be so useful because it is bogged down in history. That is, equity tends to retain simplistic or superficial definitions, even when mathematics education researchers have tried to be explicit in their theorizing. In addition, many people believe they are speaking of the same thing when, in fact, they have different definitions of equity in their heads. As such, the term fails to promote greater dialogue or clarification about the concept when individuals or groups are setting goals in their workplaces. This lack of consensus on what equity means, paired with the tendency in our field to view teaching and learning as universal, means that we often only know we are addressing equity when we are still very far from our target.

Unlike "equity," which can seem to represent a destination, "rehumanizing" is a verb; it reflects an ongoing process and requires constant vigilance to maintain and to evolve with contexts. Moreover, rehumanizing is an ongoing performance and requires evidence from those for whom we seek to rehumanize our practices that, in fact, the practices are felt in that way. For example, teachers cannot claim their pedagogy is rehumanizing without obtaining recurring evidence from their students that they agree and without giving students opportunities to offer additional approaches for rehumanizing. I use the term *rehumanizing* as opposed to *humanizing* (Paris and Winn 2013; Rosa and Orey 2016; San Pedro and Kinloch 2017) to honor the fact that humans (and other living beings) have been practicing mathematics for centuries in ways that are humane. Among other things, women in India create elaborate and symmetrical floor patterns (rangoli) with rice that adorn the doorways of homes and get swept away with the daily entry and passage of feet (Mahalingam 2000); Black women throughout the world create complex curves and spirals through cornrow designs in hair (Eglash 1999; Gilmer n.d.); Latinx jazz, mambo, and salsa musicians produce a five-stroke son clave rhythm based on geometry and least common denominators (Toussaint 2013); and young break dancers and students of capoeira use their bodies to perform geometry and calculus through various rotations in the air. In many ways, we do not need to invent something new; we simply need to return to full presence that which tends to get erased through the process of schooling.

Partly because it departs from a Western view of mathematics (Bishop 1990), rehumanizing mathematics seeks to not only decouple mathematics from wealth, domination, and compliance (O'Neil 2016); it also recouples it with connection, joy, and belonging. When people are encouraged to express themselves through the practice of mathematics, they are more likely to draw upon an innate sense of aesthetics and intuition and to seek ways that are pleasing to them. In fact, under certain conditions, rehumanizing mathematics could be considered a form of decolonizing mathematics, but only when issues of land, sovereignty, and erasure of culture and language are taken seriously (Gutiérrez 2017b; Tuck and Yang 2012).

Readers who are familiar with the Rehumanistic Mathematics movement of the 1990s (Brown 1996, 2004) may wonder how rehumanizing mathematics differs. Although these two perspectives share the goals of solving problems in society, understanding properties of objects in the world, and posing new questions, rehumanizing mathematics also squarely addresses the politics of mathematics and of mathematics education. That is, rather than assuming a neutral response or failing to attend to power dynamics, rehumanizing mathematics recognizes that challenging the status quo will likely be met with great opposition from those with privilege and high status who benefit from the system remaining the same. It also seeks to highlight where power dynamics have played out in the history of mathematics and where mathematics might come to serve the people as opposed to vice versa. Furthermore, whereas the Rehumanistic Mathematics movement tended to privilege an individual's view of the world and their relation to it so they could understand themselves better, rehumanizing mathematics begins with the power of communities and assumes a relational view is important (recognizing oneself in others and others in oneself) so that we might better understand and live alongside of one another and so that we might practice mathematics in ways that transform reality in emancipatory ways (Gerdes 1985).

■ What Might Count as Rehumanizing Practices?

Although many concepts can contribute to rehumanizing mathematics for students and teachers who are Latinx, Black, and Indigenous, eight dimensions stand out for me. They include: (1) participation/positioning, (2) cultures/histories, (3) windows/mirrors, (4) living practice, (5) creation, (6) broadening mathematics, (7) body/emotions, and (8) ownership. Rehumanizing mathematics with respect to *participation/positioning* involves recognizing hierarchies in class-rooms and society and shifting the role of authority from teacher/text to other students. That is, in terms of mathematics classrooms, we might see students responding more to each other, rather than seeking approval or evaluation from the teacher. Rehumanizing mathematics with respect to *cultures/histories* acknowledges students' funds of knowledge, algorithms from other countries, the history of mathematics, and ethnomathematics. In terms of classrooms, we might see students reconnecting with their own histories or ancestors and roots as they are learning the histories of mathematics. In this way, cultures/histories opens the door for providing students with *windows and mirrors*. That is, students can come to see themselves in the curriculum and also others or a new way of viewing the world. The Mayan concept In Lak'ech (You are another me; I am another you) helps illustrate the fact that students are not just seeking to know themselves with respect to mathematics; they are seeking to understand themselves and others in relationship. In this way, students are learning about different cultures and histories, but also taking into account particular histories that may relate to those in the classroom. Moreover, *windows and mirrors* takes up the idea that students can be taught to appreciate (not just critique, as is promoted in the mathematical practices of the Common Core State Standards) the view of others.

Recognizing mathematics as a *living practice* is another important dimension of rehumanizing mathematics, as it underscores mathematics as something in motion. When students can see mathematics as full of not just culture and history, but power dynamics, debates, divergent answers, and rule breaking, it highlights the human element and helps promote a version that is a verb rather than a noun. Moreover, seeing mathematics as living practice means individuals can recognize modern mathematics as relatively young and look to practice it in different ways, for their own purposes (not just for school or credentialing). This notion of *creation* is important, as it can encourage students to invent new algorithms or forms of doing mathematics that are consistent with their own values. In this sense, doing mathematics can mean more than simply reproducing what has come before oneself or that which has been sanctioned by mathematicians in the past, though it does not mean a kind of "anything goes" mathematics. Moreover, understanding mathematics as arising from individuals breaking rules can be a powerful incentive for forms of teaching that encourage such rule breaking. Another dimension of rehumanizing mathematics involves *broadening mathematics*. That is, currently, the mathematics to which citizens are exposed in K–12 classrooms involves primarily algebra, calculus, number sense, symbolic representation, and favoring the general case. Rehumanizing mathematics would expand that view and make room for other forms of mathematics that can allow students to see more qualitatively. Rather than viewing mathematics as culture free or value free, a more rehumanized mathematics would depart from a purely logical perspective and invite students to draw upon other parts of themselves (e.g., voice, vision, touch, intuition). By attending to emotions, individuals would be encouraged to be more in tune with themselves and less likely to succumb to pressures to ignore their senses and "just pretend" in order to do school mathematics. A critical aspect of evidence that mathematics is more rehumanized is that it conjures up feelings of joy. In a related manner, the final dimension of rehumanizing mathematics is *ownership*. When students view mathematics as something one does for oneself, not just for others, there is greater likelihood for "play," "invention," or simply "expressing oneself" through mathematics. One sign that students are feeling that mathematics is more rehumanized is when they choose to continue to grapple with mathematical problems long beyond the school bell or when they pose new questions for community problems they face and that can be addressed either partly or fully through mathematics.

■ Looking Forward

The pieces in this volume highlight different aspects of these eight dimensions. They open up a conversation about how we might move forward as a field if we care deeply about the mathematical experiences of Indigenous, Latinx, and Black students who are in our care. The chapters range in topics from emergent bilinguals who are Latinx preparing for a Thanksgiving meal to girls who are Black learning in a STEM institute. The concepts featured in this volume arise not through a set of pre-scripted practices but organically from professionals (many who share identities of their students) who put students and their needs first. Although each chapter is situated within a section topic (e.g., attending to students' identities, professional development that embraces community, and principles for teaching and teacher identity), there is great overlap. That is, each chapter has elements that could fit within other sections. For example, although the chapter by Winger, Young, Stovall, Sword, Badertscher, Gates, MacDowell, and Cuoco models a form of professional development whereby mathematics faculty educate each other as well as practicing teachers, it also showcases important principles for teaching and teacher identity. Moreover, each chapter speaks to others by highlighting recurring themes or identifying differences based upon context. For example, the chapters by Barajas-López and Bang; Caswell, Jones, LaPointe, and Kabatay; and Bunton, Cook and Tamburini all take seriously the voices of community members who are Indigenous and the power of attending to worldviews, but each location highlights how those views play out differently.

As you read through this volume, consider the following questions:

- In what way(s) does starting with students and teachers who are Latinx, Black, and Indigenous alter what counts as mathematics education or how the field might change in response?

- In each of the chapters, from whose perspective is the work rehumanizing? How do we know?

- What are some of the similarities and differences that cut across the chapters?

- How does a focus on intersectionality highlight what might otherwise be invisible?

- In what ways, if any, might these practices that are rehumanizing in their local contexts be applicable to other contexts? To other kinds of students or teachers?

Many of the rehumanizing practices we witness here—both inside and outside of school—offer a glimpse into the taken-for-granted ways in which students and teachers are repeatedly subjected to dehumanizing experiences in mathematics as well as the radical work that will be required if we intend to take seriously the lives of students and teachers who are Indigenous, Latinx, and Black. After listening to the voices of students and teachers who offer more humane practices, are we prepared to carry on as if business is usual? Or, are we up for the challenge of continuing to put Latinx, Indigenous, and Black students first in order to guide the field?

References

Aguirre, Julia, and Maria del Rosario Zavala. "Making Culturally Responsive Mathematics Teaching Explicit: A Lesson Analysis Tool." *Pedagogies: An International Journal* 8, no. 2 (2013): 163–90.

Aguirre, Julia, Karen Mayfield-Ingram, and Danny B. Martin. *The Impact of Identity on K–8 Mathematics: Rethinking Equity-Based Practices*. Reston, Va.: National Council of Teachers of Mathematics, 2013.

Anhalt, Cynthia, Ricardo Cortez, and Aliceson Smith. "Mathematical Modeling: Creating Opportunities for Participation in Mathematics." In *Access and Equity: Promoting High Quality Mathematics in Grades*

6–8, edited by Anthony Fernandes, Sandra Crespo, and Marta Civil, pp. 105–19. Reston, Va.: National Council of Teachers of Mathematics, 2017.

Anhalt, Cynthia, Susan Staats, Ricardo Cortez, and Marta Civil. "Mathematical Modeling and Culturally Relevant Pedagogy." In *Cognition, Metacognition, and Culture in STEM Education*, edited by Yehudit Judy Dori, Zemira Mevarech, and Dale Baker, pp. 307–30. Dordrecht, the Netherlands: Springer, 2018.

Berry, Robert Q., III. "Access to Upper-Level Mathematics: The Stories of Successful African American Middle School Boys." *Journal for Research in Mathematics Education* 39, no. 5 (2008): 464–88.

Berry, Robert Q., III, Mark Ellis, and Sherick Hughes. "Examining a History of Failed Reforms and Recent Stories of Success: Mathematics Education and Black Learners of Mathematics in the United States." *Race Ethnicity and Education* 17, no. 4 (2014): 540–68.

Berry, Robert Q., III, and Kateri Thunder. "Black Learners' Perseverance with Mathematics: A Qualitative Metasynthesis." *Mathematics Instruction for Perseverance* (2015). http://www.spencer.org/sites/default/files/pdfs/berry_thunder_mip_0415.pdf.

Bishop, Alan. "Western Mathematics: The Secret Weapon of Cultural Imperialism." *Race and Class* 32, no. 2 (1990): 51–65.

Brown, Kyndall A. "Culture, Identity, and Mathematics: Creating Learning Spaces for African American Males." PhD diss., University of California, Los Angeles, 2009.

_____. "Tensions and Opportunities When Implementing Social Justice Mathematics Tasks: A Commentary on Felton-Koestler's Case." In *Cases for Teacher Educators: Facilitating Conversations about Inequities in Mathematics Classrooms*, edited by Dorothy Y. White, Sandra Crespo, and Marta Civil, pp. 251–54. Charlotte, N.C.: Information Age Publishing, 2016.

_____. "Dispositions of First Year Teachers Who Teach Mathematics for Social Justice." *Journal of Multicultural Affairs* 2, no. 1 (2017): 1–9.

Brown, Stephen I. "Towards Humanistic Mathematics Education." In *International Handbook in Mathematics Education*, edited by Alan Bishop et al., pp. 1289–1321. Dordrecht, the Netherlands: Kluwer Academic Press, 1996.

_____. "Humanistic Mathematics: Personal Evaluation and Excavations." *Humanistic Mathematics Network Journal* 1, no. 27 (2004): 1–18.

Bullock, Erika C. "Beyond 'Ism' Groups and Figure Hiding: Intersectional Analysis and Critical Mathematics Education." In *Mathematics Education and Life at Times of Crisis: Proceedings of the Ninth International Mathematics Education and Society Conference*, edited by Anna Chronaki, pp. 29–44. Thessaly, Greece: University of Thessaly Press, 2017a.

_____. "Only STEM Can Save Us? Examining Race, Place, and STEM Education as Property." *Educational Studies* 53, no. 6 (2017b): 628–41.

Carraher, Terezinha N., David W. Carraher, and Analúcia D. Schliemann. "Mathematics in the Streets and in Schools." *British Journal of Developmental Psychology* 3, no. 1 (1985): 21–29.

Celedón-Pattichis, Sylvia, Sandra I. Musanti, and Mary E. Marshall. "Bilingual Elementary Teachers' Reflections on Using Students' Native Language and Culture to Teach Mathematics." In *Mathematics Teaching and Learning in K–12: Equity and Professional Development*, edited by Mary Q. Foote, pp. 7–24. New York: Palgrave Macmillan, 2010.

Celedón-Pattichis, Sylvia, and Nora Ramirez, eds. *Beyond Good Teaching: Strategies That Are Imperative for ELLs in Mathematics Classrooms*. Reston, Va.: National Council of Teachers of Mathematics, 2012.

Eglash, Ron. *African Fractals: Modern Computing and Indigenous Design*. New Brunswick, N.J.: Rutgers University Press, 1999.

Gerdes, Paulus. "Conditions and Strategies for Emancipatory Mathematics Education in Underdeveloped Countries." *For the Learning of Mathematics* 5, no. 1 (1985): 15–20.

Gholson, Maisie L. "Clean Corners and Algebra: A Critical Examination of the Constructed Invisibility of Black Girls and Women in Mathematics." *The Journal of Negro Education* 85, no. 3 (2016): 290–301. doi:10.7709/jnegroeducation.85.3.0290

Gholson, Maisie L., Erika C. Bullock, and Nathan N. Alexander. "On the Brilliance of Black Children: A Response to a Clarion Call." *Journal of Urban Mathematics Education* 5, no. 10 (2012): 1–7.

Gilmer, Gloria. "Mathematical Patterns in African American Hairstyles." http://www.math.buffalo.edu/mad/special/gilmer-gloria_HAIRSTYLES.html.

Goffney, Imani M. "Identifying, Measuring, and Defining Equitable Mathematics Instruction." PhD diss., University of Michigan, 2010.

_____. "Challenging Deficit Language." In *Cases for Teacher Educators: Facilitating Conversations about Inequities in Mathematics Classrooms*, edited by Dorothy Y. White, Sandra Crespo, and Marta Civil, pp. 389–94. Charlotte, N.C.: Information Age Publishing, 2016.

Gutiérrez, Rochelle. "Enabling the Practice of Mathematics Teachers in Context: Toward a New Equity Research Agenda." *Mathematical Thinking and Learning* 4, no. 2 and 3 (2002): 145–87.

_____. "Context Matters: Equity, Success, and the Future of Mathematics Education." In *Proceedings of the 29th Annual Meeting of the North American Chapter of the International Group for the Psychology of Mathematics Education*, edited by Teruni de Silva Lamberg and Lynda R. Wiest, pp. 1–18. Stateline (Lake Tahoe), Nevada. University of Nevada, Reno, 2007.

_____. "Framing Equity: Helping Students 'Play the Game' and 'Change the Game.'" *Teaching for Excellence and Equity in Mathematics* 1, no. 1 (2009): 4–8.

_____. "The Sociopolitical Turn in Mathematics Education." *Journal for Research in Mathematics Education* 44, no. 1 (2010/2013): 37–68. Appeared online on 2010; in print in 2013.

_____. "Embracing 'Nepantla': Rethinking Knowledge and Its Use in Teaching." *REDIMAT: Journal of Research in Mathematics Education* 1, no. 1 (2012): 29–56.

_____. *Equity: How the E-Word Helps and Hurts Our Cause in Mathematics Education*. A plenary address given in the Critical Issues in Mathematics Education Workshop. Mathematical Sciences Research Institute. March 15, 2017. Berkeley, Calif. (2017a). https://www.msri.org/workshops/836/schedules/21847.

_____. "Living Mathematx: Towards a Vision for the Future." *Philosophy of Mathematics Education Journal* 32, no. 1 (2017b). http://socialsciences.exeter.ac.uk/education/research/centres/stem/publications/pmej/pome32/index.html.

_____. "Why Mathematics Education Was Late to the Backlash Party: The Need for a Revolution." *Journal of Urban Mathematics Education* 10, no. 2 (2017c): 8–24.

Gutiérrez, Rochelle, and Sonya E. Irving. *Latina/o and Black Students and Mathematics*. A white paper commissioned by the Nellie Mae Foundation (a Jobs for the Future project). Boston: Nellie Mae, 2012. http://www.jff.org/publications/latinoa-and-black-students-and-mathematics-student-center-series.

Larnell, Gregory V., Erika C. Bullock, and Christopher C. Jett. "Rethinking Teaching and Learning Mathematics for Social Justice from a Critical-Race Perspective." *Journal of Education* 196, no. 1 (2016): 19–29.

Lave, Jean. *Cognition in Practice: Mind, Mathematics, and Culture in Everyday Life*. Cambridge, U.K.: Cambridge University Press, 1988.

Leyva, Luis. "Unpacking the Male Superiority Myth and Masculinization of Mathematics at the Intersections: A Review of Research on Gender in Mathematics Education." *Journal for Research in Mathematics Education* 48, no. 4 (2017): 397–452.

Mahalingam, Ram. "Beyond Eurocentrism: Implications of Social Epistemology for Mathematics Education." In *Multicultural Curriculum: New Directions For Social Theory, Practice, and Policy*, edited by Ram Mahalingam and Cameron McCarthy. New York: Routledge, 2000.

Martin, Danny B. "E(race)ing Race from a National Conversation on Mathematics Teaching and Learning: The National Mathematics Panel as White Institutional Space." *The Montana Math Enthusiast* 5, no. 2–3 (2008): 387–98.

_____. "Race, Racial Projects, and Mathematics Education." *Journal for Research in Mathematics Education* 44, no. 1 (2013): 316–33.

_____. "The Collective Black and Principles to Actions." *Journal of Urban Mathematics Education* 8, no. 1 (2015): 17–23.

Masingila, Joanna O. "Mathematical Practice in Carpet Laying." *Anthropology and Education Quarterly* 25, no. 4 (1994): 430–62.

_____. "Examining Students' Perceptions of Their Everyday Mathematics Practice." *Everyday and Academic Mathematics in the Classroom, Monograph Vol. 11, Journal for Research in Mathematics Education*. Reston, Va.: National Council of Teachers of Mathematics, 2002.

Myers, Marielle. *The Use of Learning Trajectory-Based Instruction in Supporting Equitable Teaching Practices in Elementary Classrooms: A Multi-Case Study*. Unpublished doctoral diss., North Carolina State University, 2014.

Myers, Marielle, Paola Sztajn, P. Holt Wilson, and Cyndi Edgington. "From Implicit to Explicit: Articulating Equitable Learning Trajectories-Based Instruction." *Journal of Urban Mathematics Education* 8, no. 2 (2015): 11–22.

National Council of Supervisors of Mathematics and TODOS Mathematics for ALL (NCSM and TODOS). "Mathematics Education through the Lens of Social Justice: Acknowledgment, Actions, and Accountability. A Joint Position Statement" (2016). http://www.todos-math.org/assets/docs2016/2016Enews/3.pospaper16_wtodos_8pp.pdf.

Nixon, Rob. *Slow Violence and the Environmentalism of the Poor*. Cambridge, Mass.: Harvard University Press, 2011.

Nunes, Terezinha, Analúcia D. Schliemann, and David W. Carraher. *Street Mathematics and School Mathematics*. Cambridge, U.K.: Cambridge University Press, 1993.

O'Neil, Cathy. *Weapons of Math Destruction: How Big Data Increases Inequality and Threatens Democracy*. New York: Broadway Books, 2016.

Paris, Django, and Maisha T. Winn, eds. *Humanizing Research: Decolonizing Qualitative Inquiry with Youth and Communities*. Thousand Oaks, Calif.: Sage Publications, 2013.

Rosa, Milton, and Daniel Clark Orey. "Humanizing Mathematics through Ethnomodelling." *Journal of Humanistic Mathematics* 6, no. 2 (2016): 3–22.

San Pedro, Timothy, and Valerie Kinloch. "Toward Projects in Humanization: Research on Co-Creating and Sustaining Dialogic Relationships." *American Educational Research Journal* 54, no. 1 (2017): 373S–394S.

Saxe, Geoffrey B. "Candy Selling and Math Learning." *Educational Researcher* 17, no. 6 (1998): 14–21.

Stinson, David W. "Negotiating the 'White Male Math Myth': African American Male Students and Success in School Mathematics." *Journal for Research in Mathematics Education* 44, no. 1 (2013): 69–99.

Style, Emily. "Curriculum as Window and Mirror." *Social Science Record* (Fall 1996). https://www.nationalseedproject.org/images/documents/Curriculum_As_Window_and_Mirror.pdf.

Tuck, Eve, and K. Wayne Yang. "Decolonization Is Not a Metaphor." *Decolonization: Indigeneity, Education, and Society* 1, no. 1 (2012): 1–40.

Toussaint, Godfried T. *The Geometry of Musical Rhythm: What Makes a "Good" Rhythm Good?* New York: CRC Press, 2013.

Turner, Erin E., Corey Drake, Amy Roth McDuffie, Julia Aguirre, Tonya Gau Bartell, and Mary Q. Foote. "Promoting Equity in Mathematics Teacher Preparation: A Framework for Advancing Teacher Learning of Children's Multiple Mathematics Knowledge Bases." *Journal of Mathematics Teacher Education* 15, no. 1 (2012): 67–82.

Turner, Erin, Higinio Dominguez, Luz Maldonado, and Susan Empson. "English Learners' Participation in Mathematical Discussion: Shifting Positionings and Dynamic Identities." *Journal for Research in Mathematics Education* 44, no. 1 (2013): 199–234.

Warburton, Trevor T. "Solving for Irrational Zeros: Whiteness in Mathematics Teacher Education." PhD diss., University of Utah, 2015.

_____. "The Overlapping Discourses of Mathematics and Whiteness: Pushing Social Justice Out of Mathematics." Paper presented at the Annual Meeting of the American Educational Research Association, San Antonio, Texas, April 2017.

PART I

Attending to Students' Identities through Learning

CHAPTER 1

Toward Indigenous Making and Sharing:
Implications for Mathematics Learning

Filiberto Barajas-López, *University of Washington, Seattle*
Megan Bang, *University of Washington, Seattle*

In this chapter, we explore the "Indigenous making and sharing" that occurred in a project called Indigenous STEAM, an ArtScience participatory design research project. The project involved Indigenous youth, families, community artists, and scientists in a summer program designed to cultivate Indigenous ways of knowing, being, and making complex socio-ecological systems through a focus on pedagogies of walking, observing, and talking about lands and waters as the foundations in making activities. We will draw from a case study that utilizes interaction analysis of ArtScience making spaces, more specifically clay work. This work seeks to expand our understandings of issues of equity in making and in mathematics learning by considering how making is necessarily a cultural activity that reflects particular epistemic practices that have consequences for how we think about and design mathematics learning environments. We specifically explore the ways in which clay making (as an embodied form of mathematics) can engage youth in humanizing mathematics and science practices as well as other disciplines as part of the making process.

■ Our Starting Point

We start by communicating our intentions for writing this chapter and by acknowledging the historical erasure of Indigenous people across continents. We begin with erasure because any conversation about equity in society, the world, education, or mathematics education needs to be situated as part of an ongoing historical, political, and social context or, in the case of Indigenous people, the project of settler colonialism (Wolfe 2006). By starting here, it is possible to consider the limitations of existing/imposed frames of learning and equity and to then consider more appropriate approaches that draw from Indigenous worldviews and cosmologies. Within this work, we position ourselves as Indigenous scholars and educators, one from the territories of central México and one from the Great Lakes, who challenge Western frames and are working to develop Indigenous-based solutions. In addition to living our lives and raising families in Indigenous communities, each of us has spent important time and effort working in both school- and community-based contexts with families and communities to develop learning environments that are transformative for our communities. Sometimes this work has been in the form of research, sometimes not, but all of it has shared a commitment to Indigenous resurgence and educational justice. An important part of this work has been the deliberate exploration and/or learning of ways to enact Indigenous-based pedagogies in various contexts—both formal and informal—with an eye toward understanding how such ways might inform and transform one another. It is from this perspective that we narrate the work undertaken in the Indigenous Science, Technology, Engineering, Arts, and Mathematics (ISTEAM) camp and consider the ways in which such work can offer expansive forms of equity and inform the field of mathematics education.

Historically, the contributions and contemporary practices of Indigenous people in mathematics have either been forgotten (erased) or positioned as deficient relative to Eurocentric conceptions of mathematics. That is, the mathematical practices and contributions of Indigenous people and other traditional cultures have largely been described as lacking the complexity or sophistication to merit higher status in the field of mathematics (Powell 2002). For example, one example often cited or acknowledged as a contribution of Indigenous people (e.g., Mayan civilization) is the concept of "0." While the conceptualization and understanding of the concept of "0" demonstrates the development of a number system and the computation of sophisticated astronomical counts (Closs 1986), such contributions remain marginal and are often excluded or devalued as major contributions to the broader field of mathematics. Such exclusion often suggests to practitioners and to learners that few cultures (mainly the Greeks) produced or developed the mathematics that are taught or practiced today in school and in society. In addition, when the contributions of Indigenous people are acknowledged, such contributions are framed as the mathematical and scientific production of Indigenous people of the past with little or no connection to the Indigenous people of today.

In the last thirty years, some researchers have attempted to make more visible the ways in which Indigenous people across continents have used mathematics and continue to do mathematics in culturally embedded forms (D'Ambrosio 1985; Eglash 2001). One area that has emerged as a productive space, both in mathematics and in mathematics education, has been ethnomathematics. Multiple definitions of ethnomathematics have been developed, but D'Ambrosio (1985) defined it as the "mathematics which is practiced among identifiable cultural groups such as national-tribe societies, labor groups, children of certain age brackets and professional classes." Bishop (1988) articulates ethnomathematics as a cultural product, whereas D'Ambrosio makes reference to cultural groups. Ethnomathematics has made explicit the relationship between culture and the development of mathematics by countering the commonly held and false assumption that mathematics is universal and culture free (D'Ambrosio 1985). From an ethnomathematics perspective, mathematics is the production of human beings and emerges from cultural activity (Bishop 1988; Lipka and Adams 2004). In addition, ethnomathematics presents a direct challenge to Eurocentric conceptions of mathematics that have been imposed and reproduced in colonized territories (Powell and Frankenstein 1997). In this chapter, we build on this ongoing research in ethnomathematics but chart another pathway that accounts for the ways in which making spaces based in youths' epistemic ecologies can enable expansive forms of making that include mathematics and are reflective of Indigenous forms of human-nature relations (Gutiérrez 2017). Put differently, our intention is to articulate ways to restore Indigenous nature-culture relationships as a direct refusal of Indigenous erasure and to uphold the epistemic authority (Booker and Goldman 2016) of Indigenous ways of knowing in mathematics learning.

■ Why Making and Sharing? Centering Indigeneity through ISTEAM Camp

We focus our attention on making because making has taken on particular meanings in the U.S. context. In the United States, a dominant view of the maker movement narrowly defines such activity as the work of individuals and groups engaging in "uniquely American activity focused on technological forms of innovation that advance hands-on learning and contribute to the growth of the economy" (Vossoughi, Hooper, and Escudé 2016, p. 207). A major assumption of this conception of the maker movement is that it privileges the creation of products, generally dealing with electronics or modern technologies, in ways that are representative of normative White culture and activities (Vossoughi, Hooper, and Escudé 2016, p. 208). We build on Vossoughi and colleagues' (pp. 213–26) critique of the maker movement to articulate Indigenous making and sharing. They suggest that the following four dimensions are critical in developing pedagogies of making that can support equitable and transformative learning for nondominant youth:

1. Critical analysis of educational injustice

2. Historicized approaches to making as cross-cultural activity

3. Explicit attention to pedagogical philosophies and practices

4. Ongoing inquiry into the sociopolitical values and purposes of making

These four dimensions are critical in developing transformative learning environments because they help to refuse approaches that reify the dynamics of erasure we mention, and they shaped how we approached our analysis and narrative. Further, the dimensions resonate with design principles Bang developed for repatriating Indigenous technologies (Bang et al. 2013) that shaped the design of the STEAM camp and guided our pedagogical practice. Since the summer of 2014, we have engaged in an ArtScience participatory design project (Bang and Vossoughi 2016) titled ISTEAM Camp. We have engaged over eighty first- to twelfth-grade Indigenous youth in complex ecological systems learning in field-based settings utilizing ArtScience pedagogies during two-week summer camps. The project was developed to engage Indigenous youth in understanding the changing lands and waters in the Pacific Northwest through direct engagement with phenomena in the world. Pedagogically, the project aimed to cultivate epistemic heterogeneity (Rosebery et al. 2010) and onto-epistemic navigation between Indigenous ways of knowing and western ways of knowing in sense making and embodied practice. The Indigenous youth participating in the camps represent a wide range of Nations across the continental U.S., Canada, and México. Such groups include Washington State tribe members from the Puyallup, Yakama, and Upper Skagit Nations (to name a few), as well as members of Nations originating outside of the state of Washington (e.g., Ojibwe, Diné, Lakota, Kiowa, Chippewa, Paiute, P'urhépecha [México]). In total, over twenty Nations are represented.

We have worked to evolve an understanding of Indigenous making and to consider the ways in which Indigenous making may afford transformative and humanizing learning opportunities for Indigenous youth. In the context of the ISTEAM camp, rehumanizing means to directly refuse Indigenous erasure by centering Indigenous knowledge systems (Cajete 2000; Kawagley 1995; Meyer 2001) as a way to counter assumptions embedded in western conceptions of knowing and knowledge production. These assumptions include an emphasis on universalism and compartmentalization of knowledge. We center Indigenous knowledge systems by historicizing the practice of making as a longstanding cultural practice with deep nature-culture relations that are enacted within the context of family and communal responsibilities.

As Indigenous scholars, we have engaged with Indigenous youth, families, and community artists by centering Indigenous nature-culture relations (as an explicit counter to western human-dominated views) to cultivate ways of knowing, being, and making through the pedagogies of storytelling and walking (observing) the lands and waters (Cajete 1999) as the foundation for the making activities. Storytelling involved communicating meanings, feelings, and ways of being, including elder storytelling. Walking (observing) entailed noticing and being present with stories in places. Finally, clay making involved the direct use of natural materials as a vehicle to contribute to and manifest the continuity of Indigenous practices and people. In the camp, the activity of making (in this case, clay work) has been established as a millenarian practice that Indigenous communities have developed as a technology in the past and in the present. Within this conception, Indigenous making is the enactment of relationships with animate materials that have life courses to fulfill communal responsibilities and as a process of knowing, being, and doing.

To document the various activities throughout the camps, we have collected video, audio recordings, and field notes of the making activities, as well as interviews with youth and adults; these materials form the basis of the data for this study. The data were logged in five-minute intervals across each summer and tagged with key markers of making, Indigenous knowledge systems, and practice configurations. The episode we present in this chapter represents a slice of a broader analysis where we examined the making activities that took place in the ISTEAM camp during the summer of 2016. As part of the analysis, we looked for instances when stories and storytelling were shared or retold in the context of the making activities. In addition, we also identified moments when youth and/or artists referenced ideas or concepts from the walking activities in the making activities. Across the data, we identified significant relationships between the storytelling, walking, and making activities; however, in this study we highlight the relationships that emerged from the clay making.

■ Making and Sharing from an Indigenous Perspective: Emergent Understandings from ISTEAM Camp

In order to understand why making and sharing reflect particular epistemic practices, it is important to understand how Indigenous communities have drawn from their own ways of knowing and relating with the world by reaffirming such relationships in daily practice. One such technology that continues to be a source of continuity, reclamation, and reaffirmation is the use of clay as one of the original technologies. Clay work continues to be used in a variety of community contexts and for varied purposes. In some contexts, like Indigenous communities in central México, clay work and the activities around it remain a central part of a community's social organization and play a strong role in the transmission of cultural practices and knowledge systems. For some Indigenous communities, clay work (most often pottery) is part of a community's specialized system of production. In these communities, families contribute to collective making, with women generally taking up key roles in the making of pots, incense burners, and other ceremonial pieces.

Clay making, as an Indigenous-based practice, involves a range of activities that integrate a variety of disciplinary domains throughout the process of making and sharing. Being in relationship with clay means understanding the science of what constitutes moldable clay throughout the mixing process. This includes an understanding of the types of organic materials (e.g., plant medicines) used, the different types of clay, the need to evenly distribute moisture through kneading and wedging, and the ways in which the elements (e.g., water, fire) come into play at different parts of the process to make a clay piece possible. In the elaboration of the clay piece, several mathematical activities also occur as embodied mathematics (Hall and Nemirovsky 2012). Nonstandard measures and proportions are used to approximate the amount of water needed to mix with dry clay. In addition, mathematical modeling is used to translate from two-dimensional (2-D) sketches to the three-dimensional (3-D) art piece. Here, the designing of the 2-D sketch allows the clay maker to conceptualize into the "real world" (i.e., the 3-D piece), somewhat similarly to the way that engineers develop models as part of an iterative process to test whether a product will work as desired (Dym 2004). The major distinction between this approach (model-based prediction) and Indigenous clay making is that the "final" clay piece (which is the only iteration) is viewed as a physical representation that captures the meanings, feelings, and ways of being that are part of the process of making and sharing.

Below, we describe one episode that highlights aspects of clay making and sharing that privilege epistemic practices that are founded on the practice of walking and clay making. It is important to note that the focus on clay emerged in the ISTEAM camp from the students' own discovery while exploring tidal pools as part of the study of beach relatives and changing waters (ocean acidification). It was there that students came in relation with a clay deposit that then prompted student-generated inquiry and a focus on clay work in year two of the camp. In our initial efforts to come in relation with clay, we approached clay work by drawing from ceremonial practices originating from Indigenous communities in central México. The ceremonial practices are the accumulation of thousands of years of oral and making transmission that are deeply based on storytelling and apprenticeship relationships. We worked to intertwine youth experiences with making relations in the natural world with processes of clay making. For example, the beach was about a half-mile walk from the community center that served as the base of the ISTEAM camp. We designed inquiries into the mathematics of the natural world for the youths to explore during these walks. In the walks, the students attended to deep observation of plant relatives and to understanding patterns in plants from various scales and perspectives. They explored symmetry, shapes, angles, tessellations, lines, and curves in plant relatives native to the Pacific Northwest. The walking episode below shows one way in which the students began to make connections between the activities of storytelling, walking, and making. In the walking episode that follows, we narrate how one nine-year-old Ojibwe/Diné youth, Dawn, began to make these connections.

Dawn: I saw many patterns and shapes.

Clay artist: You were telling me you saw many patterns and shapes. Your question was, how would I include it in clay? What are some—can you give me an example of a pattern you saw?

Dawn: This is one pattern where the leaves were kind of forward, kind of like a clover and then it would do that for like every branch.

Clay artist: Why might it all be growing out like that?

Dawn: Like sunlight. It spreads out and gets more nutrition.

Clay artist: Is that the only one [pattern] you saw or were there others?

Dawn: There was. I remember when we were telling my team and nettle goes like that and that and that.

Clay artist: So the nettle, how it was going in one direction. Cool—that's another good example.

Dawn: Oh, also I noticed that on the horsetail there would always be like a bunch around the stem and then wait and then do it again. So it's kind of over and over.

Clay artist: I noticed that too. You know what I remember about that. I actually went around and counted. And I noticed they were in groups of three and then another group of three. They were closer than I'm drawing it. I don't remember how many groups of three but about seven or eight. So this is the horsetail, the nettle, and this was some kind [*inaudible*].

In the episode above, the interaction demonstrates how children's observations/noticings of patterns in nature are conceived as part of the process of clay making. In the design of her clay piece, Dawn drew from patterns in nature (observed and noticed in the nature walks). This was a practice that paralleled one of the regional stories that was retold by an elder Indigenous storyteller on another day during a storytelling circle. In that story, a young Yakama girl persists to overcome feelings of incompetence by learning to make baskets from a cedar tree. The cedar tree guides the Yakama girl to do patterns and designs by observing nature (e.g., the rivers, the mountains).

In the walking episode, Dawn recalled the types of growth patterns that she observed between two plants. In deciding the type of design to incorporate into her clay piece, Dawn compared her observations of horsetail and nettle. She counted the branching that she observed in each of the plant relatives. Dawn also began to conceptualize why particular plants grew the way they did (e.g., exposure to sunlight) and to explore the type of relationships the surrounding plants had with each other. Furthermore, Dawn's engagement throughout the walking activities was grounded in reestablishing relationships with plant relatives with an aim to understand the knowledge (stories of reciprocal relations), medicines, and foods that plants can impart and provide to each other and for humans. As a whole, the episode demonstrates how Indigenous youth can engage in meaningful nature-culture relationships where scientific and mathematical knowledge can be constructed as part of an Indigenous knowledge system. The episode also demonstrates the role of story as an integrative part of making practices where multiple relations—such as, among others, the fulfillment of the purpose that Indigenous people have in relation to the physical world, connections to ancestors, engagement in a millenary practice, and noticings of patterns in nature—can be established.

In the post-camp reflections and interviews, Dawn and many other of the students described the meaning of their engagement across the walking and making activities as being formative experiences. For many Indigenous youth, the practice of making as a continual cultural practice and the enactment of nature-culture relations provided opportunities for youth to assert culturally based ways of being and doing. By engaging in historically rooted Indigenous practices of making, clay making was reclaimed as an original technology that continues to play a central role in the way Indigenous people manifest their relationship with the land. Indigenous youth remarked that engaging in clay making, in the same form as their ancestors had done, gave them a greater sense of responsibility for maintaining strong cultural ties through Indigenous-based making activities.

From our perspective, we interpreted this to mean that the making and observational practices represented a resurgent and humanizing form of contributing to the physical and spiritual well-being of their own communities.

It is also important to note that through Dawn's engagement with making she engaged in a variety of academic disciplines. For example, through the walking activities and her ongoing observations of plants, she also deeply engaged with mathematical concepts (e.g., patterns, symmetry) as part of her observations. This contrasts significantly with school-based western conceptions of separate academic domains, which suggest that academic disciplines can be learned separately from each other. While making, more broadly, may afford this kind of interdisciplinary work, we note that this is particularly important for Indigenous ways of knowing, causing making to be potentially fertile ground for such learning.

Figures 1.1 and 1.2 provide visual examples of clay work that demonstrate such learning. A clay bowl made by a ten-year-old Yakama girl named Lisa (fig. 1.1) shows the patterns mentioned in a Yakama Nation story. In the story, a young Yakama girl learns to make baskets from grandma cedar. The young girl in the story also learns to incorporate patterns from animals and the lands. The clay piece shows the diamond pattern learned from a snake and the triangle shapes from the mountain.

Fig. 1.1. Lisa's bowl with patterns from a Yakama Nation story

Rachel, a twelve-year-old who is Kiowa, Creek, and Cherokee, made a clay piece (fig. 1.2) focused on narrating the presence of otters in waters where otters had not been seen for many years. The first iteration of the otter was conceived as a storyboard on a two-dimensional flat piece of clay representing a linear story progression, but by the third day the concept of the otter story had evolved into a three-dimensional piece (e.g., an otter incense burner) that would be used to retell the story of otters (e.g., the elimination and return of otters in the region) and for the purpose of family and community prayer for living things including animals, plants, and water.

Fig. 1.2. Rachel's piece relating the story of otters

■ Indigenous Making: Implications for Equity and Mathematics Learning

The work that has taken place in the ISTEAM camp and our efforts to document youth restoring relationships with land, water, and communities serve as an initial articulation of how Indigenous making can expand understandings of equity and mathematics learning. We have presented an example of how making is a cultural activity that reflects particular epistemic practices that have consequences for how Indigenous youth engage with materiality and nature. Furthermore, we have made explicit the ways in which young people draw from walking and storytelling pedagogies in making. From our perspective, Indigenous making is about living nature-culture relations to establish futurity and as a direct refusal to Indigenous erasure.

In light of the design of the clay making and walking activities, engagement with Indigenous making practices suggests that scientific and mathematical knowledge is not separate or divided from a cultural activity, as seen in western thought and practice. That is, the construction of mathematical knowledge is an embodied practice in making and a part of a knowledge system. For us, engaging in mathematics learning in this way removes the imminent threat of erasure that educational spaces often impose on Indigenous people. Compared to school-based approaches to teaching mathematics, which is taught as its own discipline, productive disciplinary engagement from an Indigenous perspective can do more than teach children mathematics. Indigenous-based conceptions of making can also establish the permanence of Indigenous people as continual producers of knowledge by creating opportunities for Indigenous people to engage in interdisciplinary activity within a knowledge system that embraces nature-culture relations.

As we envision what it means to humanize mathematics, we need to be cautious of the foundational relationships that are implied or enacted in humanizing paradigms that reinscribe western forms of nature-culture relations. We also caution that trying to fit or impose Indigenous knowledge systems into western conceptions of knowledge means maintaining asymmetrical power relations and reproducing inequities and dominance. In closing, equity in mathematics education is more than providing access to normative conceptions of mathematics. Equity in mathematics education, from an Indigenous perspective, means creating spaces that contribute to the "collective continuance" of Indigenous communities (Whyte 2004). While this may include ensuring Indigenous youth can master dominant forms of mathematics, it must also mean that they are not dominated by them and that they have opportunities to engage in mathematics that contributes to our own ways of knowing and making mathematics.

Authors' Note

This work is funded by National Science Foundation grant DRL-1348494, with Megan Bang, Ann Rosebery, and Beth Warren as Principal Investigators. All opinions are strictly our own. We gratefully acknowledge the intellectual influence of our colleagues in the LIFE Center.

References

Bang, Megan, and Shirin Vossoughi. "Participatory Design Research and Educational Justice: Studying Learning and Relations within Social Change Making." *Cognition and Instruction* 34, no. 3 (2016): 173–93.

Bang, Megan, Ananda Marin, Lori Faber, and Eli S. Suzukovich. "Repatriating Indigenous Technologies in an Urban Indian Community." *Urban Education* 48, no. 5 (2013): 705–33.

Bishop, Alan J. *Mathematical Enculturation: A Cultural Perspective on Mathematics Education.* Dordrecht, the Netherlands: Kluwer Academic Publishers, 1988.

Booker, Angela, and Shelley Goldman. "Participatory Design Research as a Practice for Systemic Repair: Doing Hand-In-Hand Math Research with Families." *Cognition and Instruction* 34, no. 3 (2016): 222–35.

Cajete, Gregory A. *Igniting the Sparkle: An Indigenous Science Education Model.* Skyland, N.C.: Kivaki Press, 1999.

———. *Native Science: Natural Laws of Interdependence.* Sante Fe, N.M.: Clear Light Publishers, 2000.

Closs, Michael P. "The Mathematical Notation of the Ancient Maya." In *Native American Mathematics*, edited by Michael P. Closs, pp. 291–369. Austin: University of Texas Press, 1986.

D'Ambrosio, Ubiratan. "Ethnomathematics and Its Place in the History and Pedagogy of Mathematics." *For the Learning of Mathematics* 5, no. 1 (1985): 44–48.

Dym, Clive M. *Principles of Mathematical Modeling.* Boston: Elsevier Academic Press, 2004.

Eglash, Ron. "Indigenous Knowledge Systems." In *Reader's Guide to the History of Science*, edited by Arne Hessenbruch, pp. 372–73. London: Fitzroy Dearborn Publishers, 2001.

Gutiérrez, Rochelle. "Living Mathematx: Towards a Vision for the Future." *Philosophy of Mathematics Education* 32, no. 1 (2017).

Hall, Roger, and Ricardo Nemirovsky. "Modalities of Body Engagement in Mathematical Activity and Learning." *Special Issue on Embodied Mathematical Cognition, Journal of the Learning Sciences* 21, no. 2 (2012): 207–15.

Kawagley, Oscar A. *A Yupiaq World View: A Pathway to Ecology and Spirit.* Prospect Heights, Ill.: Waveland Press, 1995.

Lipka, Jerry, and Barbara Adams. "Culturally Based Math Education as a Way to Improve Alaska Native Students' Math Performance." Appalachian Collaborative Center for Learning, Working Paper No. 20, 2004.

Meyer, Manulani A. "Our Own Liberation: Reflections on Hawaiian Epistemology." *The Contemporary Pacific* 13, no. 1 (2001): 124–48.

Powell, Arthur B. "Ethnomathematics and the Challenges of Racism in Mathematics Education." In *Proceedings of the 3rd International Mathematics Education and Society Conference, Volume 1*, edited by Paola Valero and Ole Skovsmose, pp. 15–29. Copenhagen, Denmark: Centre for Research in Learning Mathematics, 2002.

Powell, Arthur B., and Marilyn Frankenstein, eds. *Ethnomathematics: Challenging Eurocentrism in Mathematics Education.* Albany: State University of New York Press, 1997.

Rosebery, Ann S., Mark Ogonowski, Mary Di Schino, and Beth Warren. "'The Coat Traps All Your Body Heat': Heterogeneity as Fundamental to Learning." *Journal of the Learning Sciences* 19, no. 3 (2010): 322–57.

Vossoughi, Shirin, Paula Hooper, and Meg Escudé. "Making through the Lens of Culture and Power: Towards Transformative Visions for Educational Equity." *Harvard Educational Review* (June 2016): 206–32.

Whyte, Kyle P. "Indigenous Women, Climate Change Impacts, and Collective Action." *Hypatia: Journal of Feminist Philosophy* 29, no. 3 (2004): 599–616.

Wolfe, Patrick. "Settler Colonialism and the Elimination of the Native." *Journal of Genocide Research* 8, no. 4 (2006): 387–409.

CHAPTER 2

Girls STEM Institute:
Transforming and Empowering Black Girls in Mathematics through STEM

Crystal Hill Morton, *Indiana University–Purdue University Indianapolis*
Demetrice Smith-Mutegi, *Marian University, Indianapolis, Indiana*

I was the only African American in my honors geometry class; people would look at me like why is she here? I was like, I am not going to the front. I am in AVID and we have to sit in the front, but I sat in the back. The teacher asked me why I was sitting in the back and I was like, I am not sitting in the front. During group work time, the teacher had to put them in a group with me, because the majority of the students did not want to pair up with me. When they recognized that I was as smart as they were they started to pair up with me. —*Paula*

Imagine the feeling of embarrassment when you ask a question about a problem that everyone understands. Imagine the feeling of invisibility when the posters of scientists and mathematicians in the classroom do not look like you. Imagine not getting the joke that everyone laughs at or being the last person asked to join the group. Imagine not feeling adequate to learn math, do well in math, or receive valuable feedback in math. It is unfortunate to imagine these experiences; it is more unfortunate to live them. While these experiences are dehumanizing for many children across the nation, they are not uncommon, particularly for Black girls.

■ Being Black and a Young Woman

Being a young black woman it is like he [the teacher] is intimidated by me instead of trying to teach me . . . I don't have an attitude. —*Janice*

To understand the mathematics experiences of Black girls, one must recognize the unique challenges Black girls face because of their race and gender (Archer-Banks and Behar-Horenstein 2012; Crenshaw 1991; Evans-Winters 2011; Joseph, Viesca, and Bianco 2016). Even though Black girls hold a higher value for mathematics and a higher mathematics confidence level than their White counterparts (Else-Quest, Mineo, and Higgins 2013), research has shown that teachers hold Black girls to lower expectations (Pringle et al. 2012), and they are less likely to complete advanced mathematics courses that are critical for college admission and career success (Walker 2007).

Black girls' experiences with mathematics in these dehumanizing spaces can negatively impact their image of mathematics, their identification and engagement with mathematics

(Gholston 2016), and their chances to succeed academically (Joseph 2017). As early as elementary school, Black girls are perceived as having limited mathematics knowledge and are often positioned outside of meaningful mathematics learning experiences. Black girls are disproportionately tracked into "lower-level" mathematics, which limits their access to rigorous, relevant, and high-quality mathematics instruction (NAACP Legal Defense and Educational Fund and National Women's Law Center [LDF and NWLC] 2014; Joseph 2017) throughout their high school years (Archer-Banks and Behar-Horenstein 2012).

The inequitable placement and referral practices of school personnel are often linked to their perceptions of Black girls; perceptions tainted by negative stereotypes that lead to differential treatment and expectations (LDF and NWLC 2014; Walker 2007). For example, Black girls are often stereotyped as talkative, loud, confrontational, and assertive (Joseph, Viesca, and Bianco 2016)—characteristics that clash with White-middle-class notions of femininity (National Women's Law Center and Girls for Gender Equity 2010). Therefore, teachers assume Black girls need more social correction, and more emphasis is placed on social correction than on academic development and achievement (Morris 2007). Because of the lack of access to rigorous, relevant, and high-quality mathematics instruction, Black girls leave high school not ready for college and careers, which can lead to detrimental economic consequences for them, their families, and their communities (Smith-Evans et al. 2014).

■ Learning Mathematics in a Traditional School Setting as a Black Girl

> Well, I've always got stuck with bad teachers. So it would be hard for me to, like, learn math. My last teacher would give us worksheets and have in her head that we understood the stuff on the worksheets and we didn't. She wouldn't go over it and it was kind of hard to understand what she gave us to do. . . . I hate math, but I probably would have looked at it differently if my teachers helped me understand it. —*Veronica*

When talking to Black girls about a typical day in their mathematics classrooms, the following sequence of events is a prevalent theme: Check homework, listen to a lecture, get new homework or check homework, be instructed to read sections in the textbook, and get new homework. Black students are all too often exposed to non-engaging and non-rigorous mathematics curriculum devoid of meaning and any real connections to their lived experiences (Hill 2010). Therefore, many Black girls are not challenged to think beyond facts and procedures and are denied the opportunity to engage in higher-level mathematical thinking. Because of a dehumanized, depersonalized, and decontextualized mathematics learning experiences, Black girls like Diana become disinterested and indifferent to mathematics (Gholston 2016; Joseph et al. 2017, p. 49). Diana, a first-year high school student who once loved math, shared that "when I go to geometry it is going to be the worst experience of my life."

Tarmizi, Tarmizi, and Mokhtar (2010) described mathematics teaching as a subject that is "dominated by dehumanisation, depersonalisation, and decontextualisation." To dehumanize is to deprive of human qualities. Paula, in the opening passage, spoke of dehumanizing experiences. Paula, like Veronica, Diana, and many other girls around the nation, need mathematics to be rehumanized. In a review of the literature on Black women's and girls' persistence in the Mathematics Pipeline, researchers found that *structural disruptions* to traditional systems of learning, such as co-curricular spaces and single-gender classrooms, have increased Black girls' participation in mathematics. Co-curricular spaces are an extension of the formal learning space and occur in out-of-school spaces (Joseph, Hailu, and Boston 2017). Walker (2014) found that in- and out-of-school experiences with mathematics were powerful and influential experiences for Black mathematicians.

While some researchers and mathematics educators have argued for rehumanization, traditional approaches to teaching mathematics are still dominating classrooms around the world. To promote transformation and empowerment among young, Black female students, the Girls STEM Institute (GSI), a co-curricular space, was started in 2013. This chapter will describe rehumanizing experiences in math for Black girls who participated in GSI and how these experiences help foster positive identity development and build Black girls' understanding of number and operations and their problem-solving and computational skills. (To find out more information about Girls STEM Institute, visit http://girlssteminstitute.org.)

Collectively, the impact of these experiences is of particular importance to us, the authors, as we are both Black women educators from the southeastern region of the United States who have, through many triumphs and challenges in school, found a way to love and appreciate learning mathematics. As former mathematics and science students, college mathematics and science majors, high school mathematics and science teachers, and current mathematics and science educators, we have experienced and observed mathematics instruction that lacked rigor and relevance. We found it very difficult to pull up any memories of engaging with mathematics during our myriad of courses and classes that addressed our lived experiences as young black women learning mathematics in the rural south. We have also encountered many peers who are Black women who feel "defeated" by the slightest mention of the term *mathematics*. We want to understand and help those peers. We also want to help those peers help their children excel in mathematics and beyond. Fortunately, as mathematics and science educators, we can begin this work—through Girls STEM Institute.

Through our experiences as researchers and educators, we understand that historically, Black girls and young women from low-income neighborhoods, in particular, are underrepresented in mathematics and science-related careers. Of the 27 percent of mathematics doctoral degrees awarded to women in 2015, roughly one percent were awarded to Black women (National Science Foundation [NSF] 2017, as stated in Joseph, Hailu, and Boston 2017).

We recognize that for decades, Black students and their intelligence have been framed in negative and detrimental ways. The resiliency and success of Black learners are underemphasized while underachievement and failure are emphasized (Martin 2012). Black students are positioned as deficient, underachieving, and unmotivated learners with inferior skills when compared to their White and Asian peers (Tate 1997). Positioning Black learners in this manner perpetuates the negative and often unfounded stereotype that failure among Black learners is the norm (Berry, Thunder, and McClain 2011). In our experience as former secondary teachers, we observed that Black girls, more so than girls in other racial/ethnic groups, were often quick to dismiss their mathematics and science abilities, and we believe that part of this dismissal was connected to the negative and unfounded stereotypes that teachers and administration held about their intelligence.

Through GSI we strive to provide Black girls learning opportunities to help disrupt false narratives about their intelligence and who they are as Black learners. This study is just one way to examine the impact of these learning experiences on the identity development of Black girls. From the study's conceptualization to formally writing up findings, our top priority was maintaining the integrity of the girls' voices as they shared their experiences. Therefore, throughout this chapter, we include various quotes and handwritten samples of journal entries that captured the essence of our conversations with each participant. Through this work, we hope to provide strategies to empower Black girls as learners and doers of mathematics who understand how their mathematical knowledge can be used as a catalyst for personal and social change.

Girls STEM Institute: The Study

Co-curricular programming such as afterschool STEM programming, including summer camps, has been found to contribute to improved attitudes toward STEM fields and careers, increased STEM knowledge and skills, and a higher likelihood of graduating and pursuing a STEM career (Joseph, Hailu, and Boston 2017; Krishnamurthi, Ballard, and Noam 2014). Several studies highlight the importance of informal settings on STEM learning, but few focus specifically on Black girls (McPherson 2014). To ascertain a better understanding of Black girls' informal learning experiences and the impact on their identity development, we conducted a qualitative study using semi-structured interviews and journal entries.

The sample consists of twenty-three Black girls who were participants in Girls STEM 2016 Summer Institute. During GSI, participants completed journal entries related to a variety of topics, including their experiences with mathematics in traditional school settings and their experiences in GSI. For example, students were asked to describe their best and worst math teacher. Interviews were conducted during and after GSI. They lasted between fifteen and thirty minutes in duration. The girls were asked a series of open-ended questions that included ones about their experiences in school and GSI, and their mathematics and science confidence and self-efficacy. One such question was: "What is it like being a Black girl at your school?" Interviews and journal entries were analyzed for common and unique themes using open coding.

Girls STEM Institute: The Experience

As former secondary science and mathematics teachers and current science and mathematics teacher educators, we (the co-authors) have heard stories of dehumanizing experiences in math and science classrooms from Black girls and their parents, stories like the one shared by Antoinette, an elementary student, and Daizha, a middle school student, when talking about their worst math teacher (fig. 2.1).

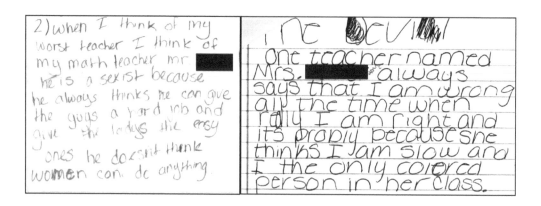

Fig 2.1. Girls STEM Institute journal entries

GSI is an informal learning program designed to provide holistic learning opportunities for girls of color like Antoinette and Daizha who are historically marginalized in STEM fields. The goals of GSI are to improve the achievement, perceptions, confidence and overall wellness and well-being of girls of color and their families. GSI's vision is to transform communities by empowering girls of color to become leaders, innovators, and educators who use STEM as a tool for personal and social change. To carry out this vision, GSI provides a rich, rigorous, relevant, and supportive context where participants have the freedom to grow interpersonally and intellectually. The theme for our summer 2016 institute was Health and Wellness. We focused on six types of health and wellness—physical, emotional, social, financial, intellectual, and environmental. To rehumanize the approach to helping young woman engage in mathematics content, GSI leaders focused on three particular elements of the institute experience: the curricular approach and the institute themes; the selection of staff and teachers; and the prioritization of parent and community engagement.

Curricular Approach and Institute Themes

The curricular approach employed by camp instructors utilized a socially transformative framework. Socially Transformative Curriculum (STC) is a curricular approach introduced by Jomo Mutegi (2011) that roots itself in 5Cs of mastery in an effort to promote critique of Western scientific ideas. The 5Cs include *content, currency, context, critique,* and *conduct.* The first level of mastery, content, speaks most directly to the subject being taught. Then, currency speaks to the relevance of the subject to human beings. Context speaks to the relevance of the subject to African people. Critique speaks to the importance of helping students use their knowledge of the subject to better understand systemic racism. Finally, conduct speaks to the importance of engaging students in a form of activism on behalf of their community. While STC began as a framework for science education, the core principles are drawn from curriculum theorists whose work is applied broadly (Mutegi 2011). Mutegi and colleagues have also applied the model to mathematics education (Pitts Bannister et al. 2017).

GSI is a four-week interdisciplinary camp with a strong focus on improving mathematics achievement. During the first week of camp, girls were administered pre-assessments in mathematics. The pre-assessments were analyzed to determine lesson structure, grouping strategies, and mathematical skills in need of reteaching. While the camp was a STEM camp, the girls spent from sixty to 240 minutes each day on mathematics skills and concepts enrichment, such as mathematical problem solving and computational fluency. The mathematics activities centered on real-life applications and aligned with several Common Core mathematical practices that most notably allowed the girls to model with mathematics, reason abstractly and quantitatively, and critique the reasoning of others.

NCTM's (2000) *Principles and Standards for School Mathematics* called for a deep and fundamental understanding of and proficiency with counting, numbers, and understanding the number system and its structure. An understanding of number and operations remains essential in the Common Core Mathematics Standards. Historically, an understanding of number has served as the cornerstone of the entire mathematics curriculum. Almost all mathematics that students encounter from prekindergarten to grade 12 is grounded in an understanding of number (NCTM 2000, p. 32). An understanding of number and structures serves as a powerful indicator of later mathematics outcomes (e.g., applied problem solving and calculation), and therefore a lack of understanding can have a negative cumulative impact on students' mathematical development (Jordan et al. 2010).

Furthermore, during GSI the mathematics concepts were grounded in socially transformative, real-world, and relevant experiences for participants. Some of the lesson topics were related to financial literacy, virtual and augmented reality, nanotechnology, entrepreneurship, HIV/STD education and prevention, the importance of seeds, and personal nutrition. Typically, the topics were introduced, prior participant knowledge was elicited and shared, and teachers implemented strategies that moved their understanding of these concepts forward mathematically. Figure 2.2 provides a sample agenda for GSI participants during the first three days of the camp.

2016 Girls STEM Institute Summer PROGRAM OVERVIEW
Theme: Health and Wellness in multiple dimensions: (physical, emotional, social, financial, intellectual, & environmental)

WEEK 1 (June 13-17)
Location: ES 1128
8:00-8:20 am each morning is pre-day teacher meeting
8:20 prepare for 8:30 arrivals

DAY/TIME	ACTIVITY/PROJECT DESCRIPTION	SPEAKERS/FIELD TRIPS	RESOURCES needed/provided
MONDAY 9-9:30	Morning Activity-Teacher Choice -. (See WEEK #1 Resources for suggestions.)	Empowerment workshop speaker will arrive at 1:00.	Team Building: Supplies: Spaghetti, tape, marshmallows, timer • Marshmallow Challenge (See link for directions) http://marshmallowchallenge.com/Instructions.html
9:30-11:00	Teambuilding - The Marshmallow Challenge		
11:15-12:15	Break and Lunch (sponsored)		
12:30-1	Financial Simulation Introduction		Financial simulation - see teacher resources Supplies: Student financial portfolio
1:00-3:45	Surviving to Thriving Empowerment workshop – Guest speaker from Wellness Office / Journal reflection		
3:45-4:00	Head to pick up location		
4:00 - 4:30	Teacher debrief and clean up		
TUESDAY 9:00-9:30 AM	Morning Activity-Teacher Choice	Algebra Project -- The Indianapolis Algebra Project (IAP) is a community-based, non-profit math literacy organization that dedicates its energies toward the construction of math competencies among Indiana's students. (http://www.indianapolisalgebraproject.org/) --Community partner will lead learning activities	Unnatural causes DVD and handouts for Place Matters ~ The Mystery: Why are zip code and street address good predictors of population health? Themes: 1. Built space and the social environment have a direct impact on residents' health. 2. Neighborhood conditions can have an indirect impact on health by making healthy choices easy, difficult, or impossible. 3. Public policy choices and private investment decisions shape neighborhood conditions.
9:30-11:00	ALGEBRA PROJECT- community partner		
11:15-12:15	Break and Lunch		
12:30-1:30	Financial Simulation (Finish day one and day two)		
1:30-1:45	Break		
1:45-3:45	Place Matters and journal reflection		
3:40 - 4:00	Head to pick up location		
4:00 - 4:30	Teacher debrief and clean up		
WEDNESDAY 9-9:25 AM	Morning Activity (Teacher choice)	Always Making Progress- AMP's programming is multifaceted in its approach by helping students develop the essential skills needed to improve academic performance and their health. Students are given individual and small group instruction which focuses on each student's academic needs. AMP works closely with students, parents, teachers, and schools to encourage community and familial collaboration (http://www.ampincindy.org/). --AMP will lead learning activities Community nutritionist will lead nutrition workshop	Need food labels for processed chips (i.e. hot fries, Takis, etc..) for nutrition workshop
9:30- 11:00 AM	Always Making Progress Power UP program – Entrepreneurship Workshop		
11:15-12:15	Lunch		
12:30-1:15	Literacy workshop		
1:15-1:30	Break		
1:30-2:35	Nutrition workshop (tracking water, sodium, and sugar intake)		
2:35-2:45	Break		
2:45-3:45	Financial Literacy Simulation		
3:40 - 4:00	Head to pick up location		
4:00 - 4:30	Teacher debrief and clean up		

Fig. 2.2. Part of week one camp overview

Also, to move the participants' understanding forward, teachers developed activities intentionally implemented to build confidence in math. For example, a series of lessons called "Get Your Money Right!" were implemented (with parenthetical and bolded references given here to the relevant 5Cs of mastery). During this series of lessons, camp participants applied problem-solving and computational fluency skills to complete a financial simulation project (**content**). This lesson required participants to further enhance their level of understanding finances by reasoning with equations, interpreting expressions, and creating equations to represent relationships between quantities. Also, participants were able to model with mathematics, reason abstractly and quantitatively, and critique the reasoning of others. As described in figure 2.3, each girl was randomly given an occupation on day one and asked to select her monthly living expenses. She was then asked to set a savings goal for the end of the simulation and create a plan, including a budget, to reach her goal. Throughout the simulations' opportunities for life, upgrades occurred, and random life events (e.g., hospital bills, car accidents, rent increases, home basement flooding) happened. All the young ladies had to assess their budgets and savings goals to determine if upgrades were a financially responsible decision, and some of them had to make budget adjustments to accommodate random life events. The girls were given autonomy in selecting methods for calculating expenses during each task, but most relied on traditional algorithms. This was not a surprise, as the majority of the girls had been introduced to the standard algorithm in school and could accurately implement it. Figure 2.4 displays student work samples of the application of traditional algorithms from a middle school (grade 6) and high school (grade 11) participant. They calculated their monthly salary, living expenses, upgrades to living expenses, and savings goal, and they balanced them with each task. The sixth grader used two strategies to calculate her monthly pay from her biweekly amount. Throughout the simulation, she used multiple strategies as a way to check her calculations while other girls checked their work with a calculator. The eleventh grader used traditional algorithms throughout the simulation as well. For most participants, errors in their calculations stemmed from miswriting values and not from a lack of understanding. For example, when the sixth grader calculated the money left over after subtracting her monthly expenses, she wrote her monthly income as \$1111.54 instead of \$1211.54, which left her with \$100.00 less in her savings for the month. In this case, she did not check her work and never caught her error. It was clear from the simulation that she understood how to add, subtract, multiply, and divide multidigit numbers. We recognized her error was the result of a careless mistake and not from a lack of understanding. In a follow-up conversation, she was encouraged to look back over her work to check for accuracy and to determine the reasonableness of her solutions.

Day 1:

Occupation Choosing

Have students either select an occupation from the pre selected options, or choose a level of education and be assigned an occupation from that category at random.

Students need to record the financial information from their occupation sheet and/ or paycheck stub onto their tracking sheet.

Student loan debt monthly bills are roughly 10% of a paycheck. This is lower than average. (This assumes the students have some scholarships/good grades in high school. This also helps balance the fact that the simulation ends before the typical 10 year payment period for a student loan.)

Choosing Expenses

Students complete the initial expense questions and research expense options or select expenses from a preselected options. Students need to record their choice on their tracking sheet.

Students then can choose additional expenses in the same manner.

Day 2:

Make a Financial Plan

Each student needs to come up a budget, set a goal for the end of the simulation, and create a plan for meeting their goals. All information should be recorded on their on their tracking sheets. Students should calculate the raw amount for each item, as well as the percentage of the budget.

Fig. 2.3. Part of Get Your Money Right! lesson procedures

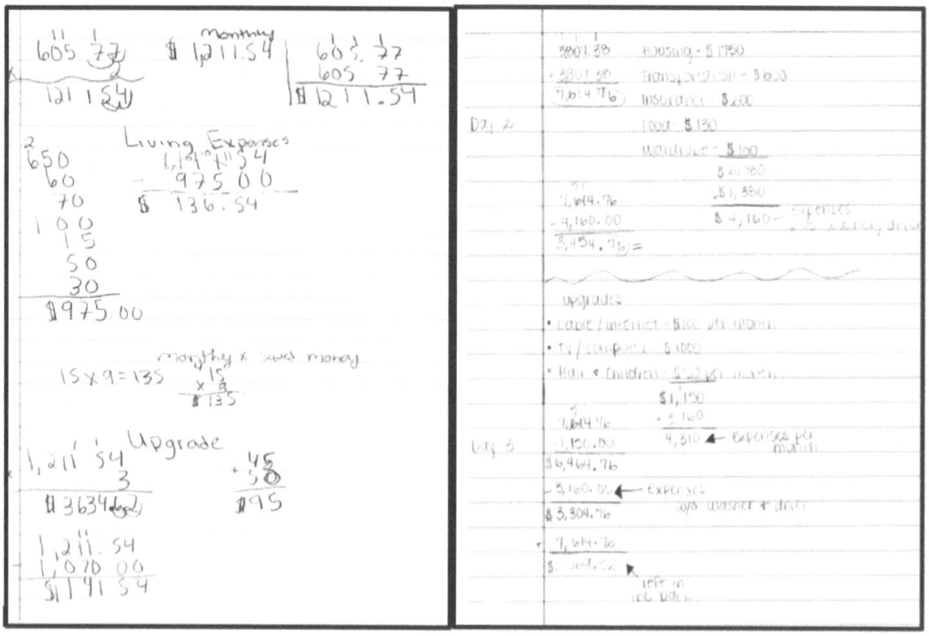

Fig. 2.4. Calculations from Get Your Money Right! from a sixth grader (left)
and an eleventh grader (right)

Throughout the two-week simulation, the girls were asked to reflect on their progress toward their financial goal as well as the progress of their peers (see fig. 2.5). Participants answered questions such as: "Are you making enough money or are you needing more?" "Are you on track to meet your financial goal at the end of the simulation?" "How is your current budget working out for you?" and "What ways could you change for the better?" Those who had lower-paying jobs because of their education levels commented on the importance of completing high school and postsecondary education. Across the spectrum of high- and low-paying jobs, all the girls spoke about the importance of budgeting and saving money to provide for their families. Incorporating time for reflection provided each young lady a space to think about and discuss the importance of financial responsibility, financial wellness, and the impact of educational attainment on their future earning potential.

This simulation was about much more than keeping a household budget (**currency**); it helped young women understand how systemic racism and gender discrimination can serve as barriers to their financial wellness and the financial wellness of their families and communities (**context and critique**). During the simulation, they were introduced to concepts such as income disparities, budgeting, responsible credit usage, banking practices, predatory lending practices, and earning potential based on education level. The goal of the curriculum is to provide a real-life experience that empowers young women with the tools to understand how to better plan for their financial futures and the future of their families and communities (**conduct**).

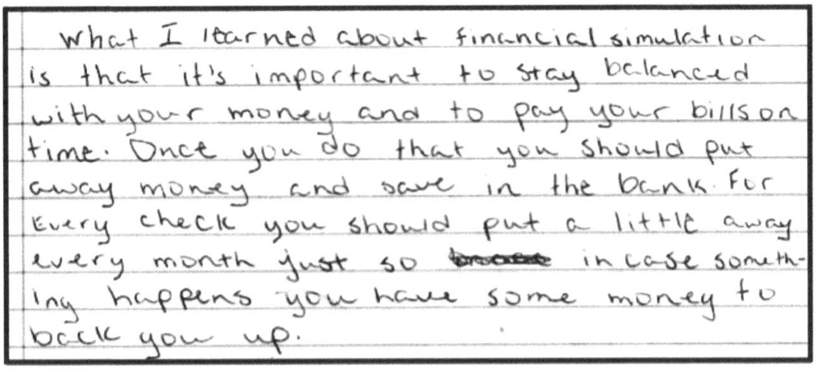

What I learned about financial simulation is that it's important to stay balanced with your money and to pay your bills on time. Once you do that you should put away money and save in the bank. For Every check you should put a little away every month just so ~~because~~ in case something happens you have some money to back you up.

Fig. 2.5. Financial simulation reflection

The mathematical thinking and skills used during the financial simulation were expanded upon through the girls' interactions with the Indy's Algebra Project and with Always Making Progress (AMP). A sample of standards addressed during mathematics enrichment exercises with the Indy's Algebra Project included but were not limited to solving unit rate problems (i.e., unit pricing and constant speed); solving real-world and mathematical problems involving the four operations with rational numbers; and deriving formulas for the sum of a finite geometric series and using the formula to solve problems. When creating business plans as a part of their entrepreneurship development with AMP, GSI participants created budgets, analyzed profit and losses, discussed different investment options, and analyzed return on investments (ROI).

Selection of Staff and Teachers

Secondly, while it is understood that teachers from any ethnic background can effectively and successfully teach Black girls (Cooper 2003; Gay 2000; Ladson-Billings 1994, as cited in Milner 2006, p. 10), fewer than 4 percent of traditional classroom teachers are teachers of color. Additionally, a recent study by Gershenson, Jacknowitz, and Brannegan (2017) found a causal relationship between Black students with exposure to Black teachers and educational attainment. Black students were less likely to drop out and more likely to pursue college when exposed to a Black teacher. GSI leadership was very intentional about hiring program staff who reflect the demographics of the girls served in the Institute. Unlike in many traditional spaces, the teachers and the program manager selected by GSI leaders build culturally informed relationships with participants, and they serve as role models (Milner 2006, p. 93). Both the teachers and the program manager have similar levels of interaction with program participants. The leadership also ensures that participants interact with a diverse range of professionals and community members throughout the program. The access to and interactions with a diverse range of professionals (e.g., teachers, chemists, bankers, nutritionists, engineers, nurses) can inform students' professional decisions and help participants visualize possibilities for their lives.

Prioritization of Parent and Community Engagement

Lastly, GSI prioritizes parent and community engagement because it is understood that it is not enough to support the learning of the Black girl; families and communities must also be engaged for critical systemic and long-term change to occur. Girls STEM Institute's curricular approach, selection of staff and teachers, and prioritization of parent and community engagement, when coupled with an overall holistic approach, provide humanizing experiences for Black girls. These experiences are crucial to fostering positive development of mathematics and science identities.

■ Girls STEM Institute: Study Results

The impact of Girls STEM Institute on Black girls' identity was related to their surroundings and interactions with other girls during the institute, the teachers and staff, and the program curriculum. Some of the major themes emanating from the data included an environment of comfort and care, collaboration and relationships, and confidence and empowerment.

Environment of Comfort and Care

> This is the best camp I've been to because I feel loved and welcomed here instead of like a regular kid who joined a camp. I am glad that I was able to be here because there are no funny-acting teachers, like what I mean everybody is treated the same. —*Janice*

In their interviews and journal entries, participants provided insights into their perception of GSI's environment. Many of the girls echoed Janice's sentiments about the love and hospitality they felt each day. They enjoyed being in the environment and building relationships with caring and compassionate peers and teachers. This environment provided Black girls with an opportunity to learn and engage with mathematics and science while being their authentic selves. They were not worried about being stereotyped and treated differently because they were Black and female. An environment in which teachers care about the learning and overall well-being of students is what Malloy (2009) viewed as important for improving the mathematical understanding and performance of Black students. This sense of comfort the girls felt made it easier for them to build relationships with the teachers and other girls in the program.

Collaboration and Relationships

The camp offered opportunities for the girls to work in collaborative teams to conduct mathematics and science investigations, solve problems, and discuss phenomena. Fortunately, this experience was unlike their traditional school experiences. Veronica shared this during an interview: "I've never been with like a great group of girls. Like last week I felt like I could be myself around them [the girls in the camp] without them making fun of me." The comfortability of the camp environment also translated to increase participants' confidence in advocating for themselves in times of need.

> Like when I guess just being like around some of the girls and then knowing that they don't care if you are wrong or right. They don't care. They share their opinions too. Being around that environment for a while kind of makes you feel like, oh, since they are doing it you can do it too. You don't have to, like, keep all that inside. You can share your opinion about this too. —*Veronica*

Confidence and Empowerment

In their interviews, camp participants also talked about how their participation in the program helped to increase their mathematics and science confidence.

> My confidence increased because the Algebra Project taught us new stuff that we did not cover last year. At first, I didn't understand it, but then it clicked and made sense. They taught us about vectors and other things we have not learned in Algebra 2 or Geometry. So I was able to do material that I will do when school starts. —*Kamilah*

Additionally, several young ladies discussed how their overall confidence was impacted. Many girls shared a perspective similar to Kourtney's:

> I feel like I'm more confident, yeah. I feel like because you guys tell us every day no matter what color you are you can do anything you like. And the people you bring in like that one lady on the first day, she was bullied when was young. Like now she is successful, and you know she is not getting bullied and everybody is looking at her like, you did that? So I feel like the people you bring in and the teachers encourage us to become whatever you want in life. —*Kourtney*

■ What Teachers Think

Teachers and program managers for GSI have unique perspectives on the impact of the program. Teachers acknowledged the need to provide a holistic approach to educating these girls and young women, as well as making sound curricular decisions to engage learners in STEM content. A staff member for GSI, who is a local school district employee, compared her experience in a traditional setting to that of GSI:

> Working in the public school district for years, I am primarily afforded the chance to work with students and parents within the parameters of their educational purposes only. This limitation can sometimes be frustrating and unsatisfying. As it relates to GSI, not only is the student being served educationally and socially, it also encompasses parental participation. Parents, as well as students, are constantly engaged in processes to improve the students and their families. Some examples include parents and students attending leadership and development sessions, fun times with one another with something as simple as bowling, and of course several STEM activities. All of these examples are impactful, because they are inclusive in developing a well-rounded young lady, while also keeping the family involved. —*Ann*

The sentiments shared by Ann are consistent with the literature on Black parent involvement (Winters 1994). Additionally, teachers described the content taught during the camp as curriculum with humanistic value. The camp provided opportunities for teachers to "keep it real," unlike the constraints brought by traditional classroom settings. One instructor from the camp describes one of her most positive experiences:

> One thing I appreciate about the program was the chance to "keep it real." We were able to talk to the ladies about real-life issues in a safe and open environment. The girls learned lessons they could use to improve their academics and their everyday lives as well.

Other instructors shared their thoughts on the appropriateness of the curriculum provided by the camp, as well as the career connections with professionals:

The implementation of culturally relevant curriculum permeated this camp. The students were able to connect with what was being taught, and the faculty knew how to work with them on their level. Not only was the program educational, but it provided many opportunities for the ladies to be influenced by positive role models. The guest speakers allowed the students to glimpse potential careers and ask questions of professional adults. I specifically remember two detectives, a cosmetologist, banker, and two college professors speaking to the students. All of these speakers were of diverse backgrounds, reflecting the students in the program. —*Anissa*

■ Conclusions

Providing key experiences for young Black girls is crucial to fostering positive development of mathematics identity. This study provides a model of a rehumanized approach to learning mathematics for Black girls. Designing and implementing rehumanized mathematics is key for several reasons. First, there is a growing interest in STEM at both the national and international level, as well as the persistence of racial disparities in educational achievement. Secondly, as former math students, we often reflect on our experiences and the experiences of other Black women. This helps us to understand the importance of providing more welcoming opportunities to learn and study mathematics and science. Opportunities such as the Girls STEM Institute are designed to support the positive development of Black girls as learners and doers of mathematics and science. More specifically, the goal of GSI is to provide learners who identify as Black girls an opportunity to develop an understanding of mathematics and other STEM concepts in a meaningful and culturally grounded out-of-school context.

Participants report positive experiences with GSI and its curricular approaches. Some of them return year after year. Some of them bring friends. It is a place where they can be girls. Where they can be students. Where they can be learners of mathematics and feel human! Imagine that!

I am so blessed and honored to be a part of GSI. With its hard work coupled with compassion and tenacity, this is an entity that is truly a caring facility for students and families and its positive impact will be felt for years to come. —*Ann*

Dr. Crystal Morton has truly created a fantastic program that can affect generations of women to come. She and her staff truly cared about the students and treated them with respect and care. Although professional, the environment was relaxed and fun, producing great results. The girls leave valued, cultivated, and educated. —*Anissa*

Positive experiences with mathematics should not be limited to out-of-school programs. Students in mathematics classrooms should be challenged with exploring mathematics through a culturally relevant, socially transformative approach. Teachers can provide these positive and humanizing experiences by developing a strong and sincere rapport with Black girls and their families. It is important for teachers to affirm who Black girls are as mathematics learners. This includes but is not limited to pre-assessing to understand what Black girls know (not what they don't know) (Ladson-Billings 2009). Aguirre, Mayfield-Ingram, and Martin (2013) recommend that teachers *affirm learners' mathematics identity* (i.e., encourage students to see themselves as problem solvers capable of making valuable contributions to mathematics and validate students' knowledge and lived experiences as learners) and leverage *multiple mathematics competencies* (i.e., present mathematical tasks with multiple entry points) (p. 46). This leveraging will provide Black girls the autonomy to use mathematical strategies that they are comfortable using to solve problems. It is also important for teachers to teach mathematics in context for Black learners. Aguirre, Mayfield-Ingram, and Martin (2013) discuss the importance of *challenging spaces of marginality* (i.e., centering students' lived experiences and knowledge as intellectual spaces for exploring mathematical concepts and ideas) (p. 47). The 5Cs framework helps to contextualize mathematics learning experiences. To move beyond content mastery, it is necessary for teachers to integrate authentic learning experiences (i.e., simulations, in-and-out-of-school community-based projects) and experiences that can be extended to their communities.

In addition to mathematics learning experiences, the classroom environment is of equal importance when rehumanizing mathematics. Girls STEM Institute participants benefited from a collaborative, inviting, and supporting space—a space where they developed bonds of sisterhood. It is imperative for teachers to create a community of learners within their classrooms. "Rather than achieving success at the cost of others, success is experienced by individuals only when success is experienced by the class as a whole. In an environment where competitive individualism is not the norm, students are respected for the knowledge they bring to the classroom, and they work together to support, teach and take responsibility for one another" (Wagner et al. 2000, p. 110). It is also essential for school and district administrators to explore ways to increase the number of teachers who reflect the students that they serve. Implementing these strategies can help transform the teaching and learning of mathematics in schools.

Imagine how great it would be to have Black girls talk about their mathematics schooling experiences the way Sophia described her first week at Girls STEM Institute, as shown in figure 2.6.

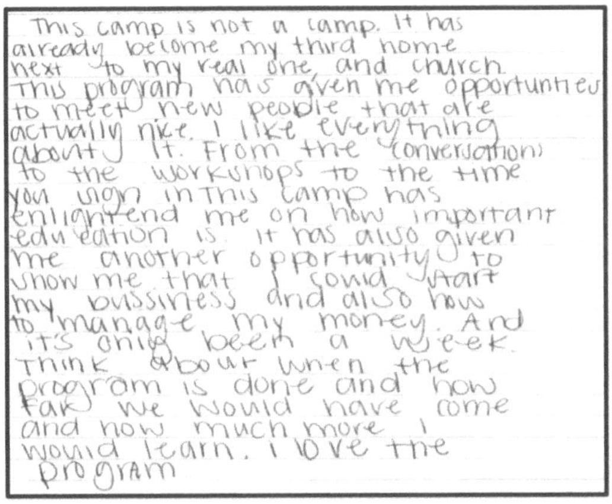

This camp is not a camp. It has already become my third home next to my real one and church. This program has given me opportunties to meet new people that are actually nice. I like everything about it. From the conversations to the workshops to the time you wan in This camp has enlightend me on how important education is. It has also given me another opportunity to show me that I could start my bussiness and also how to manage my money. And it's only been a week. Think about when the program is done and how far we would have come and how much more I would learn. I love the program

Fig. 2.6. Girls STEM Institute journal entry

In order to advance these practices, further work studying the role of out-of-school programs in rehumanizing STEM subjects for students should be explored, as well as an examination made of the longitudinal impact on students' identity and engagement with mathematics.

References

Aguirre, Julia, Karen Mayfield-Ingram, and Danny Martin. *The Impact of Identity in K–8 Mathematics: Rethinking Equity-Based Practices.* Reston, Va.: National Council of Teachers of Mathematics, 2013.

Archer-Banks, Diana, and Linda Behar-Horenstein. "Ogbu Revisited: Unpacking High Achieving African American Girls' High School Experiences." *Urban Education* 47, no. 1 (2012): 198–223.

Berry, Robert, Katheri Thunder, and Oren McClain. "Counter Narratives: Examining the Mathematics and Racial Identities of Black Boys Who Are Successful with School Mathematics." *Journal of African-American Males in Education* 2, no. 1 (2011): 10–23.

Crenshaw, Kimberly. "Mapping the Margins: Intersectionality, Identity Politics, and Violence against Women of Color." *Stanford Law Review* 43 (1991): 1241–99.

Else-Quest, Nicole, Concetta Mineo, and Ashley Higgins. "Math and Science Attitudes and Achievement at the Intersection of Gender and Ethnicity." *Psychology of Women Quarterly* 37, no. 3 (2013): 293–309.

Evans-Winters, Venus. *Teaching Black Girls: Resiliency in Urban Classrooms.* New York: Peter Lang Publishing, 2011.

Gershenson, Seth, Alison Jacknowitz, and Andrew Brannegan. "Are Student Absences Worth the Worry in U.S. Primary Schools?" *Education Finance and Policy* 17, no. 2 (2017): 137–65.

Gholson, Maisie. "Clean Corners and Algebra: A Critical Examination of Constructed Invisibility of Black Girls and Women in Mathematics." *The Journal of Negro Education* 85, no. 3 (2016): 290–301.

Hill, Crystal. "When Traditional Won't Do: Experiences from a 'Lower-Level' Mathematics Classroom." *The Clearing House: A Journal of Educational Strategies, Issues and Ideas* 83, no. 6 (2010): 239–43.

Jordan, Nancy, Joseph Glutting, Chaitanya Ramineni, and Marley Watkins. "Validating a Number Sense Screening Tool for Use in Kindergarten and First Grade: Prediction of Mathematics Proficiency in Third Grade." *School Psychology Review* 39, no 2 (2010): 181–98.

Joseph, Nicole, Kara Viesca, and Margarita Bianco. "Black Female Adolescents and Racism in Schools: Experiences in a Colorblind Society." *The High School Journal* 100 (2016): 4–25.

Joseph, Nicole, Meseret Hailu, and Denise Boston. "Black Women's and Girls' Persistence in the P–20 Mathematics Pipeline: Two Decades of Children, Youth, and Adult Education Research." *Review of Research in Education* 41 (2017): 203–27.

Krishnamurthi, Anita, Melissa Ballard, and Gil G. Noam. "Examining the Impact of Afterschool STEM Programs." Afterschool Alliance. June 30, 2014. https://eric.ed.gov/ ?q=source%3A%22Afterschool%2BAlliance%22&id=ED546628.

Ladson-Billings, Gloria. *The Dreamkeepers: Successful Teachers of African American Children.* 2nd ed. San Francisco: Jossey-Bass Publishers, 2009.

Malloy, Carol. "Instructional Strategies and Dispositions of Teachers Who Help African American Students Gain Conceptual Understanding." In *Mathematics Teaching, Learning, and Liberation in the Lives of Black Children*, edited by Danny Martin, pp. 87–122. New York: Routledge, 2009.

Martin, Danny. "Learning Mathematics While Black." *The Journal of Educational Foundations* (Winter-Spring 2012): 47–66.

McPherson, Ezella. "Informal Learning in Science, Math, and Engineering Majors for African American Female Undergraduates." *Global Education Review* 1, no. 4 (2014): 96–113.

Milner, Richard. "The Promise of Black Teachers' Success with Black Students." *Educational Foundations* 20, no. 3-4 (2006): 89–104.

Morris, Edward. "'Ladies' or 'Loudies'? Perceptions and Experiences of Black Girls in Classrooms." *Youth and Society* 38, no. 4 (2007): 490–515.

Mutegi, Jomo W. "The Inadequacies of 'Science for All' and the Necessity and Nature of a Socially Transformative Curriculum Approach for African American Science Education." *Journal of Research in Science Teaching* 48 (2011): 301–6.

National Council of Teachers of Mathematics (NCTM). *Principles and Standards for School Mathematics.* Reston, Va.: NCTM, 2000.

NAACP Legal Defense and Educational Fund and National Women's Law Center (LDF and NWLC). "Unlocking Opportunity for African American Girls," 2014. https://nwlc.org/resources/unlocking-opportunity-african-american-girls-call-action-educational-equity/.

National Women's Law Center and Girls for Gender Equity. "Listening Session on the Needs of Young Women of Color," 2015. https://nwlc.org/resources/what-young-women-of-color-in-nyc-need/.

Perry, Brea, Tanja Link, Christina Boelter, and Carl Leukefeld. "Blinded to Science: Gender Differences in the Effects of Race, Ethnicity, and Socioeconomic Status on Academic and Science Attitudes among Sixth Graders." *Gender and Education* 24, no. 7 (2012): 1–19.

Pitts Bannister, Vanessa R., Julius Davis, Jomo Mutegi, LaTasha Thompson, and Deborah Lewis. "'Returning to the Root' of the Problem: Improving the Social Condition of African Americans through Science and Mathematics Education." *Catalyst: A Social Justice Forum* 7, no. 1 (2017): Article 2.

Pringle, Rose, Katie Brkich, Thomasenia Adams, Cirecie West-Olatunji, and Diana Archer-Banks. "Factors Influencing Elementary Teachers' Positioning of African American Girls as Science and Mathematics Learners." *School Science and Mathematics* 112 (2012): 217–29.

Smith-Evans, Leticia, Janel George, Fatima Graves, Lara Kaufmann, and Lauren Frohlich. "Unlocking Opportunity for African American Girls: A Call to Action for Educational Equity." *The NAACP Legal Defense and Educational Fund and National Women's Law Center*, 2014. https://nwlc.org/resources/unlocking-opportunity-african-american-girls-call-action-educational-equity/.

Tarmizi, Mohd Ariff Ahmad, Rohani Ahmad Tarmizi, and Mohd Zin Bin Mokhtar. "Humanizing Mathematics Learning: Secondary Students' Beliefs on Mathematics Teachers' Teaching Efficacy." *Procedia—Social and Behavioral Sciences* 8 (2010): 532–6. ISSN 1877-0428, http://dx.doi.org/10.1016/j.sbspro.2010.12.073.

Tate, William. "Race-Ethnicity, SES, Gender, and Language Proficiency in Mathematics Achievement: An Update." *Journal for Research in Mathematics Education* 28 (1997): 652–79.

Walker, Erica. "Why Aren't More Minorities Taking Advanced Math?" *Educational Leadership* 65, no. 3 (2007): 48–53.

_____. *Beyond Banneker: Black Mathematicians and the Paths to Excellence.* New York: SUNY Press, 2014.

Wagner, Lesley, Francine Roy, Elena Ecatoiu, and Celia Rousseau. "Culturally Relevant Mathematics Teaching at the Secondary School Level." In *Changing the Faces of Mathematics: Perspectives on African Americans*, edited by Marilyn Strutchens, Martin Johnson, and William Tate, pp. 107–22. Reston, Va.: NCTM, 2000.

Winters, Wendy Glasgow. "Working with African American Mothers and Urban Schools: The Power of Participation." Paper presented at the Safe Schools, Safe Students Conference: A Collaborative Approach to Achieving Safe, Disciplined and Drug-Free Schools Conducive to Learning, Washington, D.C., 1994. (ERIC Document Reproduction Service No. ED 383959).

CHAPTER 3

Shades of Blackness:
Rehumanizing Mathematics Education through an Understanding of Sub-Saharan African Immigrants

Oyemolade Osibodu, *Michigan State University, East Lansing*

Missy D. Cosby, *Michigan State University, East Lansing*

The mathematics education experiences of Sub-Saharan African (SSA) immigrants in the United States remain under-researched, even as this population continues to increase. As a result of this limited base of research literature, the experiences of African immigrants are often conflated with those of African Americans, a practice that ignores their culture and conceals their African, Black, and immigrant identities. Inspired by characters from novels—Yaa Gyasi's *Homegoing* (2016) and Chimamanda Ngozi Adichie's *Americanah* (2013)—this chapter examines the schooling experiences and the positioning of SSA immigrants in mathematics education as a way to highlight the complexities of attending to multiple versions of Blackness for classroom teachers. Additionally, the first co-author is an African immigrant from Nigeria who has lived in the United States for ten years studying mathematics education and can speak to the experience. The second co-author is an African American high school mathematics teacher discussing her experiences with African immigrant students in her high school. This work seeks to expand our understanding of Blackness and the Black experience in mathematics education and to help teachers see their Black students as more than just a monolithic Black group, encouraging that recognition through the idea of the particularity of the African immigrant experience.

■ Oyemolade's Story

"Algebra, geometry, FOIL, and parentheses." What do these have in common? I first heard these words in 2002 when I emigrated to the U.S. from Nigeria to begin my undergraduate studies. Despite being educated in English while growing up in Nigeria and having English as my primary spoken language, I found myself having to relearn both the vocabulary and the symbology of mathematics in order to communicate in this supposed "universal language." For example, Nigerians (as do most Africans) use brackets to signify both () and [], so this differentiation was also unfamiliar to me. Not only was this mathematics lingo foreign, I had also only studied maths (not math) instead of algebra, geometry, or calculus. These subsets of mathematics did not exist in my primary and secondary school education, given the integrated nature of the curriculum used during my schooling in Nigeria.

Upon arrival at my undergraduate institution in the U.S., my academic advisor recommended that I begin my mathematics requirements with college algebra because she "did not think I could handle calculus," given that my incoming grades appeared quite low after the conversion from the Nigerian system. I am not sure how I found the courage to advocate for myself, but I demanded that I enroll in calculus because I had the appropriate foundation despite what my grades reflected. I was placed on academic probation before I began my course work, but after earning a 4.0 grade point average at the end of my first semester and being placed on the dean's list the probation was lifted. Additionally, several of my cousins who emigrated to the U.S. and enrolled in K–12 schools were held back a grade level because the schools did not believe they could perform at grade level. This experience of being placed **below ability** is not limited to my family's experience; it is a recurring issue as captured by Awokoya and Clark (2008). It was only years later that I realized that we were *racialized*. That is, our identities were made racial through social interactions, positioning, and discourse—because of our skin color (Nasir 2002; Waters 1999). Before coming to the U.S., I had not "believed myself to be Black." (Ta-Nehesi Coates nuances the racial construction by using the phrase "those who believe themselves to be . . ." [Coates 2017].) I was not coming from a racialized society but one that emphasized ethnicity; therefore, my Yoruba identity took precedence over my Blackness.

After completing my undergraduate studies and earning a master's degree in 2010, I relocated to South Africa to teach mathematics at a school with students from about forty-one African countries. As a result of my previous experience, it was important to me that students were placed in the correct level of mathematics class. I trusted students who said they felt prepared to be in an advanced mathematics class because of my prior experience with mathematics placement in the U.S. and from knowing the vastness of mathematics curricula across the continent. Nevertheless, I realize now that I focused primarily on students who exercised agency. I also realize that I made decisions about student placement based on the historical precedence of the student's country of origin. For instance, if a Kenyan student asked to be moved up a level, I was more willing to allow this if prior Kenyan students had succeeded in the course. Both of these practices were problematic.

The students in my class were diverse culturally, linguistically, and mathematically. I allowed students to use the forms of mathematical representation that they learned in their home countries while also ensuring that they knew the representation validated by the Cambridge International Examination—the examining body to whom we were held accountable. Stated a different way, I was allowing students "access to both the culture of power and the power of culture" in mathematics (del Carmen Salazar, 2013, p. 145).

■ On the Need for Shades of Blackness

Statistics from the Pew Research Center (Anderson 2017) state that the African immigrant population is the fastest-growing immigrant population in the U.S., increasing by more than 40 percent from 2000 to 2013, with more than two million African immigrants living in the United States by 2015. More specifically, most members of this growing African immigrant population hail from Sub-Saharan Africa. The number of immigrants from SSA grew by 8 percent from 2014 to 2015 (Hernandez 2012). Considering this increase, and given the dearth of mathematics education research focused on African immigrants in the U.S. save for a few examples (e.g., Staats 2009), we sought to examine the schooling experiences and mathematics learning of these students. In this chapter, we use two works of fiction, *Homegoing* (2016) and *Americanah* (2013), critically acclaimed books written by SSA immigrants centering SSA immigrant experiences in the U.S., as our starting point. Both books address the experiences of SSA immigrant students in U.S. schools by focusing on challenges encountered. These experiences of schooling can inform mathematics educators and mathematics teachers to rehumanize their mathematics experiences, experiences that have been dehumanized by racialization and cultural and linguistic conflation. Phakeng (2017) emphasized that discussions of immigrants in U.S. education tend to prioritize those who are English language learners, yet those who emigrated from primarily English-speaking countries with linguistic and cultural differences also need their stories to be highlighted, especially considering the racialization steeped in anti-blackness they face in the U.S., where racism is endemic (Delgado and Stefancic 2012).

We use the learning experiences of SSA immigrant characters from Yaa Gyasi's *Homegoing* and Chimamanda Ngozi Adichie's *Americanah*, Oyemolade's and Missy's stories, and what little is known from academic literature as means for demonstrating the ways in which African immigrant students have been experiencing mathematics education in the U.S. in dehumanizing ways. Attending to their experiences of racialization and cultural insensitivity, we end with suggestions that are worth considering along with an adaptation of a framework that can be used to better support rehumanization for the mathematics learning experiences of this growing and under-researched population of learners.

■ On Figure Hiding

Homegoing (2016) tells the story of the lineage of two Ghanaian stepsisters: one who lived out her life in Ghana and another who was kidnapped and sold into slavery to the U.S. The tale begins in the eighteenth century during the colonization of Ghana and follows the family lineage of each sister through to the twenty-first century, where two of their descendants meet on a college campus in the U.S. Though *Homegoing* is fiction, it illuminates the complicated lived experiences and the need for nuancing the various "shades of Blackness" of Black people living in the U.S. Likewise, *Americanah* (2013) depicts the story of a Nigerian family emigrating to the U.S. for educational pursuits. It follows the lead character, Ifemelu, on her journey as she experiences racism. Erika Bullock, critical mathematics educator, in her plenary talk at the ninth Mathematics Education and Society conference, proposed the use of intersectionality to avoid what she termed *figure hiding* in our scholarly pursuits on social justice (Bullock 2017). (Her term is a play on the title of the film *Hidden Figures* [Melfi 2016].) Similarly, Mamokgethi Setati Phakeng (2017) stated, "There is diversity among people who share the same race and so focusing only on visible diversity ignores this fact and treats silenced voices as a homogeneous group" (p. 20). To this end, our purpose in this chapter is to use our personal experiences and those of the characters in *Homegoing* and *Americanah* to highlight the figure hiding of SSAs who are Black, African, and immigrants whose cultures are silenced in mathematics classrooms, particularly given the current anti-immigrant climate in the U.S.

■ On African Immigrants in the U.S. Educational System

In *Homegoing* (2016), the character Marjorie is a Ghanaian immigrant in the U.S. Her English teacher, Mrs. Pinkston, asks Marjorie to write a poem about what it means to be African American. The following conversation ensued:

Marjorie: But I'm not African American.

Mrs. Pinkston: Listen, Marjorie, I'm going to tell you something that maybe nobody's told you yet. Here, in this country, it doesn't matter where you came from first to the white people running things. You're here now, and here black is black is black. (Gyasi 2016, p. 273)

While we do not disagree with this classification as Black because we do believe that *there is so much beauty in being Black* (as stated by by Tina Knowles in the "Tina Taught Me" interlude on Solange Knowles's 2016 album *A Seat at the Table*), we highlight the danger of conflating the experiences of African Americans with that of SSA immigrants—experiences that could not be farther apart in reality (Allen, Jackson, and Knight 2012). We use the charge stated by Allen and colleagues (2012) that for "African immigrant students to benefit from pedagogy that is culturally relevant for them, teachers must recognize the diversity among and within people of African descent, particularly in terms of their identities" (p. 3).

Kumi-Yeboah and Smith (2016) investigated the school learning experiences of sixty Ghanaian immigrants attending an urban public school and found that a number of factors contributed to their academic experiences. Though Ghanaian immigrant students conveyed various views of their U.S. schooling experiences, they expressed that teachers would often categorize them as African American, as in Marjorie's story in *Homegoing* (Kumi-Yeboah and Smith 2016; Gyasi 2016). Here we see an example of figure hiding—though they are receiving some mathematics support, their cultures are not highlighted and epistemologies not attended to in their mathematics learning. With regards to mathematics learning, specifically, the Ghanaian immigrants referenced being successful in mathematics in the U.S. because of their Ghanaian mathematics learning experiences. One student stated "I would say that I have good grades in all of my science courses and mathematics because I studied most of the topics in Ghana before coming to the States. I have good grades in school because I work hard and want [*sic*] to proof [*sic*] to those who made fun of me when I first came to the States wrong" (Kumi-Yeboah and Smith 2016, p. 13). Here, this student utilizes some of the advanced aspects of the Ghanaian mathematics curricula to his advantage.

SSA immigrants have at times been viewed as needing special education services and may also be pushed back one grade level (Awokoya and Clark 2008), as captured in Oyemolade's story. In *Americanah* (2013), the main protagonist is a Nigerian woman who came to the U.S. to study and who lived briefly with her aunt and nephew, who had emigrated some years before when her nephew, Dike, was just a baby. Adichie recounts a story where Aunty Uju and Ifemelu discussed a phone call from Dike's middle school teacher recommending him for special education services due to his "aggression." Aunty Uju refused, because she felt that Dike was being singled out as one of only two Black children in the entire school and because she had been warned by a fellow African immigrant mother that this would happen.

Adichie (2013) also speaks to the notion of mathematics education being more advanced in Nigerian schooling than it is in the United States through dialogue between Ifemelu and Dike. The conversation progresses as follows:

Once, she [Ifemelu] asked Dike what he had done in school before summer, and he said "Circles." They would sit on the floor in a circle and share their favorite things. She was appalled. "Can you do division?" He looked at her strangely. "I'm only in first grade, Coz." When I was your age I could do simple division. (p. 138)

Ifemelu found it silly that Dike's teacher had given students homework coupons and that he was not learning more advanced mathematics, so she spent the rest of that summer teaching him *maths*. She focused on long division and made sure he was proficient, because she believed he would have learned it by this point had he been in Nigeria. In fact, Ifemelu had very strong views on American education in general. She stated that "American children learned nothing in elementary school" (p. 138). As a result of this interaction, Dike later found mathematics to be easy and attributed this change to his summer experience with Ifemelu. Though we know that the American elementary experience can be quite valuable, this point was used to illustrate Ifemelu's perspective. Recognizing that *Americanah* is fiction, we use this narrative as an illustrative example of what Kumi-Yeboah and Smith (2016) highlighted earlier: The ways that mathematics is taught in both Nigeria and Ghana are not necessarily deficient but, in some ways, are more advanced. This story also shows the high level of standards held and is a counternarrative to the racialization and deficit mindset approach that colors many of the SSA immigrant experiences previously described.

■ On Rehumanizing Educational and Mathematics Learning Experiences

According to Freire (2003), humanizing pedagogy has the power to alter and change oppressive systems such as those found in schools. This can only happen if the pedagogy builds upon students' cultural and linguistic repertoires, centers student experiences, focuses on raising students' critical awareness and higher-order thinking skills, and emphasizes trust between the teacher and students (Zisselsberger 2016). However, Black people (a racial categorization that includes members of the African diaspora) in the U.S. are continually dehumanized in their interactions with social institutions such as schooling (Langer-Osuna and Nasir 2016). It can be argued that Black students and, even more so, SSA immigrants have been coerced to divest themselves of their cultural resources and assimilate in order to succeed in U.S. public schools, as is also the case with Mexican immigrant students (del Carmen Salazar 2013). In order for this to change, we must consider the role of race, culture, and identity in education and must include the ways in which society has functioned to dehumanize those who have been considered "Other." Schools and education must be viewed as sites of rehumanization where high expectations are held for Black students in conjunction with a caring and supportive environment as students learn to deal with racism and racialization in broader society (Langer-Osuna and Nasir 2016).

■ Missy's Story

"It's clear that we have some white classes and some brown classes in this school." As the only African American teacher at this high school, I was taken aback when I heard this comment. It came from a White colleague at the suburban area high school where I currently teach mathematics in response to her spending several days observing teachers throughout the building. During my seventeen years of teaching there I have worked with students from many backgrounds, including a number of students from Nigeria, Ethiopia, Cameroon, Uganda, and Zimbabwe. I have observed that these students are rarely placed in advanced or honors track mathematics courses and that those who are placed in on-level mathematics courses are moved into the remedial track at some time throughout their tenure in high school.

The dehumanization, racialization, and devaluing of their cultural funds of knowledge (Moll et al. 1992) begins at enrollment, as parents and students are left with no other option to select for race and ethnicity categories other than to mark "African American." These placement experiences both racialize African immigrant students and/or make them invisible as learners with distinct characteristics and cultural needs. When it comes time to select the student's schedule and mathematics class, the counselor asks to see a transcript from any previous schooling and uses that to select the mathematics course. This is not always easy, because courses in Cameroon or Nigeria are not always delineated by content (algebra, geometry, precalculus, etc.), as was evident in Oyemolade's story. Courses at this high school are not only classified by content, they are also stratified by level (remedial, on-level, honors, advanced placement). This makes for a confusing selection process that culminates with having the parents and students look through a series of textbooks used at the high school to decide which content the student is familiar with. Again, when an integrated approach is taken in another country and not at the receiving school, it is quite possible that chunks of familiar content will be scattered throughout several texts, leaving the parent, the student, and the counselor with a dilemma. The resolution is usually to place the student in a mathematics course that is below their needed level so as to not overwhelm them. For example, if a student is placed in geometry and encounters a mathematics problem that requires factoring, content learned in a previous algebra course, this student is seen as not having the necessary prerequisite skills. Many of my colleagues have not resorted to culturally sensitive ways of resolving issues like this. It is simply recommended that the student is misplaced and they are then moved to a lower-level course.

I recall having one Cameroonian student, Abeni (a pseudonym), for whom this was the case. She and her parents were devastated by her being told that she "could not handle" the mathematics in her geometry honors course. Everything that she had previously believed about herself as a confident mathematics learner was being challenged in this new cultural context as she was moved from geometry honors into my geometry class. Due to my previous conceptions of the general experiences of African immigrant students in this school context, I did my very best to work with her and her parents and help her to see her strengths as a mathematics learner. This included providing multiple and varied opportunities to assess her mathematics knowledge; open and regular communication with both her and her parents via phone, email, and parent-teacher conferences; and using teaching methods such as the flipped classroom model that allowed for an increase in class time spent talking with students about mathematical ideas. In a card given to me at the end of year, she wrote, "Thanks for helping me do much better in math than I had thought possible and for not making me feel stupid." It was all that I could do to keep from crying, knowing that the previous ordeal had made a student who previously saw herself as a competent mathematics learner "feel stupid."

Having taught my entire career at this high school, it would be quite easy to begin to operate under the myth of meritocracy and the veil of whiteness. It would also be quite easy for me to have projected an African American sense of Blackness onto the SSA immigrant students as well. Though I cannot be certain, I do not think that I did this for Abeni. If anything, I might have invited Abeni to attend a Black Student Union (BSU) meeting not fully recognizing that those gatherings largely address issues of being Black in the U.S. context. This is not to say that she should not have attended a BSU meeting, but perhaps I could have also guided her in forming an African Student Alliance with the other SSAs at the high school. Over the years, I have worked to be more self-reflective and aware of my own projection of Blackness onto students. I also ask many questions of my students and their parents in an effort to better understand their needs and perspectives. Furthermore, I ask questions of my colleagues to challenge their assumptions and to prompt them to consider the impact of our policies and procedures. This, I believe, is a step in the right direction to combatting the racialization of SSA immigrant students and others. Though change is difficult and slow, it is for Abeni and many other students with similar stories that I continue to push for changes within our current system and rehumanizing the process.

■ On Shading Blackness: Toward Rehumanizing Mathematics Education for SSA Immigrant Students

Does life imitate art or does art imitate life? As we read Gyasi's *Homegoing* and Adichie's *Americanah*, we reflected on our own experiences as an SSA immigrant learning mathematics in the U.S. and as an African American person teaching mathematics to SSA immigrants. The stories and experiences shared in these novels brought issues of racialization and cultural insensitivity in U.S. schooling to the forefront. We turned to mathematics education literature for empirical documentation of these experiences even though, as we mentioned earlier, there is a dearth of research in mathematics education in the U.S. related to the experiences of SSA immigrants. We find this to be problematic because of this group's intersectional identities as Black, African, and immigrant. To avoid *figure hiding* (Bullock 2017), it is important that we, as a scholarly community, strongly consider this group, given its prominent identity triad. Other research has shown that this population is vulnerable in U.S. schooling (Allen, Jackson, and Knight 2012; Awokoya and Clark 2008; Kumi-Yeboah and Smith 2016; Njue and Retish 2010), so there is reason to believe that they are not being well served in mathematics education. Recall that in *Homegoing*, Marjorie's teacher stated that "black is black is black," and although we agree with this statement in the U.S. context, having this attitude is problematic because it hides the rich and distinct cultures of this diverse population given the many shades of Blackness that exist. These shades of Blackness come from the creation of African diasporas resulting from both immigration and the Trans-Atlantic slave trade (e.g., SSA immigrants, Afro-Caribbeans, Afro-Latinx, Jamaican Americans). Although our goal in writing this chapter is to point out the figure hiding of SSA immigrants in mathematics education research in the U.S., we offer a few suggestions for classroom teachers and researchers as we seek to rehumanize mathematics education for these students.

First, the U.S. education system employs a narrow view of citizenship that trickles down into the mathematics classroom. For example, according to Bajaj and Bartlett (2017), U.S. social studies classes are focused on preparing all students (including immigrants) to be citizens, not of their country, but of the U.S. This, in turn, affects classroom discourse, where students like Marjorie are seen only as American Black and thus are stripped of their citizenship and all that it entails. Second, it needs to be acknowledged that schooling in the U.S. context is normed to White, middle-class values with a focus on standards, including high-stakes testing, and assumes that most or all students are college bound (Bajaj and Bartlett 2017). As such, symbology is normed and many other ways of knowing and representing mathematical ideas are marginalized, including the integrated curricula previously experienced by many SSA immigrant students. In order to better serve SSA immigrants and all students, a rethinking of the foundational assumptions of U.S. schooling is in order (Bajaj and Bartlett 2017). Milner (2007) conceptualized a framework for educational researchers engaged in research centering race and culture. We posit that aspects of this framework are applicable for research and practice in mathematics education.

It could aid in thinking about these fundamental assumptions in mathematics education, what is normalized, and whose epistemologies matter. Milner's framework suggests the following: *researching the self, researching the self in relation to others, engaged reflection,* and *shifting from self to the system.* Taking each in turn, we conclude by examining the role that these concepts could potentially play in the rehumanization of mathematics learning experiences for SSA immigrants.

Researching the self and the self in relation to others could be both for individual mathematics educators and researchers as well as for the broader mathematics education community as a whole. This could consist of a deepening of one's knowledge of their own race and culture and of those in the communities they endeavor to educate (Milner 2007). For the mathematics community, more broadly, this includes exploring the ways in which it is racialized, gendered, and exclusionary, contrary to the widely accepted notion of neutrality with regard to race and culture (Joseph, Hailu, and Boston 2017). The dialectical process of researching the self and the self in relation to others serves to acquire the cultural knowledge necessary to accurately interpret the experiences and expressed commentary of SSA immigrant students and to disrupt deficit discourses and the practices operationalized by them. Consider Missy's story: As an African American teacher, part of what was necessary was for her to reject the *black is black is black* narrative, explore her own positionality, and address the ways in which her student's experiences were markedly different in order to better serve her. Operationalized, this could look similar to Oyemolade's demonstration of advocacy, without which dehumanizing practices would continue.

Engaged reflection would require mathematics educators and members of the broader mathematics education community to create opportunities to work together with the members of various communities that they serve—in this case, SSA immigrant students and families—in order to understand their experiences and their shades of Blackness. These voices and perspectives, their counterstories, should deepen the understanding of their experiences and the ways in which they are racialized, dehumanized, and marginalized (Milner 2007). Such validation for their counter-stories helps to decenter the normalized voice, no longer privileging one over the other (Solorzano and Yosso 2001). Therefore, this would allow mathematics educators and mathematics teachers alike to explicate the experiences of SSAs, thus avoiding the "danger of a single story" (Adichie 2009) and creating awareness of the varied shades of Blackness that exist. Additionally, the connection to parents and families would provide opportunities to draw on their funds of knowledge (Moll et al. 1992) and enrich the mathematics learning experiences for all.

When **shifting from self to the system** or from the individual classroom level to widespread practice and policy, there are a myriad of considerations, such as curricula, student placement and tracking, and referrals to special education, as was mentioned in Adichie's *Americanah* and elsewhere. Bajaj and Bartlett (2017) posit that a critical transnational curriculum could address the problems encountered by immigrant students. As such, they promote the inclusion of heterogeneous grouping, inquiry-based learning, a social justice orientation, and building on culturally relevant and sustaining pedagogies. As Bajaj and Bartlett (2017) note, "Pedagogies are deeply cultural" (p. 29). Therefore, even the use of pedagogies such as social justice mathematics, project-based learning, and inquiry-based learning have cultural elements that are often unfamiliar to SSAs. As a result, mathematics educators and teachers need to be mindful of this. Furthermore, Bajaj and Bartlett suggest avoiding tracking in order to allow immigrants to thrive. Thus, schools like the one where Missy teaches should embrace diversity as a valuable tool for students to express their unique identities and in order to allow for an easier transition. Moreover, the students should be allowed the opportunity and space to develop projects related to their cultural contexts.

Another consideration would be for schools to amass a small library of textbooks from other countries. As in Missy's story, students were asked to look through the school's textbooks to help decide placement. However, exploration of and familiarity with textbooks and curricula from other countries could only serve to expand the knowledge base of mathematics educators, allow them to understand mathematical symbology and nomenclature in these countries, and aid them in understanding and promoting broader engagement in mathematics.

■ On Embracing Sankofa

Sankofa is a word from the Twi people of Ghana that roughly means "going back to retrieve what was lost" (Temple 2010; Watson and Knight-Manuel 2017). In this chapter, we embraced the spirit of Sankofa by reflecting on our past experience as an SSA immigrant mathematics student in the U.S. (Oyemolade) and an African American teacher of SSA immigrant mathematics students (Missy) to inform the mathematics education community of the dehumanizing ways SSAs have experienced mathematics in the U.S. Our expressed purpose was to use our personal experiences, those from the characters in *Homegoing* and *Americanah,* and existing empirical research to highlight the figure hiding of SSAs living at the intersection of Black, African, and immigrant, whose cultures are silenced in mathematics classrooms. Drawing on literature from sociology and educational research, more broadly, we were able to illustrate some ways in which SSA immigrant students with English proficiency experience the U.S. schooling context, though we do not know nearly enough about how they experience mathematics learning. As we look forward, we hope to conduct an empirical study with SSAs having English proficiency—heeding Phakeng's (2017) call—in Missy's school to add to this body of literature. Given that our goal is to further rehumanize SSAs' experiences, we will embrace humanizing research (Paris 2011) methodologies that emphasize the "building of relation-ships of care and dignity for both researchers and participants" (p. 140). To further nuance the dis-cussion, Watson and Knight-Manuel (2017) also indicate that teachers have placed SSAs as "Black model minorities," and we seek to uncover this practice in our study. For us, this practice of creating a chasm between SSAs and their African American counterparts adds to the dehumanization of mathematical experiences and should be addressed in this work.

In closing, we purport that shades of Blackness is essentially doing intersectional work. Kimberlé Crenshaw, a legal studies and intersectionality scholar, expressed it well when she stated that "treating different things the same can generate as much inequality as treating the same things differently" (Crenshaw 1997, p. 285). Therefore, it is important that we acknowledge the Black, African, and immigrant identities that SSA immigrant students hold and endeavor to unhide them, thus rehumanizing their mathematics learning.

References

Adichie, Chimamanda Ngozi. "The Danger of a Single Story." TED Talk, Oxford, England (2009).

_____. *Americanah.* New York: Anchor Books, 2013.

Allen, Keisha McIntosh, Iesha Jackson, and Michelle G. Knight. "Complicating Culturally Relevant Peda-gogy: Unpacking West African Immigrants' Cultural Identities." *International Journal of Multicultural Education* 14, no. 2 (2012): 1–28.

Anderson, Monica. "African Immigrant Population in U.S. Steadily Climbs." Pew Research Center *Fact Tank Blog,* February 14, 2017. http://www.pewresearch.org/fact-tank/2017/02/14/african-immigrant-population-in-u-s-steadily-climbs/.

Awokoya, Janet Tolulope, and Christine Clark. "Demystifying Cultural Theories and Practices: Locating Black Immigrant Experiences in Teacher Education Research." *Multicultural Education* 16, no. 2 (2008): 49–58.

Bajaj, Monisha, and Lesley Bartlett. "Critical Transnational Curriculum for Immigrant and Refugee Students." *Curriculum Inquiry* 47, no. 1 (2017): 25–35.

Bullock, Erika C. "Beyond 'ism' Groups and Figure Hiding: Intersectional Analysis and Critical Mathematics Education." In *Proceedings of the Ninth International Mathematics Education and Society Conference,* pp. 29–44. Volos, Greece: University of Thessaly Press, 2017.

Coates, Ta-Nehisi. "Revisiting the Case for Reparations" [Lecture]. The World Lecture Series, East Lansing, Michigan, April 3, 2017.

Crenshaw, Kimberlé Williams. "Color Blindness, History, and the Law." In *The House that Race Built*, edited by Wahneema Lubiano, pp. 280–88. New York: Pantheon, 1997.

del Carmen Salazar, María. "A Humanizing Pedagogy: Reinventing the Principles and Practice of Education as a Journey Toward Liberation." *Review of Research in Education* 37, no. 1 (2013): 121–48.

Delgado, Richard, and Jean Stefancic. *Critical Race Theory: An Introduction*. New York: NYU Press, 2012.

Freire, Paulo. *Pedagogy of the Oppressed*. New York: Continuum, 2003.

Gyasi, Yaa. *Homegoing*. New York: Knopf, 2016.

Hernandez, Donald J. "Changing Demography and Circumstances for Young Black Children in African and Caribbean Immigrant Families." Washington, D.C.: Migration Policy Institute, 2012.

Joseph, Nicole M., Meseret Hailu, and Denise Boston. "Black Women's and Girls' Persistence in the P–20 Mathematics Pipeline: Two Decades of Children, Youth, and Adult Education Research." *Review of Research in Education* 41, no. 1 (2017): 203–27.

Kumi-Yeboah, Alex, and Patriann Smith. "Cross-Cultural Educational Experiences and Academic Achievement of Ghanaian Immigrant Youth in Urban Public Schools." *Education and Urban Society* (2016).

Langer-Osuna, Jennifer M., and Na'ilah Suad Nasir. "Rehumanizing the 'Other' Race, Culture, and Identity in Education Research." *Review of Research in Education* 40, no. 1 (2016): 723–43.

Melfi, Theodore, director. *Hidden Figures* [motion picture]. Los Angeles: 20th Century Fox, 2016.

Milner, H. Richard, IV. "Race, Culture, and Researcher Positionality: Working through Dangers Seen, Unseen, and Unforeseen." *Educational Researcher* 36, no. 7 (2007): 388–400.

Moll, Luis C., Cathy Amanti, Deborah Neff, and Norma Gonzalez. "Funds of Knowledge for Teaching: Using a Qualitative Approach to Connect Homes and Classrooms." *Theory into Practice* 31, no. 2 (1992): 132–41.

Nasir, Na'ilah Suad. "Identity, Goals, and Learning: Mathematics in Cultural Practice." *Mathematical Thinking and Learning* 4, no. 2–3 (2002): 213–47.

Njue, John, and Paul Retish. "Transitioning: Academic and Social Performance of African Immigrant Students in an American High School." *Urban Education* 45, no. 3 (2010): 347–70.

Paris, Django. "'A Friend Who Understand Fully': Notes on Humanizing Research in a Multiethnic Youth Community." *International Journal of Qualitative Studies in Education* 24, no. 2 (2011): 137–49.

Phakeng, Mamokgethi Setati. "Visible and Invisible Diversity in Academic Publishing." *For the Learning of Mathematics,* 37, no. 1 (2017): 19–20.

Solorzano, Daniel G., and Tara J. Yosso. "Critical Race and LatCrit Theory and Method: Counter-Storytelling." *International Journal of Qualitative Studies in Education* 14, no. 4 (2001): 471–95.

Staats, Susan. "Somali Mathematics Terminology: A Community Exploration of Mathematics and Culture." In *Multilingualism in Mathematics Classrooms: Global Perspectives*, edited by Richard Barwell, pp. 32–46. Bristol, U.K.: Multilingual Matters, 2009.

Temple, Christel N. "The Emergence of Sankofa Practice in the United States: A Modern History." *Journal of Black Studies* 41, no. 1 (2010): 127–50.

Waters, Mary C. *Black Identities: West Indian Immigrant Dreams and American Realities*. Cambridge, Mass.: Harvard University Press, 2009.

Watson, Vaughn W. M., and Michelle G. Knight-Manuel. "Challenging Popularized Narratives of Immigrant Youth from West Africa: Examining Social Processes of Navigating Identities and Engaging Civically." *Review of Research in Education* 41, no. 1 (2017): 279–310.

Zisselsberger, Margarita Gomez. "Toward a More Humanizing Pedagogy: Leveling the Cultural and Linguistic Capital of Students in a Fifth-Grade Writing Classroom." *Bilingual Research Journal* 39, no. 2 (2016): 121–37.

CHAPTER 4

We Fear No Number:
Humanizing Mathematics Teaching and Learning for Black Girls

Nicole M. Joseph, *Vanderbilt University, Nashville, Tennessee*
Norman V. Alston, *eMode Learning Foundation, Seattle, Washington*

Black girls' experiences in mathematics remain invisible and largely untheorized. Their intersectional identities and collective historical experience with interlocking systems of oppression in United States society render their experiences important for understanding dehumanization and how we might reconstruct humanizing pedagogy. This invisibility results in obscurity for most mathematics education researchers, teachers, and anyone else interested in improving Black girls' educational outcomes. One of the co-authors, Norman V. Alston, founder of Seattle-based eMode, works to tackle the deficit-laden messages Black girls often receive in school mathematics. In this chapter, we will incorporate interviews of Alston and of a focus group of five Black girls who have participated in eMode for one to five years. We will describe his unorthodox teaching practices, where he models unequivocal faith, love, and care for the Black girls participating in eMode. Their stories reveal his strong mathematical knowledge coupled with emancipatory pedagogies that promote deep meaning-making of mathematics and Black culture. Due in part to their participation, eMode Black girls resist assimilation while navigating an oppressive public school system. These are dispositions necessary to teach social justice and mathematics. Aiming to humanize the research process, we amplify Black girls' voices and highlight how their experiences in eMode help us better understand rehumanization in mathematics spaces for underrepresented groups.

■ How and Where We Enter

We are Black mathematicians, mathematics teachers, and mathematics educators committed to critical and transformative scholarship and teaching. Together, we bring over forty years of mathematics teaching of Black students in many different settings, mainly low-income and underresourced schools. Our interests merged in 1999 when we first met (it was Sister Nicole's first teaching job) and began teaching side by side at Zion Preparatory Academy, founded by the religious leader Bishop E. Drayton, pastor of the Zion United House of Prayer. Zion was a faith-based education program for primarily low-income African American students, and we taught with the conviction that all Black children could learn mathematics. Zion's mission was to ensure academic excellence in a supportive

Afrocentric, Christian-based environment whereby Black children could realize their fullest potential, with integrity, and become responsible and contributing members of society. Although there were many students who had been turned away from public schools, we were trained to leave no student behind regardless of their circumstances. Zion believed in every child.

Over the years, we deepened our mathematics content knowledge, attended mathematics conferences, eventually became frequent facilitators of professional development for other teachers—inside and outside of Zion—and even became Washington State Supplemental Service providers for mathematics enrichment, running summer camps in Alston's parents' church basement. We commonly refer to each other as "brother" and "sister" for two important reasons: We have a shared cultural and spiritual experience teaching at a faith-based institution, and we are part of a collective history that has specific significance in the U.S. because we are "descendants of slaves" who had their identities stolen from them during one of the most horrific holocausts in world history. In an effort to provide ourselves with some semblance of unity and solidarity where our ancestors were held hostage, we have adopted each other as brother and sister.

It has been eighteen years since our first meeting, and we have chosen different pathways but remain connected through our belief in the importance of centering Black children and their experiences in mathematics. I (Brother Alston) have watched Sister Nicole's career skyrocket in part because of her love and devotion for our people and her unrelenting mission to (*a*) improve mathematics education for Black girls and women by challenging metanarratives and stereotypes that position them as inferior and deficient and (*b*) reclaim Black women's and girls' math identities to include valued Black femininities and intersecting identities coupled with strong math content knowledge. And I (Sister Nicole) have watched Brother Alston engage in "boots on the ground" transformative work with Black children. He regularly demonstrates their genius, and he guides them to fall in love with learning while helping them to see themselves as conscious and critical learners of mathematics. Brother Alston teaches in community classrooms, classrooms that are outside of the four walls of schools, whereby he can practice steadfastness with Black children and their families in deep cultural ways.

After spending twelve years in the K–12 education system as a math teacher and instructional math coach, I, Sister Nicole, took the path of an education researcher in higher education, taking up an agenda about the underrepresentation of Black women and girls in mathematics and the roles that race, gender, and interlocking systems of oppression play in shaping their underrepresentation. I, Brother Alston, simply chose to confine myself exclusively to teaching mathematics to children outside of formal schooling. The "e" in eMode—represents the mode in which I teach by engagement, enrichment, and experiential learning. This mode undergirds my teaching philosophy regarding mathematics (enrichment) because it allows my students and me to experience the elegant majesty and mystery of what it means to do mathematics.

When we saw the theme for this volume of *Annual Perspectives in Mathematics Education* (*APME*), we both immediately thought about coauthoring a chapter. We draw from research and personal experience in humanizing mathematics experiences for Black students, and we have compelling evidence and examples of ways to reach, teach, and transform mathematics learning for Black girls. We know that our shared understandings about these issues influenced the design of our study. When Sister Nicole called me to share the theme of the call, I immediately told her that my Saturday class this year had a majority of Black girls and that examining their experiences would make for an important study that could contribute to this *APME* volume.

Together, we decided that Nicole would interview me to unpack how my teaching philosophy and pedagogies illuminate conceptualizations of humanizing pedagogies (Freire 1970). We also decided that it would be important to hear the voices of the girls through a focus group in order to triangulate our data. Thus, we do this work committed to illuminating Black girls' intersectional experiences and agency in mathematics, where they fear no number. "Fear no number" is a metaphorical way to show that these young ladies act upon the world with confidence while learning math at eMode. The epigraph below is followed by Brother Alston speaking about his early experiences with mathematics. For the remaining sections of the chapter, we write from Nicole's perspective as she interviews Brother Alston and provide perspectives gained from the focus group of eMode students.

> I have always loved learning. My father taught me that. But school tried to destroy it and drive it out of me. So I learned to figure things out on my own, at home away from teachers. Serving children is my life's work, and only by death will I ever retire.
> —*Norman V. Alston*

I never learned to read at school. My father taught me how to read at age three, so by the time I was four years of age, I was a very fluent reader. Daddy spent a lot of time teaching me phonics, and he had me reading words in the dictionary, big words all the time. At age five, I went to kindergarten, and I can distinctly remember that I was reading on a second- or third-grade level easily. I went to school a confident young Black man prepared to be a great student. Early on I was touted as being "smart." Reading with my father instilled this in me. My ability to read, and comprehend what I had read, gave me a great sense of confidence and competence. I saw myself as being able and accomplished. Being called upon to read aloud was very affirming. However, knowing for myself that I was smart was really the intrinsic feedback that I valued most. In third grade, something traumatic happened in school. I remember coming into my classroom at Madrona Elementary School at the corner of 33rd and Union. I went in the classroom, and we had to stand behind our chairs, our backpacks still on, and we couldn't be seated until we answered a multiplication fact. I'm almost sixty years of age and I remember this vividly. My teacher asked me what three times three was. I didn't like playing that game because I felt like if you made a mistake you would get laughed at so I didn't want to answer too quickly. I paused to "think" and she started making comments about how I should have quickly known that basic fact! She laughed at me, and the other students joined in the laughter. She went on to the next person as I stood there feeling humiliated. At that moment, at that very precise moment in time, I began to hate school and not like to participate in mathematics. I liked mathematics. I liked learning. But I decided at that very moment in time, I could not learn at school. I became instantly convinced that schools were not a safe place for me to learn anything. I withdrew, made myself small, but I reckoned that if I would learn anything, I could only learn it at home away from schools and especially away from teachers.

■ The Mission of eMode Foundation Acts as Critical Praxis of Humanizing Pedagogy

The previous section demonstrates Brother Alston's lived experiences of dehumanization in mathematics classrooms that later served as the impetus for his thirty-year career teaching mathematics to "little Black and Brown brothers and sisters" in ways that aim to humanize the learning of mathematics. I asked Brother Alston how he might respond to the "Where is the mathematics?" question that is so prevalent in the mathematics education community, and he stated:

So I actually think when I go to teach mathematics on a Saturday for three hours, that—and the demographic that I'm serving, I mean, again, a lot of the females, African American girls, that that is social justice work. When I talk to them [the Black girls] about mathematics, I don't let them whisper at me or give me a quiet answer . . . I need boldness from you. I need a big voice from you. As I'm teaching mathematics in that context on a Saturday, I'm doing social work with mathematics as a backdrop, meaning I'm coaching these girls to have a voice, to be independent, to know how to debate and to argue, and they come to understand that debate and argument is a form of logic and it's a form of getting to proof and understanding and clarity. By debate and discourse we use mathematics as a tool. I'm equipping African American girls to do mathematics and to be strong mathematicians when nobody else is in such an environment apart from their normal school experience.

Brother Alston views his teaching as grounded in mathematics content, mathematics processes, and social justice simultaneously, and this quote suggests that he is engaging Black girls in their liberation through mathematics. He understands that the school system will not equip them to think critically about how to name oppressive conditions affecting their own lives, their communities, and the world. Brother Alston does not just teach mathematics, he brings it to life and inspires a love for learning. This quote also suggests that he reclaims the social stereotypes about Black girl femininity—being loud and independent (Epstein, Blake, and González 2017)—to show them that such qualities as "a big voice" are valued while learning math.

With more than two decades of teaching mathematics after many years of self-study in algebra, calculus, physics, and all things numerical, Brother Alston dedicates his life to Black children. eMode is his nonprofit organization dedicated to providing math enrichment to children in kindergarten through fifth grade, focusing especially on those from underserved communities. Brother Alston is a teacher-activist who begins with the belief that children are highly capable in math, promoting the idea that they can learn and enjoy learning math well beyond their grade level by using active thinking and cooperative learning. Coupled with active thinking and cooperative learning, Brother Alston helps Black girls develop early numerical literacy and love of math through fun and culturally relevant programs. This mission serves as a strategy for doing humanizing and social justice work that is also critical praxis (Collins and Bilge 2016). The teaching and learning at eMode is critical praxis because not only does Brother Alston apply scholarly knowledge to the social problem of Black girls' invisibility, dehumanization, and underperformance in math, he also uses the knowledge learned within everyday life, particularly knowledge from historical and pop Black culture. Therefore, critical praxis includes scholarship and practice speaking to and informing each other for the purpose of getting at more equitable outcomes in math for underrepresented minorities, particularly Black girls. eMode is a place where teachers can learn about rehumanizing teaching and learning for Black girls and other underrepresented students.

■ Black Girls Fear No Number

Kaliya (kindergarten), Turner (fourth grade), Ebony (fifth), Essence (fifth), and Gabrielle (sixth) participated in a ninety-minute focus group that asked them about their experiences at eMode Saturday mathematics academy. These young ladies have been taught by Brother Alston from one to five years at the academy and have the experience to speak to what makes eMode a special place to learn mathematics. Logic puzzles and games are a part of their warm-ups, and the girls were working on operations of fractions, decimals, and percent at the time of the focus group. In addition to mathematics, the Saturday academy also integrates time for science, the arts, maker-space engineering, and experiential project-based learning. Their discussion, coupled with Brother Alston's interview, can help mathematics teachers envision what it could mean to rehumanize mathematics for Black girls.

■ Fun Can Rehumanize the Teaching and Learning of Mathematics

Brother Alston discussed how he never teaches a mathematics lesson without laughter. He demonstrates a childlike love of learning, and no student is thinking about how rigorous the mathematics is. Fun was salient in the girls' discussion of their experiences. Essence shared that, from her perspective, she likes eMode because "we are always doing really fun activities that barely anyone has ever tried before." Kaliyah agreed and added that Brother Alston is a great mathematics teacher. Kaliyah stated that science is her favorite subject, and it's fun because "if you mess up, you can—there is some way that you can fix your experiment." Ebony described the "three hot seats" game as being fun. Three Hot Seats is a logic and critical thinking game the girls and Brother Alston play using deductive reasoning to arrive at a truthful conclusion of fact. Typically, three students are assigned a numerical identification that is unknown to themselves, while the rest of the class knows the number that each student has been assigned. Play begins with the girls using their number sense and classification skills to reason from general to specific about their number. They ask the student audience interrogatives that can only be answered with "Yes," "No," or "Irrelevant." The games sharpen the girls' minds by forcing them to think logically and sort out the responses by ruling out information that cannot be the case until they are left with only one or a few limited possibilities.

Essence talked about the Family Lineage game in which students learn to think about their ethnicity and family tree as a horizontal number line divided first into two segments, Mama's side and Daddy's side. Then the game begins, and it is all visual estimation of fractions fraught with stories about "Big Mama" and "Papa" and their ancestors. "Often, I infuse history and the Black experience into the narrative," explained Brother Alston. Essence discussed a game involving fractions on a number line when she commented:

> He'll [Brother Alston] do this thing where we have a number line, and he'll be like when we get to the center, I want you to tell me to stop. And so he'll—when he starts preparing to do it, he's like when I get to the center, I want you to tell me to and we all say stop. He's like barely one-fourth of the way there.

What Essence does not explicitly articulate is that Brother Alston layers in additional conditions, such as "I want you guys to stop when we're 50 percent of three-quarters of the way." Essence stated that these "tricks" do not hurt her feelings but instead challenge her brain. The girls learn arithmetic through games and computational strategies. (They sometimes refer to such strategies as "tricks.")

Some of the computational games and strategies lessons include the use of real money. Money is a tool and a great way to learn lots of arithmetic. For instance, when learning about decimal division lessons, real cash and coins are used rather than play money. Using real money prompts great thinking and motivation. The students learn that it is possible, for instance, that four girls can share a quantity like 75 cents, a situation that could be real for them given the complexities around low-income families' financial resources. Students also learn the time value of money by playing the compound interest game. They are given a dollar to keep. That dollar's serial number is recorded, and the girls earn a weekly compounding interest for a select period of time, the "maturity date." Using money this way is hugely important to the girls because they quickly conceptualize the time value of money, and the mathematics and computation involved is reinforced for a very real-world purpose. Additionally, they learn the discipline of holding on to money and letting it work for them. The girls manage the growth of their money using a spreadsheet, but they are also required to work out future principal and interest payments with pencil and paper. One of the girls has had the same dollar Brother Alston gave her over four years ago. Students at eMode truly enjoy using real money.

Brother Alston aims to develop the full humanity in his Black girls because it is important for rehumanization (Salazar 2013). The focus on the whole person in humanizing pedagogy is based on Freirean notions that "education is more than technical training because it involves the full development of the person; it has a humanistic orientation" (Schugurensky 2011, p. 67). This means that teachers need to help Black girls come to know themselves as creators of new thoughts, problem solvers, and individuals with imaginations able to recognize and appreciate different perspectives. In figure 4.1 (all photos are included with permission), Brother Alston is helping this Black girl detect patterns by finding the digital root of natural numbers, while she is learning to measure lengths on a ruler. He is on the floor, or wherever his students need him most, but he never teaches from behind a desk.

Fig. 4.1. Brother Alston using math tools to teach

■ Why Black Girls Come to a Saturday Mathematics Class: The Centrality of Relevance and Thinking

Brother Alston quoted Dr. Martin Luther King, Jr., in his interview, saying, "Rarely do we find students who willingly engage in hard, solid thinking. There is almost a universal quest for easy answers and half-baked solutions. Nothing pains some students more than having to think."

Five-year-old Kaliyah shared candidly about why she comes to eMode: "Why I come is because I—when I first started school, I didn't even know what *plus* meant and then when I came on Saturday, Brother Alston showed me what that meant and he showed me math." Kaliyah and Ebony came to eMode following their older brother Kenneth, who completed Saturday Mathematics Academy as a sixth grader and is now a ninth-grade mathematics mentor teacher teaching for eMode. Kaliyah has grown up to report how much she loves fractions. Brother Alston remembers telling Kaliyah that to hate fractions is like saying you hate your mama and your daddy because they are a part of your whole being. That appalled her: She said, "I love my parents!" At six years old, Kaliyah is exceptionally adept at creating physical models that represent mathematical situations, and especially fractions. In figure 4.2, Kaliyah is at the board presenting a lesson review to the class modeling with Cuisenaire rods.

Fig. 4.2. Kaliyah modeling fraction relationships using Cuisenaire rods

"I think one reason why I come here is because every time I come here I realize there's one other thing in this world that's related to mathematics," explained Essence. She mentioned that what she learns in the Saturday mathematics classes are ways mathematics is integrated into her life and everyday activity. From a humanizing pedagogy perspective, helping Black girls see the utility of math in their lives dismantles banking education models (Freire 1970) because the girls are active in making connections between home life and mathematics.

Ebony spoke with confidence as she explained why she attends:

> For one, I love mathematics. It's one of my favorite subjects. Second, it just helps me. It always makes me a step or two ahead in my class. Other kids might be struggling or falling behind. But when I come here every Saturday, it gives me a couple of extra steps ahead.

Both Brother Alston and Ebony understand the importance of being "a couple of extra steps ahead" for a Black student in U.S. schools. Her love of mathematics is fostered by Brother Alston and that contributes to rehumanizing teaching for Black girls because rarely are they viewed as intelligent and belonging in mathematics (Gholson 2016; Joseph, Hailu, and Boston 2017). Additionally, this quote suggests that Ebony realizes that struggling and falling behind is a normative experience for many students in mathematics classrooms; getting additional support from eMode can therefore help her position herself as being ahead, which can bring about validation from teachers, peers, and families. Gabrielle explained:

> Well, I like it because it's fun and also although it's not a social group, you get to talk to people about the different relations and stuff with mathematics and other stuff. And also you can find that there's always another way to do something. I was really bad at decimals so Brother Alston taught me another way to do it and it was so much easier because my teacher, she really—it felt like it was overcomplicated to me. Now it's like when Brother Alston showed me this way and I was like—and he was like okay, that's right. So you do that. And I was like, yeah, because it works better for me the way Brother Alston shows me. It's not overcomplicated and it's fun. Mathematics can be fun. It's one of the subjects that you dread it before you come to his class and then when you get to his class, everything clicks.

This quote first suggests that Black girls value being able to talk while also doing math. Gabrielle's perspective pushes back on notions of sanitized math classroom expectations where students who are quiet and working are somehow learning. Brother Alston does not expect nor require his students to leave their identities at the door but instead welcomes all the varying aspects of their personhood. These practices are more inclusive and humanizing, and they move beyond research-based student-centered practices that can fall short of transforming Black girls' perception of competence when used without a disposition for equity and social justice (Dunleavy and Joseph, under review). This is an example of the ways that intersecting identities can support math learning. This quote also helps us to understand that mathematics problems can have multiple pathways to a solution and why that is important for Black girls' perspectives of success both in their everyday lives and in school mathematics. Overall, when a teacher is in pursuit of humanization, it is a synergistic experience and journey between the individual and collective (Freire 1970).

■ The Urban Mathematics Renaissance Concept: Black Children Falling in Love with Learning

Brother Alston wants to help bring about an urban mathematics renaissance. He imagines building the most fantastic institute for mathematics and science. It would be the intellectual crown jewel of the city of Seattle. It would be filled with exhibits that children would be drawn to and inspired by. It would be staffed by people who love children, teaching, and learning. He went on to explain that our country needs a revival, a rebirth of simply learning and doing mathematics for its own sake. He poignantly stated, "Not for a test score, not for a grade, and not for admission into some college. We simply need to learn that mathematics can be enjoyed the same way you'd enjoy literature, the arts, entertainment, or athletics."

eMode is a microcosm of this renaissance concept because the Black girls in the program are inspired and love to learn mathematics. Brother Alston takes into account the social realities of our Black girls, such as the negative stereotypes society places upon them. He understands that the development of a rehumanizing pedagogy should counteract these realities and be inclusive of the sociohistorical, sociocultural, and sociopolitical contexts of our Black girls' lives both inside and outside of school (Bartolomé 1994; Huerta 2011; Roberts 2000). Educators who desire to enact rehumanizing teaching of mathematics must commit to exploring the varied macro- and micro-level elements that affect Black girls and other marginalized students' learning, thereby interrogating multiple forms of oppression in their students' lives (Collins and Bilge 2016; Fránquiz and Salazar 2004).

This renaissance is important for Black children who do not have resources at home. This type of experience addresses the structure and psychosocial dimensions of human liberation, where it would be intentionally focused on the academic, but also the affective domain (Bell and Schniedewind 1989). The affective is ever-present at eMode. For example, the girls love that Brother Alston calls them "sister." Ebony described it as "kinda like a relationship. When you know someone like that, it's kinda like they are related to you. You know them." Essence chimed in and said, "It just kinda feels normal. . . . A lot of people call each other sister or brother because it just feels normal and we are kind of all related by blood if you go back far enough." Turner emphatically stated:

> Well, I'm gonna have to go to the Bible on this. It's—there's a good speech in the Bible where it says we're all made from the same blood, the blood of Christ. We all have the same blood and we might not all share the same DNA but we all—in one way we are all the same.

Ebony's and Turner's comments point out that the language of "brother" and "sister" has deep meaning for them as it relates to family and sharing a bond. This connects back to why we call each other brother and sister—a unity that bonds us, given that our ancestral origins are black boxes. Having a bond to show affection for one another is something that appears important to our Black girls. Analogously, Brother Alston explained in his interview that he views the girls as his little sisters whom he respects and feels a sense of responsibility for.

■ What Teachers Can Do: Toward Rehumanizing Teaching Mathematics for Black Girls

We close this chapter by giving hope to mathematics teachers. To engage in the pursuit of rehumanizing the teaching and learning of mathematics for Black children, having a clear ethical and political commitment to transforming oppressive conditions for many of these children is necessary (Freire 1970). All pedagogy is political and requires radical reconstruction of teaching and learning, and that pedagogy must be meaningful and connected to social change by engaging students with the world so they can transform it (Giroux 2010). Thus, beginning with moral conviction for humanization, the following recommendations overlap and can support teacher development in rehumanizing mathematics:

1. Rely less on traditional methods of mathematics teaching and seek to forge a cultural democracy where Black girls are treated with respect and dignity (Macadeo and Bartolome 1999). Brother Alston models this when he chooses to use Black culture as a frame of reference for all the girls' mathematics engagements. Typically, problem-based learning situations are constructed using popular culture, themes, music, and language that the girls themselves clearly identify as their own. Brother Alston offers a whimsical and informal social environment to invite girls to engage in doing mathematics while "socializing" and enjoying each other's company. Lecture and direct instruction are not a part of his classroom; instead, collaborative small groups and inquiry-based learning happen. He does very little traditional "teaching," but he asks lots of questions. The girls themselves, working in concert, do the real teaching and learning.

2. Understand that a rehumanizing pedagogy is a co-constructed experience and that it is critical for Black girls' academic and social resiliency for school success (Fránquiz and Salazar 2004; Reyes 2007). This means that teachers need to be prepared to experience vulnerability in letting go of the power to better support Black girls' development of themselves as knowledge producers. Brother Alston provides problem types that lend themselves to deep mathematical thinking and the use of manipulatives. Girls are asked to take control of their learning experience. He sometimes interjects with more questions and guidance, but he does not lead or control the students. The girls often report that they wish they could learn mathematics in this way at school.

3. Engage in consciousness raising through dialogue using knowledge grounded in personal experience, relationship building, and a view of students as emotional and social beings, not solely cognitive learners (Jennings and Da Matta 2009). This means teachers must help Black girls name oppressions they experience in their lives and help them understand that how they know what they know is real and legitimate and that they have agency to challenge things in their lives that are negative. In Brother Alston's classroom, spontaneous conversations often arise that might seem unrelated to the mathematics. These are moments that the girls share lots of meaningful information about school and their personal lives. Therefore, they become conditioned and accustomed to doing mathematics while reflecting on their lives.

4. Give Black girls more mathematics, not less. Require that they think and engage with rigorous mathematics for a purpose but also allow them simultaneously to be social (Frymer 2005). This means that teachers must move beyond a textbook and trust that the girls will come up with powerful ideas. Brother Alston rejoices and loudly cheers the girls when they make mathematical discoveries or derive proofs and when they explain their thinking in ways that persuade, or dissuade, others. Brother Alston explained

that what is truly inspiring is when the girls stand up to him and use reason and sound argumentation to refute him. Teaching Black girls to resist passivity is enacting rehumanization.

Mathematics teachers who challenge themselves to adopt these dispositions, beliefs, and practices can increase the likelihood of Black girls feeling that they are valued and they belong in the mathematics space. These recommendations are consistent with eMode's mission to create unique and productive humanizing ways of teaching mathematics that empower Black girls.

■ Conclusion

eMode inspires and empowers Black girls as they progress through their public schools. They remember and regard their experiential learning from one of their community's elders. This helps to strengthen their overall confidence and participation in their classrooms. While much lament and hand-wringing occur over the achievement gap, the opportunity gap, and all the other gaps, we believe that the real gap is the love or caring gap (Noddings 2013). Black girls in eMode thrive because they are in an environment of love and care. They know Brother Alston would lay down his life for any one of them at any time. They know that he is not motivated by remuneration. They know that their teacher loves to see them learn and enjoy doing mathematics. They know that their teacher considers them to be his role models and that he looks up to them. This kind of devotion cannot help but to build trust and true relationship with students. In an environment such as this, resilience, rigor, and deep mathematical thinking will burgeon because when love and care are present, so then is a strong teacher-student bond. This bond allows the teacher great moral authority to challenge the great potential in every Black girl.

References

Alston, Norman V. "Blacks at Garfield Not Getting a Proper Education." *Seattle Times* (1979).

Bartolomé, Lilia. "Beyond the Methods Fetish: Toward a Humanizing Pedagogy." *Harvard Educational Review* 64 (1994): 173–95.

Bell, Lee, and Nancy Schniedewind. "Realizing the Promise of Humanistic Education: A Reconstructed Pedagogy for Personal and Social Change." *Journal of Humanistic Psychology* 29 (1989): 200–23.

Collins, Patricia Hill, and Sirma Bilge. *Intersectionality: Key Concepts*. Malden, Mass.: Polity, 2016.

Epstein, Rebecca, Jamila Blake, and Thalia González. "Girlhood Interrupted: The Erasure of Black Girls' Childhood" (June 27, 2017). https://ssrn.com/abstract=3000695.

Fránquiz, Maria E., and Maria del Carmen Salazar. "The Transformative Potential of Humanizing Pedagogy: Addressing the Diverse Needs of Chicano/Mexicano Students." *High School Journal* 87, no. 4 (2004): 36–53.

Freire, Paolo. *Pedagogy of the Oppressed*. New York: Continuum, 1970.

_____. *The Politics of Education: Culture, Power and Liberation*. New York: Bergin & Garvey, 1985.

Frymer, Benjamin. "Freire, Alienation, and Contemporary Youth: Toward a Pedagogy of Everyday Life." *InterActions: UCLA Journal of Education and Information Studies* (2005). Retrieved from http://escholarship.org/uc/item/5wd2w4gs.

Gholson, Maisie. "Clean Corners and Algebra: A Critical Examination of the Constructed Invisibility of Black Girls and Women in Mathematics." *The Journal of Negro Education* 85, no. 3 (2016): 290–301.

Giroux, Henry. "Lessons to be Learned from Paulo Freire as Education Is Being Taken Over by the Mega Rich" (2010). Retrieved from http://www.truth-out.org/archive/component/k2/item/93016:lessons-to-be-learned-from-paulo-freire-as-education-is-being-taken-over-by-the-mega-rich.

Huerta, Teresa M. "Humanizing Pedagogy: Beliefs and Practices on the Teaching of Latino Children." *Bilingual Research Journal* 34 no. 1 (2011): 38–57.

Jennings, Louise, and Cynthia Smith. "Examining the Role of Critical Inquiry for Transformative Practices: Two Joint Case Studies of Multicultural Teacher Education." *Teachers College Record* 104 (2002): 456–81.

Jennings, Louise, and Gylton Da Matta. "Rooted in Resistance: Women Teachers Constructing Counter-Pedagogies in Post-Authoritarian Brazil." *Teaching Education* 20, no. 3 (2009): 215–28.

Joseph, Nicole M., Meseret Hailu, and Denise Boston. "Black Girls' and Women's Persistence in the P–20 Mathematics Pipeline: Two Decades of Children, Youth, and Adult Education Research." *Review of Research in Education* 41, no. 1 (2017): 203–27.

Macedo, Donaldo, and Lilia Bartolomé, *Dancing with Bigotry*. New York: St. Martin's Press, 1999.

Noddings, Nel. *Caring: A Relational Approach to Ethics and Moral Education*. Los Angeles: University of California Press, 2013.

Reyes, Reynaldo. "Marginalized Students in Secondary School Settings: The Pedagogical and Theoretical Implications of Addressing the Needs of Student Sub-Populations." *Journal of Border Educational Research* 6 (2007): 3–5.

Roberts, Peter. *Education, Literacy, and Humanization: Exploring the Work of Paulo Freire*. Westport, Conn.: Bergin & Garvey, 2000.

Salazar, Maria del Carmen. "A Humanizing Pedagogy: Reinventing the Principles and Practice of Education as a Journey toward Liberation." *Review of Research in Education* 34 (2013): 121–48.

Schugurensky, Daniel. *Paulo Freire*. New York: Continuum, 2011.

CHAPTER 5

Every Penny Counts:
Promoting Community Engagement to Engage Students in Mathematical Modeling

Jennifer Suh, *George Mason University, Fairfax, Virginia*
Lauren Britton, *Westlawn Elementary School, Falls Church, Virginia*
Kristen Burke, *Westlawn Elementary School, Falls Church, Virginia*
Kathleen Matson, *George Mason University, Fairfax, Virginia*
Linda Ferguson, *Westlawn Elementary School, Falls Church, Virginia*
Spencer Jamieson, *Fairfax County Public Schools, Virginia*
Padmanabhan Seshaiyer, *George Mason University, Fairfax, Virginia*

This chapter shares the voices of classroom teachers, an administrator, and mathematics educators, who collectively designed and implemented an innovative strategy of using mathematical modeling to engage students, their families, and their community to link mathematics as a powerful tool to make an impact in their lives. Gutstein and Peterson (2013) advocate students using mathematics as a tool for empowering themselves to make judgments and potentially change the world around them. However, mathematics has been a "dehumanizing" experience for many, being viewed as a subject taught in a fashion that "inflicts psychological damage on students" and where there is only one right answer or only one right way to carry out a computation (Greer, Mukhopadhyay, and Roth 2012, p. 6). Greer and colleagues go on to state that to (re)humanize mathematics and mathematics education it is necessary to "connect with students' lived experience, their bodies, their immediate experiences, their emotions, needs, and desires" and to understand that mathematics is "inherently social" and that education is fundamentally "about interpersonal relations between students and teachers" (pp. 6–7). Reform mathematics proponents have advocated for mathematics to be more related to students' lives by building on community and cultural knowledge and practices with issues that matter to them, which then helps students view mathematics as a vehicle through which they learn to be active change agents for social justice (Aguirre et al. 2013; Bartell et al. 2017; Berry 2008; Civil 2007; Wager 2012).

Mathematical modeling has several attributes of an approach that "(re)humanizes" mathematics. By tapping into students' funds of knowledge, mathematics becomes personally relevant (Gutiérrez and Irving 2012), and real-world problems illustrate the usefulness of mathematics to students' everyday situations (Pollak 2012). Mathematical modeling can help create a small piece of the real culture of mathematics within a classroom as students choose what mathematics to use, decide how they might use it, and justify their choices (Civil 2007). Mathematical modeling bridges the different uses of mathematics because mathematics is connected to students' lived experiences, problems, and needs; results must also make sense in the real world (Pollak 2012). Additionally, mathematical modeling "(re)humanizes" mathematics by becoming a tool through which both students and teachers can affect social change (Gutiérrez and Irving 2012). Finally, mathematical modeling "(re)humanizes" mathematics by drawing on Bartell and colleagues' (2017) Equitable Mathematics Teaching Practices.

Utilizing students' out-of-school knowledge and experiences and their "funds of knowledge" (Moll et al. 1992) is one approach to (re)humanizing mathematics and mathematics education. Civil (2007) highlighted the importance of teachers' learning about the knowledge and resources of their particular students and their households as they initiate innovations in teaching. She investigated how teaching innovations might be developed to "enable students to advance in their learning of the prescribed school mathematics in ways that are true to mathematicians' mathematics while building on students' knowledge of and experiences with everyday mathematics" (p. 41). Our work with mathematical modeling builds on the idea of bridging different uses of mathematics—i.e., the mathematics of everyday, ordinary settings, school classrooms, and the mathematics used by mathematicians (Civil 2007; Masingila, Davidenko, and Prus-Wisniowska 1996). Starting with students' interests and experiences, teachers developed a mathematical modeling task that was relevant and authentic to students. Familiarity with food drive initiatives and with planning a family celebration meal accessed the mathematics of students' everyday settings; addressing mandated standards used the mathematics of school classrooms; and the messiness and openness of the mathematical modeling task corresponded with the way mathematicians use mathematics.

In addition to using students' funds of knowledge, we see our use of mathematical modeling aligning with Social Justice Pedagogy (Gutiérrez and Irving 2012). Social Justice Pedagogy moves beyond simply engaging students in relevant mathematics; it uses mathematics as a tool to examine issues that affect students' lives and to effect change (Gutiérrez and Irving 2012). In our project, members of the student population at the school directly benefit from local food drive initiatives making the issue of childhood hunger one that is relevant to students. The goal of Social Justice Pedagogy in mathematics education is to involve students in developing mathematical arguments that will help convince others of action (Gutiérrez and Irving 2012). Beyond increasing engagement, motivation, and interest, applying mathematics to students' personal or community issues is also a way to highlight the mathematical competencies of students from nondominant communities (Gutiérrez and Irving 2012).

Bartell and colleagues (2017) proposed nine Equitable Mathematics Teaching Practices to promote equitable opportunities for students as they engage in the Common Core State Standards for Mathematics (CCSSM) Standards for Mathematical Practice (SMP) (National Governors Association Center for Best Practices and Council of Chief State School Officers [NGA Center and CCSSO] 2010). They advocated for connecting the goals for students with research on effective pedagogy for students from nondominant communities, and they provided examples of how their equitable practices can intersect with the different SMP. Our mathematical modeling project focused specifically on SMP.4 (model with mathematics) (NGA Center and CCSSO 2010). In our project, we saw how Bartell and colleagues' Equitable Mathematics Teaching Practice 1 (draw on students' funds of knowledge), Practice 3 (position students as capable), and Practice 5 (attend explicitly to race and culture) were interwoven with SMP.4 on modeling. In addition, we saw how mathematical modeling supported the other SMP, including SMP.1 (make sense of problems and persevere in solving them), SMP.3 (construct viable arguments and critique the reasoning of others), and SMP.5 (use appropriate tools strategically).

In our project, we describe how we build on and move beyond the existing concepts of (re)humanizing mathematics as discussed above. We see the theme of (re)humanizing mathematics through mathematical modeling emerge through students' experience with service learning, their community engagement, and the way they build a metaphoric relationship with mathematics. Service learning provides students an opportunity to apply mathematics to contexts that they care about. Community engagement works to draw families and schools together through mathematics, breaking down the barriers that often exist between them. As students learn to appreciate the usefulness of and gain an interest in mathematics, we see the focus of mathematics shift from achievement to include the affective aspects of mathematics. Through mathematical modeling, students can develop a positive disposition toward and build a metaphoric relationship with mathematics.

■ The Positionality of the Authors, and Working Collaboratively as Designers

A Mathematical Modeling Design Institute gave the authors of this chapter a chance to work together. For the three authors who are mathematics educators, this research interest stems from their connections as members of a cross-cultural community that drive their social justice pedagogy. One was born to Korean immigrant parents, one immigrated from India as an adult, and the third grew up in Ecuador and Mexico and closely identifies with the Latinx community; all of them work on practices to advocate for and advance children who have been historically underrepresented in mathematics education. The two authors who are classroom teachers are committed to their school's population, believing that all students deserve access to high-quality instruction. Another author is the district's mathematics specialist, who has worked in supporting Title I schools for over twenty years. He believes that all students can reach their potential given the access and opportunity and that all students can be successful with the proper experiences. The author who is a school principal is a Black woman who identifies with and values the historical tenets of the civil rights movements. She sees value in how successful education can lift and propel children out of poverty.

Westlawn Elementary, the school for this project, has a diverse ethnic population of students: Latinx (63 percent), Asian (19 percent), White (11 percent), and Black (3 percent), with 4 percent of the families identifying themselves as "other." Sixty-nine percent of this Title I elementary school's students qualify for free/reduced breakfast and lunch. Fifty-three percent of its students receive English language services; 12 percent receive special education services. Of the ninety-nine teachers, twenty are bilingual in either Spanish, Vietnamese, French, or Farsi. The teachers' classrooms represented in this chapter mirror the school's demographics.

The school is viewed by the parents as a hub where early literacy programs begin with three-year-olds, where Latinx parents engage in school leadership opportunities to advocate for themselves and their children, and where parents can come to find refuge and direction for services for their daily lives. This school-community connection creates caring and trusting bonds among the parents, teachers, administrators, and students, and it personifies the school's vision of developing the total child while fully engaging, and collaborating with, all stakeholders.

The school culture is one where the teachers' and principal's partnership work with the parents is enhanced by its social and community connections. Throughout the year, family-oriented curriculum events, both during the day and at night, are planned. These events include Math Night, Partners in Print (Literacy), and STEM Night. At these events, teachers, parents, and students interact. Teachers demonstrate learning strategies and coach parents on how to use the strategies with their children. Parents and their children practice the strategies with specific activities and develop a shared sense of responsibility. These events help the parents understand what is occurring at school and how to support their children.

Within the school, teachers and administrators have high academic and social growth expectations for their students. The teachers plan and deliver such best practices as using differentiated instruction, activating prior knowledge and building background knowledge, working on vocabulary development, and evoking creative and critical thinking, including real-world connections to the curriculum, technology-based activities, and assessment for learning and application. Teachers implement best practices with language and culture in mind. Teachers use various scaffolds to include sensory (real-life objects, pictures), graphic (graphic organizers, charts), interactive (explicit modeling, think-alouds, cooperative learning) and linguistic (sentence frames, word walls, leveled texts).

The teachers strive to tap into their students' cultural backgrounds and celebrate their cultural differences in the educational setting. Teachers recognize that students from other countries may come with different algorithms or approaches to solving problems, which are valued and celebrated. One teacher shared, "I identify with these students because I was a student here myself, and I am personally invested in this school and community because I have lived in the neighborhood for twenty-two years." As a school community, Westlawn utilizes and celebrates cultural differences with an annual International Fair where families display and explain key aspects of their traditions, demonstrate dances and songs, and share in culture-specific meals.

Our project focused on implementing mathematical modeling in elementary classrooms while attending to equitable math teaching practices. The Institute used mathematical modeling as a process of posing an authentic, personally relevant problem where mathematics was used to make decisions and solve real-world problems (see fig. 5.1).

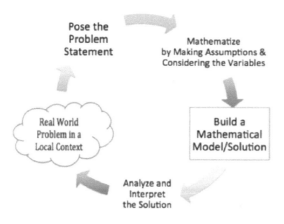

Fig. 5.1. Mathematical modeling process in the elementary grades

The following narrative shares the voices of a first-grade teacher and a fourth-grade teacher who collaboratively planned and launched a community-based learning project using mathematical modeling. Teachers asked students to think of ways they could help their community combat hunger, leading to a coin drive and "Thanksgiving" meal-planning budget project.

While we use the term "Thanksgiving" in this chapter, we put it in quotation marks as a way to recognize that its common use in a school context is oppressive and problematic for many families and communities. Sentimentalized stories about the first Thanksgiving don't address issues of domination or speak out against the effects of Whites on Native American cultures. Stories associated with "Thanksgiving" that gloss over the impact of colonialism promote racism by "functioning to dissolve cultural differences and distort history" (Spina 1997, p. 32).

Inspiration through a Community-Based Math Learning Project

The teachers were inspired by a project at a neighboring school where students researched solutions to address childhood hunger in the United States. The teachers felt that this type of service project would fit in well with the community outreach initiative at their local site. Teachers understood that some of their student population directly benefited from local food drive initiatives, making this project powerful for their school population. Teachers wanted a task that was appropriate for first through fourth grades. They discussed topics relevant to each grade's standards (decimals, money, counting collections, skip-counting, rounding) and saw the potential for the meal-planning budget project to cover these standards.

The teachers proposed the "Thanksgiving" meal community-based learning project to the principal. After learning about the prevalence of childhood hunger in the United States, students would lead a school-wide coin drive to raise money to purchase "Thanksgiving" meal baskets for local families in need. First- and fourth-grade students were tasked with planning all of the logistics of the fundraiser. They determined how to inform the rest of the school about their "Coin Harvest" project, and they created flyers and commercials to spread the word. They also decided that each teacher should have a jar in the classroom to make it easier for students to donate coins. The coins would be collected on a weekly basis so that a running total could be displayed on a number line in the school lobby. At the end of the Coin Harvest, students created "Thanksgiving" meal plans and presented them to the principal. These meal plans represented students' ideas of the best way to use the money raised. The principal used these ideas to determine the contents of the meals to be provided. The principal, parent liaison, and teachers collaborated to establish the possible number of meals and school families to whom the meals would go. Historically, the school provided "Thanksgiving" meals to twenty-five to fifty school families with the assistance of donations from business and faith-based partners and local food pantries. Now, the number of meals provided from the school has doubled. The school provided twenty-five to fifty meals both at the Thanksgiving break in November and for the winter break in December. All families who requested assistance received it.

The Launch of the Coin Harvest Project

Both the teachers launched the task by showing students a video presenting the fact that one in five children in the United States go hungry. Fourth-grade students then discussed their reactions to the video, which included shock, confusion, and sadness. Many did not yet understand that food insecurity is a problem within their immediate community, that children do not have to be homeless to go hungry, or what the statistic of one in five children actually looks like. To make this concrete for the first-grade students, the teacher asked five students to stand up. Then one sat down to represent a child who wouldn't have dinner that night. To see what that would look like in the whole classroom, students played a familiar math routine game, count around the circle, but every time they got to a multiple of five, someone else had to sit down. At the end of the circle, there were four students sitting down who represented those would not have dinner. The class then tried to imagine what that would mean for the whole school, and in turn the entire community. The first-grade students had originally thought the video was just a cute clip to watch, but they became very upset when they realized that this was a real issue that affected people in their own neighborhood, people they might even know. They were saddened and concerned, and from there, we did not even have to convince them to try to help—they had decided right then that they wanted to.

The fourth-grade teacher also wanted students to gain a better understanding of what "one in five children" might look like in their community. To accomplish this, the fourth-grade students analyzed population data and created and extended number patterns. Students had access to hundreds charts, and many approached the task by coloring multiples of 5 to determine that 20 out of 100 children might be hungry. Students estimated this was about one classroom of kids. Students then figured out they needed ten hundreds charts to reach 1,000 and counted multiples of 20 to see that 200 out of 1,000 children, or about one grade level, might not have enough food to eat. Students used similar strategies to see how many children could be affected out of 10,000 and 100,000. Students concluded that out of the approximately 200,000 children living in the county, 40,000 do not know where they will get their next meal.

After understanding the magnitude of childhood hunger, students were motivated to help these families. Both classes compiled lists of ideas for how they could help (see fig. 5.2). First-grade students came up with ideas such as "share our food," "invite them over for dinner," and "buy food for them." Popular themes for the fourth graders also were to donate food and money. Students concluded that many people have spare change, leading to the idea of a school-wide Coin Harvest. Because the Coin Harvest was launched in October, students decided the money collected could be used to buy "Thanksgiving" meals for local families in need. Some enthusiastic students started telling teachers about the project in the hallway as they went home that day, and a number of them brought in coins the next day, before the Coin Harvest had even been officially planned or announced to the school.

Fig. 5.2. Brainstorming ways to help fight childhood hunger

Students were eager to get the whole school involved in this project and created flyers to hang around the school explaining how everyone could participate (see fig. 5.3). Both grades worked together to make commercials for the school morning news channel. Seeing their flyers displayed and their commercials gave students a sense of ownership with their project.

Fig. 5.3. Spreading the word to the school community

Snapshot of the Mathematical Modeling Task in First Grade

Once the school had begun collecting money for the Coin Harvest, the first-grade students participated in a variety of number-sense activities using the change in their classrooms, counting and manipulating the money as they raised it. This project was easily differentiated with math tasks that appealed to students with diverse interests, prior knowledge, and abilities. Tasks included estimating, sorting, counting, skip-counting, and more. To estimate, students counted small handfuls of change from the classroom collection jar, and they tried to guess how much was in the whole jar. The students also began exploring money by sorting coins to identify them and their corresponding values. Some groups discovered efficient strategies by skip-counting by 5s and 10s after sorting, while others counted mixed collections of coins.

Leading up to this task, the class participated in cross-curricular activities relating to nutrition, health, and traditions. They learned about holidays around the world. The teacher wanted to tap into her students' specific cultural and family traditions, so the class did activities where students brought in flags, food, clothing, or other items to share something about their own traditions. Since they were planning a "Thanksgiving" meal, the teacher had the students make their own "Thanksgiving plate," and she emphasized that if they don't celebrate Thanksgiving, it could be any other meal they have for important holidays, parties, or anything else. Once each child had made his or her own ideal plate, the teacher asked the students to share what types of foods they like to eat for "Thanksgiving" or any other traditional family meal. After the class compiled a list, the students' ideas were explicitly used in the teacher-made grocery store circular for the final mathematical modeling task. Students came up with a mix of traditional foods, healthy items, and desserts, including rice, beans, carrots, fresh fruits, pies, cakes, and more. The discussions focused on planning well-balanced, healthy meals, but since many traditional meals do have some sort of dessert, students included a treat, which pleased them.

The first grade's mathematical modeling task was "How can we plan the best meal for $20?" They had to decide what the "best" meal was within a $20 budget constraint. The first-grade teacher provided students with a teacher-made circular that included most of the food items that students had suggested, with rounded dollar prices. Students created a grocery list or plan so that they could tell the principal and the teacher managing the food drive what to buy with the money they raised. Students were given the choice to work through and present their ideas in any way, including but not limited to writing a grocery list, drawing a picture, cutting out the circular and gluing the items onto a picture of a basket, or making a poster. Students were able to use any resources or manipulatives they thought might help them and were given the choice of working individually or in pairs.

The first graders used a wide variety of strategies; these included using their fingers, cubes, money, number lines, hundreds charts, tally marks, pictures, and more. A common strategy that the first-grade teacher noticed in her classroom was how a few groups used a combination of cubes and the cutout pictures from the circular to keep track. They cut out the pictures and then counted cubes for each item, making a stack or a tower for each. They would then go back and count them all together each time, until they got to 20.

Many students came in under budget at first. This was technically correct, but it was a challenge for students to figure out if they could afford to add anything else. A few students had gone over budget, giving them a chance to check their work, revise their thinking, and share how they fixed their mathematics (see fig. 5.4). Students would suggest things like "he could take some away" or "switch it with a $1" (exchange one food item for another one that cost less).

Fig. 5.4. Learning that mathematical ideas can be revised and enhanced

One student in the first-grade class had an individualized educational program (IEP) that included math and communication goals. She generally struggled with understanding multistep directions, as well as with communicating her own understanding. During this task, she struggled with remembering how much money she had spent (and how much she was allowed to spend). The teacher asked her what she could do to make sure she only spent $20. She told the teacher that she should count. The teacher knew this student worked best with manipulatives, so she gave her twenty one-dollar bills, and the student acted out buying each item on her list (see fig. 5.5).

Ms. Burke: Grapes. How much do they cost?

Tania: 2.

Ms. Burke: Okay, so what do you need to do?

Tania: [*counting*] 1, 2. [*Hands teacher two dollars*]

Ms. Burke: Great, now what?

Tania: Pie! 5. 1, 2, 3, 4, 5.

She continued handing the teacher the money for each item until she ran out of money. She realized she had too many things, saying "Uh-oh! No more!" The teacher responded, "That's right, you don't have any more money. So what do you need to do?" Tania then pulled off the last pictures she hadn't counted yet: macaroni and cheese and apples.

Fig. 5.5. Making the math modeling task accessible to all students

The first-grade teacher reflected on how mathematical modeling impacted her students:

> I believe this project empowered my whole class to be more confident, motivated mathematicians for a number of reasons. The real-world issue, the realistic math modeling task, the open nature of the task itself, and even the fact that the students had personal, cultural, and creative input into the content of the circular itself. The real-world problem that hit close to home got the kids legitimately concerned for the members of the community around them. I have never seen six-year-olds work so hard at something in the four years I have been teaching. They were so proud of their work planning the Coin Harvest. They told their families, their friends—they were even walking down the hallway telling other teachers.

The first-grade teacher's comment highlights how the project attended to the issues of identity. The design of the activities aligned with Gutiérrez's (2007) window/mirror metaphor, where students had "opportunities to see themselves in the curriculum (mirror) as well as have a view onto a broader world (window)." For example, using mathematics to analyze their favorite family meal offered a mirror to the use of mathematics within their lives while providing a window to see the world around them by helping with the community with the "Thanksgiving" meals.

Snapshot of the Mathematical Modeling Task in Fourth Grade

The fourth-grade mathematical modeling task took place about a month after the initial launch, and yet students were still so invested in this project. A number line was displayed in the lobby of the school to track how much money had been raised, and students would come in excitedly announcing the new totals. Every time someone dropped coins in the class jar, the entire class would erupt in wild cheers. The project not only helped build community and empathy in the classroom, but students were empowered by the fact that they had mobilized such a large-scale effort within the school. In one month, students raised a total of $1,300!

At the end of the school Coin Harvest, the fourth-grade teacher posed the following problem to students: "Based on the Coin Harvest money, how can you plan the best meal to feed the most families?" Student parameters were a well-balanced meal that would feed a family of four. Students could spend the money any way they chose, but they had to justify why theirs was the "best" meal. They also had to estimate how many meals could be purchased based on their plan.

Students worked in small groups to create grocery shopping lists. They made decisions on how much of each item to buy to have enough food for a family of four. Students of all mathematical ability levels were able to participate due to the open-ended nature of the task. The teacher observed students coaching their partners with computations and checking each other's work. Groups used strategies such as rounding decimals to whole numbers and repeated addition or subtraction to estimate how many meals could be purchased using their plan.

Each group presented their meal plans and justifications to their principal, who would be purchasing the food, and answered the principal's questions about their meal proposals. Some groups determined their meal was the best because it included a mix of healthy and traditional "Thanksgiving" foods, while others reasoned that they had looked for inexpensive items to feed the most families possible. One group included more expensive organic foods. They felt that since these families do not have enough to eat, they should have the best-quality ingredients in their meal. The students' menus influenced the purchase of new items for the bags that had not been purchased in the past. The new items included bags of carrots, juice boxes, and an assortment of pies (pumpkin, apple, and sweet potato). Additionally, the principal asked the students how they traditionally spent "Thanksgiving" and if they included any of their favorite family meal items in their proposed menus. The students saw the holiday as an opportunity to spend time with their families. Some liked the traditional "Thanksgiving" foods; others said that their families substituted turkey with fish or had beans and rice along with the mashed potatoes. The students were selfless in their comments as they were focused on making sure their persuasive argument to the principal was convincing enough to influence her to purchase their menu items. After the principal purchased the meals, she explained to students how their ideas influenced her decisions about which foods to buy. The presentations were an important part of the project as students felt their input about how to spend the money was valued. Students also helped the principal fill the Thanksgiving bags going to families so they could see the end result of their hard work. With the money raised, twenty Thanksgiving meals were purchased for families in the community.

Reflecting on how the mathematical modeling project empowered her students, the fourth-grade teacher commented:

> I was inspired by the compassion and empathy I saw in my students throughout this project. They were so motivated to solve this problem that they didn't view the math as an obstacle or a chore. They were able to experience how mathematics can be used in the real world through this authentic task. On several occasions, students would ask, "When are we having math?" This was so different from the way they are used to doing math. I felt a positive shift in their attitudes toward mathematics through this project. It has inspired me to incorporate more open-ended, creative tasks into my curriculum, as I observe students are more invested when they feel a sense of ownership in their work and are given choices.

The fourth-grade teacher's comment highlights the shift in her thinking as she saw herself as a change agent for social justice and documents the evolution of the teachers seeing themselves as agents of social justice through their teaching. They created the learning environment that not only honored what their students brought to the table (their excitement, skills, and motivation to learn) but also honored their cultural backgrounds and their concern for their community. This empowerment for teachers and the ownership sensed by students is what "rehumanized" mathematics in our mathematical modeling project.

■ Considerations for Teachers and Future Mathematical Modeling Tasks

Knowing that not all families celebrate "Thanksgiving," the teachers talked about traditions around the world, as well as students' personal family traditions before approaching the topic of American "Thanksgiving." First-grade students brought items from home to share their family and cultural traditions so that all students would feel included, even if they do not specifically celebrate "Thanksgiving." Both grade levels discussed different kinds of meals for various holidays, celebrations, and special occasions. Students were encouraged to incorporate food items from their personal traditions when creating their meal plans. Classes also discussed the difficulties that holiday breaks can present for some families, as many children depend on the breakfast and lunch provided at school. Not having access to those meals over break might put an additional burden on families who struggle to put food on the table.

With the knowledge that school breaks can be especially problematic for families struggling with food insecurity, the teachers have discussed the possibility of doing future coin drive projects closer to winter break. Students on free and reduced meal plans spend up to two weeks over the winter holiday without school breakfast and lunch. Providing food baskets to families during this time might have a bigger impact. The teachers have also talked about how to involve the community, so less of the burden falls on students and parents at the school who might be directly affected by the problem. This could include having students write letters to local businesses in hopes of receiving additional monetary or food donations.

In attempting to rehumanize mathematics in our classrooms, our main goal was for all students to feel successful at this project and to gain confidence as mathematicians. To accomplish this, both classroom teachers utilized mathematical manipulative libraries to ensure students had access to a variety of problem-solving tools. The skills needed were also explicitly taught, explored, or integrated into lessons leading up to the final mathematical modeling task.

The mathematical modeling task was open in the ways mentioned earlier, but the teachers plan to adjust the task in the future to include even more freedom for the students. The teachers would also like to incorporate a graphing component to track how much money is collected each week. Based on the data, students could estimate how much might be collected by the end of the Coin Harvest.

In first grade, the final mathematical modeling task could then include different *potential* budgets, to allow for differentiation. Since all students were successful with a $20 budget, teachers could propose this as well as a larger budget for some students to work with, which would allow for the task to offer more of a challenge for those students who would benefit from it.

Fourth-grade students were given some parameters in the final budget task, such as a plan that would feed the most possible families and a well-balanced meal that would feed a family of four. The fourth-grade teacher plans to remove these parameters in future projects to see what assumptions and constraints the students make on their own. While students will need varying degrees of scaffolding with these types of open-ended tasks, the fourth-grade teacher acknowledges that she continues to work on allowing students to experience productive struggle. This often feels uncomfortable and messy, but it is empowering for students to have the freedom to explore solutions through their own creative approaches and contributes to their feelings of success in mathematics.

■ Implications

Our narrative contributes a picture of how mathematical modeling provided an innovative way for teachers to rehumanize mathematics by (1) naturally building on students' funds of knowledge, (2) allowing a bridge between mathematics and the real world, (3) becoming a tool through which both students and teachers can affect social change (Gutiérrez and Irving 2012), and (4) implementing an equitable practice that gave diverse learners access to mathematics.

The features of mathematical modeling, as articulated above, naturally connect mathematics to social justice issues by bridging students' lived experiences, needs, and desires to school mathematics. For this project, teachers positioned students' cultural backgrounds as funds of knowledge by discussing traditions around the world as well as students' personal family traditions before approaching the topic of American "Thanksgiving" and using this to draw students closer to mathematics. Students were able to see their own ideas concretely used in the project. Our work speaks to the importance of students' experiences and funds of knowledge as a starting place for school mathematics. By learning about their students and what motivated them, teachers connected mathematics with students' interests. The school administrator reflected:

> Our teachers always think about how they can connect the learning for our students to real-world experiences. The Coin Harvest represented two key values of our school community, *caring culture* and *giving back*. Our teachers cultivate these values each and every day as they teach. It was natural for the students to embrace the Coin Harvest as an opportunity to help others. The teachers recognize that every child has a talent, skill, and ambition. Our teachers inspire and help their students to find their unique talent, skill, and ambition!

Our project showed how mathematical modeling bridges mathematics and the real world (Pollak 2012). We found that teachers do not need to choose between a focus on mathematics or a focus on social justice. By bridging the mathematics of students' everyday settings to school mathematics we saw mathematical modeling as a tool that motivated and engaged students while developing their confidence as mathematicians. We highlighted that while students were motivated by a problem that was socially and emotionally relevant to their lives, mathematics learning remained central to the project. Combining the community engagement project directly with the mathematical modeling task made mathematics come alive for students—beyond problems on a 2-D worksheet into 3-D reality. The problem-based activities of saving money with a project goal, making optimal choices of meal items, and budgeting money were important mathematics for students but also part of the process to help families in need. The hands-on work of packing the Thanksgiving baskets for families in their community further brought this project to life. We feel that our project showed that both the social justice aspect and the mathematics can be addressed without sacrificing either.

Mathematical modeling in this project also highlighted the involvement of teachers and students in affecting social change (Gutiérrez and Irving 2012). We documented the evolution of teachers who started to see themselves as agents of social justice by using authentic tasks that mattered to students' lives and recognizing and acting upon the power that both teachers and students had in making positive change. Students were empowered to act about an issue that not only saddened and concerned them but one that was relevant to them and their community. Students used mathematics to develop practical actions by which they and other stakeholders could address hunger in their community.

Lastly, we saw mathematical modeling as an equitable teaching practice that gave access to diverse learners. Our experiences with this project confirmed that young students' mathematical learning can be enriched and extended by activities that feature low floors, high ceilings, and wide walls (English 2017)—all features of mathematical modeling. The task was open in multiple ways, making it accessible for diverse learners. Being able to use any resource or manipulative helped concrete, hands-on learners and those who struggled with visual memory. Freedom to represent their model in any form allowed for creativity. First graders could cut and paste pictures, supporting children who struggled with the fine-motor skills of writing and reducing the language barriers that many students faced. Fourth-grade students had the freedom to choose what they purchased and the type of mathematics used to justify the choices for their "best" meal. Mathematical modeling in the elementary classroom is a creative endeavor, offering many solutions to real-world problems where mathematics can be used as a tool for social action. Mathematical modeling provided space for teachers and students to have a collective experience through the iterative process of making sense of and building knowledge of important mathematical ideas while engaging in the critical twenty-first-century skills necessary in our complex modern world (Suh, Matson, and Seshaiyer 2017). Our narrative shows that mathematics can be a part of service learning but can also be a great lesson for students in how math can serve them as mathematicians.

References

Aguirre, Julia M., Erin E. Turner, Tonya Gau Bartell, Crystal Kalinec-Craig, Mary Q. Foote, Amy Roth McDuffie, and Corey Drake. "Making Connections in Practice: How Prospective Elementary Teachers Connect to Children's Mathematical Thinking and Community Funds of Knowledge in Mathematics Instruction." *Journal of Teacher Education* 64, no. 2 (2013): 178–92.

Bartell, Tonya, Anita Wager, Ann Edwards, Dan Battey, Mary Foote, and Joi Spencer. "Toward a Framework for Research Linking Equitable Teaching with the Standards for Mathematical Practice." *Journal for Research in Mathematics Education* 48, no. 1 (2017): 7–21.

Berry, Robert Q., III. "Access to Upper-Level Mathematics: The Stories of Successful African American Middle School Boys." *Journal for Research in Mathematics Education* 39, no. 5 (2008): 464–88.

Civil, Marta. "Building on Community Knowledge: An Avenue to Equity in Mathematics Education." In *Improving Access to Mathematics: Diversity and Equity in the Classroom*, edited by Na'ilah Suad Nasir and Paul Cobb, pp. 105–17. New York: Teachers College Press, 2007.

English, L. D. "Advancing Elementary and Middle School STEM Education." *International Journal of Science and Mathematics Education* 15, no. 1 (2017): 5–24. https://doi.org/10.1007/s10763-017-9802-x.

Greer, Brian, Swapna Mukhopadhyay, and Wolff-Michael Roth. "Celebrating Diversity, Realizing Alternatives." In *Alternative Forms Of Knowing (in) Mathematics*, pp. 1–8. Rotterdam, the Netherlands: Sense Publishers, 2012. https://www.sensepublishers.com/media/1466-alternative-forms-of-knowing-in-mathematics.pdf.

Gutstein, Eric, and Bob Peterson, eds. *Rethinking Mathematics: Teaching Social Justice by the Numbers*. Milwaukee, Wis.: Rethinking Schools, Ltd., 2013.

Gutiérrez, Rochelle. "Context Matters: Equity, Success, and the Future of Mathematics Education." In *Proceedings of the 29th Annual Meeting of the North American Chapter of the International Group for the Psychology of Mathematics Education*, edited by T. Lamberg and L. R. Wiest, pp. 1–18. Reno: University of Nevada, 2007.

Gutiérrez, Rochelle, and Sonya Irving. "Student Centered Learning: Latino/a and Black Students and Mathematics." Boston: Nellie Mae Education Foundation, 2012.

Masingila, Joanna, Susana S. Davidenko, and Ewa Prus-Wisniowska. "Mathematics Learning and Practice in and out of School: A Framework for Connecting These Experiences." *Educational Studies in Mathematics* 31, nos. 1/2 (1996): 175–200.

Moll, Luis, Cathy Amanti, Deborah Neff, and Norma Gonzalez. "Funds of Knowledge for Teaching: Using a Qualitative Approach to Connect Homes and Classrooms." *Theory into Practice* 31, no. 2 (1992): 132–41.

National Governors Association Center for Best Practices and Council of Chief State School Officers (NGA Center and CCSSO). *Common Core State Standards for Mathematics*. Washington, D.C.: NGA Center and CCSSO, 2010. http://www.corestandards.org.

Pollak, Henry. "Introduction." In *Mathematical Modeling Handbook*, edited by H. Gould, D. R. Murray, and A. Sanfratello, pp. viii–xi. Bedford, Mass.: Consortium for Mathematics and Its Applications, 2012. http://www.comap.com/modelingHB/Modeling_HB_Sample.pdf.

Spina, Stephanie Urso. "Demythifying Multicultural Education: Social Semiotics as a Tool of Critical Pedagogy." *Teaching Education* 9, no. 1 (1997): 27–36. https://doi.org/10.1080/1047621970090104.

Suh, Jennifer M., Kathleen Matson, and Padmanabhan Seshaiyer. "Engaging Elementary Students in the Creative Process of Mathematizing Their World through Mathematical Modeling." *Education Sciences* 7, no. 62 (2017). doi:10.3390/educsci7020062.

Wager, Anita A. "Incorporating Out-Of-School Mathematics: From Cultural Context to Embedded Practice." *Journal of Mathematics Teacher Education* 15, no. 1 (2012): 9–23

PART II

Professional Development
That Embraces Community

CHAPTER 6

"We Don't Think of It in Terms of Math, It's Just the Way of Life"

Bev Caswell, *Ontario Institute for Studies in Education, University of Toronto, Ontario, Canada*
Jason Jones, *Nigigoonsiminikaaning First Nation, Rainy River District School Board, Fort Frances, Ontario, Canada*
Marjolaine LaPointe, *Kawartha Pine Ridge District School Board, Peterborough, Ontario, Canada*
Tracy Kabatay, *Seine River First Nation, Ontario, Canada*

When we ask what it means to *rehumanize* mathematics, we might also ask, "When has there been a time when mathematics was humanizing?" We acknowledge that, for many people, school mathematics has never been a humanizing experience. Here, we outline how humanizing mathematics is about creating spaces for voices that have previously been silenced and marginalized, building meaningful and mutually beneficial relationships, and finding ways to relearn and observe mathematics as a human endeavor. Within this framework, the challenge of "rehumanizing mathematics" requires addressing power imbalances in a variety of contexts: in classrooms, in schools, at the district level, and in the way professional development (PD) in education is negotiated.

This chapter demonstrates the contributions to mathematics and to the humanization of mathematics that are made possible when Indigenous language teachers, First Nation Educational Counsellors, and Elders are included in collaborative mathematics teacher professional development. (The chapter's title is a quote from Elder Mike Kabatay of Seine River First Nation.) This work is part of a larger PD research project, the Math for Young Children project, that invites teams of educators to design and rethink the foundation of an early-years mathematics curriculum by prioritizing spatial and embodied aspects of mathematics in kindergarten to grade 3 classrooms (Moss et al. 2016).

This chapter will provide readers with our account of the sociohistorical context that underlies the current paradigm shift to rehumanize mathematics. To honor the concept of rehumanization, we take a nontraditional approach by introducing the individual experiences and perspectives of the authors and by giving narrative accounts from community members of how the mathematics focus on geometry and spatial reasoning impacted mathematics literacy, cultural connection, and language revitalization within their communities. We hope that, by the conclusion of this chapter, educators will be persuaded to rethink typical hierarchies in PD and consider the broad implications and application of this approach to other PD programs aimed at integrating aspects of equity and education within critical gateway subjects.

■ Sociohistorical Context

In Canada, beginning in the 1870s, more than 150,000 First Nations, Métis, and Inuit children were taken from their homes, their communities, and their parents and placed in Indian residential schools. These government-funded, church-run schools had a stated policy to "kill the Indian in the child." Many students, forbidden to speak their language and practice their own culture, suffered emotional, physical, and sexual abuse (Truth and Reconciliation Commission [TRC] 2015).

In 2008, the Truth and Reconciliation Commission (TRC) was formed in Canada to gather statements and "document the truth of survivors, families, communities and anyone personally affected by the Indian Residential School experience" (TRC 2015, p. 7). Canada's Prime Minister made a public apology on behalf of the government. A final report was issued in 2015, calling for a commitment to a process of reconciliation defined as "an ongoing process of establishing and maintaining respectful relationships" (TRC 2015, p. 16). The report resulted in 94 Calls to Action, focusing efforts toward language revitalization, land reclamation, and recognition of the devastating legacy of residential school experience. The tenth Call to Action serves as a relevant example with its specific recognition of the need for a new commitment to "education legislation with the full participation and informed consent of Aboriginal peoples" (TRC 2015, p. 197). This includes but is not limited to the following:

i.   Improving education attainment levels

ii. Developing culturally appropriate curricula

iii. Protecting the right to Aboriginal languages

iv. Enabling parental and community responsibility, control, and accountability

v.   Enabling parents to fully participate in the education of their children. (p. 197)

■ (Re)Humanizing Mathematics

In its simplest form, this legislation outlines a mandate to *rehumanize* education. What would happen if we focus on "establishing and maintaining respectful relationships" (p. 16) and brought this spirit of reconciliation into our mathematics teaching, research, and teacher professional development? Rochelle Gutiérrez (2012a) speaks about how a "more humanistic conception of mathematics requires teaching that moves beyond the ability to perform well on standardized tests or measures of conceptual knowledge" (p. 31) and argues that "it is not enough to call it equity if mathematics as a field and/or our relationships on this planet do not change" (p. 20).

■ Rehumanization of Mathematics Educators

In this spirit of rehumanization, we begin by positioning ourselves in relation to the research.

Bev Caswell is a mathematics education professor who works with educators to design inquiry-based learning environments. Bev aims to create collective spaces in which each educator within the PD circle can bring expertise based on their own ways of knowing and lived experiences. Within this framework, Bev recognizes her privilege as a White/settler mathematics education professor and has committed her position of authority to disrupt typical hierarchies in PD, which includes creating space for educators who have been historically excluded from positions of power within school districts and for voices that have been previously silenced. Her work is inspired by activist scholars such as Rochelle Gutiérrez, Eric Gutstein, Kyndall Brown, Marta Civil, Lisa Lunney Borden, Indigo Esmonde, and Joan Moss.

Jason Jones is the Anishinaabemowin (Ojibwe language) coordinator for a district school board in Treaty #3 territory in Northwestern Ontario. Jason's parents are residential school survivors, and, although they are Ojibwe speakers, their experiences of language suppression in residential school led them, as with others, "to decide not to teach their children an Aboriginal language" (TRC, p. 84). At age 19, Jason took it upon himself to learn the language. He is now considered a "language warrior" who plays an integral role in revitalizing Anishinaabemowin.

Marjolaine LaPointe is of the Deer clan, from Ardoch Algonquin First Nation, and is an Anishinaabemowin teacher. Marjolaine provides this perspective on the long-term effect of language suppression from the residential school system: "The colonial system that is Canada was quite successful with my family, and I'm the first in three generations to pick the language back up again." Her work aims to show students how Anishinaabemowin functions as a profoundly mathematical and scientific language.

Tracy Kabatay is of the Jackfish clan and is an Anishinaabe Educational Counsellor who acts as liaison between students from her First Nation community and the public school they attend, providing both support and advocacy. In her words, she has chosen this path "for the love of our children. Everything is for our children and for our futures." Tracy describes herself walking "in both the Anishinaabe world and the non-Anishinaabe world." Her own school experience was a lesson in "learning how to survive school in the White world, while at the same time making sure I didn't lose who I was." She relates that although she encountered many barriers and challenges in school, she did not lose her voice, culture, beliefs, and morals. She now works with Anishinaabe Educational Assistants and her community to develop educational policies to limit the barriers and challenges students face in school and to protect and promote students' cultural identities.

In this chapter, we will refer to individual authors, their stories, and their experiences in the third person, using first names only. We also refer to mathematics education researchers in this chapter by their first and last names rather than citing their findings in more conventional reference terms; we intend this as a mechanism to rehumanize the researchers and present the mathematics education community in its most inclusive and inviting form.

■ PD Location, Structure, and Approach

Our PD approach to rehumanize mathematics incorporates elements of Japanese lesson study, which authentically places all members of the PD community as curriculum designers and researchers contributing to mathematics education. While traditional Japanese lesson study can be a tightly structured process with strongly formalized rules and procedures, we adapted a more fluid, context-responsive version of this approach (Moss et al. 2015).

Our project was situated in northwestern Ontario, in both provincial public schools serving predominantly Anishinaabe students and federally funded First Nation schools on reserves; it took place over a six-month period. All PD sessions were videotaped and audio-recorded. Excerpts of conversations were transcribed and children's artifacts were saved.

Together, members of the working collective—Anishinaabe and non-Anishinaabe educators, Elders, and university researchers—participated in a variety of geometry and spatial reasoning activities as learners, designed and conducted task-based clinical interviews with children, co-designed and collaboratively carried out exploratory lessons in classrooms with children, engaged with mathematics education research, and created resources for other educators (Moss et al. 2015). (For examples of the materials from the project, see this article's page on NCTM's More4U website.)

The multiplicity of voices and the growing relationships among people who had previously operated in separate spheres were remarkable to witness. As Tracy puts it, "I've been working as the First Nation Education Counsellor for ten years, and that was the first time I was actually invited at an administrative level to a meeting with the district school board. It was actually nice to have that welcome and to walk into that room that day and to be a part of the discussion." Linda Tuhiwai Smith (2012) describes changes of this type as marking the shift between Indigenous people "being viewed as research objects . . . and becoming our own researchers" (p. 187).

Tracy highlights how this PD was different: "Before this PD, community was always separate from school. There was never any effort to bring community and school together." Tracy continues, "Cultural sensitivity was never explored. PD was created based on non-Anishinaabe people's assumptions about what we may feel or get out of the PD, but it wasn't us there at the table. Even the non-Anishinaabe teachers involved weren't given voice."

Typical PD in schools is often a top-down process in which outside "experts" deliver a message or program for teachers in a district to implement regardless of its relevance to the realities of the community. As an alternative approach, our PD invited key community leaders and educators to join in the process of figuring out new ways to foster enhanced mathematics learning. This created buy-in for teachers in the PD. As one numeracy coach described:

> It was amazing how non-threatening this PD was. You weren't just telling us the best way to do math. You gave us the chance to try some of the math activities, then invited us to go together into the classrooms and try it. Typically in PD, we don't work in classrooms with children and have the work happen before our very eyes. We don't see teachers co-teaching and collaborating with researchers, but in this PD, that is how it worked. We all felt like we were contributing to something greater.

Throughout this PD, the fluidity of both roles and working spaces—academic researchers co-teaching young children with classroom teachers, classroom teachers presenting their work in academic settings, young children joining in to test ideas in progress, and intense discussions of the complexities of mathematics and language at local festive gatherings—radically upended the relational hierarchies and divisions so commonly entrenched in school settings and the broader community. This site-based approach to PD enabled ongoing interplay between lesson and curriculum design; this allowed participants to move into classrooms to try something out, return to the drawing board to rethink the lesson in light of children's responses or an informed suggestion from a community member, and then try out the redesigned lesson with a new grade or group of children. Quickly, teachers began to view themselves as curriculum designers who were creating a bank of resources for other educators within the community. Seeing their students so engaged, thoughtful, and keenly responsive to mathematical learning was transformative for many teachers, setting in motion a dynamic upward continuum of designing, teaching, and learning.

The inclusion of Elders, language and cultural teachers, and community members provided an unprecedented opportunity for non-Ashininaabe educators to form new relationships, build awareness of the continuities and disjunctions between Indigenous (e.g., Anishinaabe) and Western mathematical understandings, and gain new understanding to inform their way of teaching.

■ Community Connections

In addition to engagement and learning, community connections were critical for the success of this project. Not only were Tracy and Jason involved in creating new spatial math activities grounded in their culture, but from the very beginning of the project they played an integral role in providing direct connections with the communities, organizing social gatherings and cultural celebrations. Tracy explains her intentions for community connectivity:

> I wanted the research team to know where our kids come from and the knowledge that we carry already, which was validated when you look at the research results—that our kids are very smart—which is really an awesome thing for us. My father did a blessing for the whole project. And it was bigger than what you might consider a blessing. We invited the spiritual part of being an Anishinaabe person to the research. He said we need to take care of the people who are going to be taking care of the children. That was the beginning of our partnership.

This created opportunities for non-Anishinaabe PD members to understand protocols; develop awareness and understanding of Anishinaabe knowledges, histories, and perspectives; and experience the "funds of knowledge" (Civil 2016) within each First Nation community. For many of the non-Anishinaabe teachers and school district leaders, this was the first time they had stepped foot in the First Nation communities, even though their classrooms and schools were made up predominantly of children from those communities.

■ Our Mathematics Focus: Spatial Reasoning in the Early Years

Motivated by research pointing to the importance of early years mathematics in providing a strong foundation for overall school achievement, Bev and her colleague Joan Moss were invited to work within a school district in northwestern Ontario to strengthen the teaching and learning of mathematics in kindergarten through grade 3 classrooms. In their previous work in urban centers, Bev and Joan had observed how young children thrived in a rigorous yet play-based, spatially enriched mathematics program (developed collaboratively by Bev and Joan with classroom teachers and district numeracy coaches).

The focus on developing children's spatial reasoning and geometric thinking aligns closely with NCTM expectations (NCTM 2000, 2006). Spatial reasoning provides an equitable entry point to school mathematics for children as it often develops ahead of number sense, grounds mathematics understanding through body-related experiences, and offers aesthetic appeal through the use of symmetries. This focus often reveals spatial abilities that can go unnoticed in classrooms exclusively focused on number and arithmetic (Moss et al. 2015). However, research shows that spatial skills are both malleable and highly correlated with mathematics achievement (Bruce et al. 2015; Uttal et al. 2013).

From a rehumanizing perspective, Tracy spoke about the mathematics focus with her father, Elder Mike Kabatay:

> I had explained to him that the project was about spatial geometry, symmetry, and he was like, "What is that?" The more I talked to him about it, he was like, "Oh, that's our way of life. And that's the way it is for Anishinaabe people. We don't think of it in terms of math, it's just the way of life."

For everyone involved in the PD, the realization that mathematics is deeply embedded in cultural practice and is deeply connected to Anishinaabe ways of thinking and being was profound. It clearly showed how mathematics is part of what it means to be human.

■ Family Math Events

Mathematics also became a rehumanizing activity by including voices of the community in planning family math events, which combined Anishinaabe and Western ways of knowing. (For a list of these activities, see this book's page at NCTM's More4U website.) The focus on spatial reasoning afforded ways of connecting with cultural practices and generating culturally responsive math activities. For example, during one of our PD sessions, we explored the use of tangrams to strengthen students' skills in composing and decomposing 2-D shapes—an important concept in geometry. From this, Tracy and colleague Shelly Jones came up with the idea for children and families to use tangrams to represent their distinct clan animals, an important system within Anishinaabe culture. During the family math event, families created their clan animals from the tangram shapes and clan animal outlines provided. They then recreated and printed the images on a square of cloth with fabric paint using larger wooden tangram shapes that had been built specifically for the event by older students in a woodworking class. Elders then sewed each square into a tangram quilt that combined all the clan animals. The quilt was placed on display in the school entranceway, providing students and families with a daily opportunity to see their culture and mathematical ingenuity proudly reflected within the school. This is but one example of a humanizing way to see math as an inclusive, playful, engaging, accessible, and honored endeavor that incorporates important aspects of family and cultural identity.

In addition to raising awareness of geometry and measurement concepts embedded in local cultural practices, family math events helped to build trust between the school system and the community. For some parents who were residential school survivors, this was the first time they had set foot in a school since their own school days. This event provided an opportunity for parents to observe their children's ways of knowing being respected and showcased while co-participating in the mathematical process. This integrated approach became a model for the entire school district.

■ Language Revitalization through Mathematics

A key and unique feature of the PD has been the inclusion of Anishinaabemowin teachers. According to Marie Battiste (2013), "Indigenous language revitalization is the most significant factor in the survival of Indigenous knowledge and culture" (p. 146). In the words of a PD participant: "When I listen to the Elders and to the leadership, they want to have Ojibwe language. Language is more than just a language. It's the culture. The traditions, histories, perspectives are embedded in the language."

We explicitly used mathematics as a subversive tool to promote language revitalization. We were inspired by the work of Lisa Lunney Borden (2011, 2013, 2014) who transformed her mathematics teaching practice by learning and incorporating the verb-based grammatical structure of the Mi'kmaw language taught to her by Elders. Her mathematics teaching became more action-oriented when compared to the typical and predominantly noun-based Western approach to school mathematics (Lunney Borden and Munroe 2016). Lisa argues that "verbification holds promise as a means of supporting Aboriginal students in mathematics learning" (Lunney Borden 2011, p. 13). As Jason pointed out early in the PD, "Ojibwe language being 80 percent verbs, and us wanting math to be a verb-based activity, that connection was pretty simple to make." Marjolaine points out how the nature of the PD allowed for reciprocal learning and for thinking about mathematics in a new way: "Through the math project, I'm learning the deep understanding of the language along with my students. In our language, most of our words are verbs so when we do math, we're not doing math, we're mathing!"

Over the course of the PD, Jason contributed an Anishinaabemowin word that encapsulates a (re)humanizing way of thinking about mathematics: *Gaa-maamiwi-asigaginendamowin*. Loosely translated, this word means "gathering to learn and do mathematics together, collectively performing useful action." This is reminiscent of *mawikinutimatimk*, or "coming together to learn," a Mi'kmaw term that Lisa Lunney Borden (2011, p. 9) learned from Elders, which implies "that everyone comes to the table with gifts and talents to share—everyone has something that they can learn. It conjures an image of a community of learners working in a circle where all members are equally important and necessary" (p. 9). Similarly, Dwayne Donald, Florence Glanfield, and Gladys Sterenberg (2011) describe "culturally relational education . . . based on the Cree concept of *miyo-wichitowin*, a healing energy or medicine that is generated when we are actively together with the intention of honouring and respecting the relationships we are enmeshed within" (n.p.).

■ Spatial Reasoning and Anishinaabemowin

Anishinaabemowin is structured in relation to movement, and spatial relationships are embedded in the sounds of the language. One adaptation of lesson study that was introduced in the PD was a teacher-led interview with individual children that focused on composing and decomposing 2-D shapes (Sarama and Clements 2003). As Marjolaine highlights:

> We talked about the location of things and how they are described not only in the location but in reference to other things. So if you are going to slide it [a geometric shape], are you going to continue to slide it? Because if you are going to continue to slide it, then you are going to add more sounds than if you are going to slide it and then stop. If you are going to turn it, and just keep turning it, you are going to use a different verb or a different series of sounds after that core idea than if you are to turn it a bit and then stop. There would have to be an end point where you either use that *g* or the *k* sound.

This description reinforced for the teachers that slides and turns are central ideas relating to geometric transformation (NCTM 2000, 2006; Ontario Ministry of Education [OME] 2014) and highlights the need for children "to understand the idea of *relative* location, namely that any location can be described only in relation to them or something or someone else" (Moss et al. 2016, p. 175). It also highlights perspective taking, a central skill in the development of spatial reasoning and a way of visualizing the continuity of a slide and of a turn, connecting the idea that "visualization is a particularly powerful, and at times essential tool for scientific and mathematical thinking" (Moss et al. 2015, p. 30).

Our PD marked the first time that Anishinaabemowin teachers were invited to co-teach mathematics lessons with classroom teachers. In doing so, we found that Anishinaabemowin (Ojibwe language) provided a way in to think about the importance of visualization, a foundational process in developing students' spatial reasoning that was not previously appreciated within the traditional school system. As an example lesson, children were shown a paper rectangle followed by a paper square (equivalent to 1/8 of the area of the rectangle). Students were asked to think about or visualize how many such squares they would need to cover the rectangle.

During the lesson debrief, Jason introduced the Anishinaabemowin word for rectangle: genoo-gakagaag. As Jason stated, "The literal meaning is 'rectangle.' But it means elongated square with points moving on there. So it's talking about how it visually looks." Jason's use of genoo-gakagaag illuminated the concept, which is sometimes difficult to grasp, that a square is a special rectangle. The Anishinaabemowin word provided children with an opportunity to visualize the movement of a shape, rather than define an image in its static form. This ability to visualize movement is a key component of spatial reasoning.

The unique capabilities of Anishinaabemowin for highlighting critical features of geometrical shapes is further illustrated by Marjolaine. In her words:

> I was thinking of this word, *kakadeyaa*, which means a square, but it's not a noun. It's a verb which means it's squaring itself. And *kakadeyaa* has this *k* sound which is a cutting, a grouping, a separating, and when we break the language down into those sound-based parts, we start thinking in three dimensions as opposed to binaries of "this is this and this is that,'" and we see relationships between many things. And the language really lends itself to spatial reasoning and math inquiry. That word also implies that what you're looking at has grouped or separated itself in a way that is different from its natural state. Which is kind of what a square is because if you look out onto the land, what we see are not really squares—we see things that are of all kinds of different shapes but that very harsh squaring off is an odd thing to see. And so that's why we have a very specific word for it.

Not only did the Anishinaabemowin language offer new insights into spatial concepts, but mathematics offered Jason a deeper understanding of the language:

> Working in this math project helps me to understand the language a lot better. Some of these new math concepts that were introduced to us when I tried to translate really helped me to understand more about the language. It helps me to be proud of my own language and understand the vitality that it has and its ability to create new words, which inspires me to think—wow—our language can go a long way in developing conceptual understandings.

■ Elders Rehumanize Mathematics

Elders Ogimaawigwanebiik (Nancy) Jones, Mike Kabatay, and Nora Atlookan offered ceremonial opening protocols to begin research, PD, and family math nights "in a Good Way." (*Mino-bimaadiziwin* is the Anishinaabe philosophy of how to live life in a Good Way.) There was an understanding that the work would involve seeing children in a good light and hearing children in a compassionate way. Bringing this kind of humanity into the project became a sacred promise that inspired new levels of commitment.

The spatial thinking focus provided opportunities for Anishinaabe educators and elders to connect to cultural practices from their home communities, further rehumanizing mathematics. For example, one activity invited learners to predict designs that would appear after holes were punched in a folded piece of paper that was then unfolded. According to Joan Moss and colleagues (2016), the activity requires spatial visualization to "generate, maintain, and manipulate a mental image" (p. 33). This activity sparked Elder Nora Atlookan to share stories about her mother, who practiced the cultural art form of birch bark biting, which involves visualizing and then creating symmetrical designs by folding and biting the birch bark. (See this chapter's page on NCTM's More4U website.) Nora describes the cognitive and physical processes of birch bark biting: "My mother would bite and think at the same time. She would fold up the birch bark, bite it, but not opening it, folding, then biting and biting again. When the bark was unfolded, it would be amazing to see all kinds of intricate designs she had created."

Lines of symmetry appear as the square, rectangle, or circle of thin birch bark is repeatedly folded. The finished product reveals rotational, reflection, and point symmetry. Lisa Lunney Borden (2014) describes how birch bark biting demonstrates "understanding of fractions as part of a whole, of geometric properties of 2-D shapes, of symmetry, and of transformational geometry" (p. 192).

At one point, Nora referred to an earlier conversation in the PD about how people with strong spatial visualization skills tend to do well in mathematics and how "this ability to perceive complex spatial patterns and comprehend imaginary movements in space" (Mix and Cheng 2012, p. 200) is foundational in geometric thinking. She was emotionally moved by the realization that her mother must have possessed not only artistic talent but impressive spatial talent as well. Rehumanizing mathematics validated Nora's cultural knowledge, honored her mother, and contributed a new and important understanding of geometric and spatial possibilities through art forms that had been nearly forgotten in her home community. Her interest in sharing this art form with children (and teaching the paper folding/hole punch activity in Ojibwe) created an opportunity for her to work with teachers and authentically share knowledge in classrooms.

■ Results

In addition to the project honoring Anishinaabe mathematics in its own terms, there was shared consensus within the group of Elders, teachers, parents, and researchers that it was important to learn whether this approach facilitated children's learning in general mathematics. The schools in which we worked had been identified by the district as "the lowest performing" on provincial standardized tests. To assess the progress of children in kindergarten to grade 3, we administered individual pre- and post-tests including measures of geometry, spatial reasoning, spatial language, and numeration. After our first year together in the project, the results were very encouraging. Children not only demonstrated significant progress in measures of geometry and spatial thinking, but they also performed significantly better in numeration than did a control group for that year. (See Hawes et al. 2017 for details of the measures and results). These results provide an encouraging counternarrative to the hegemonic messages permeating the media about the gap between Indigenous and non-Indigenous student achievement.

When these research results were shared with the community, Elder Mike Kabatay remarked, "You've reawakened something that is already in our children." This statement highlights an understanding of the knowledge that lies within Anishinaabe people, knowledge that was suppressed during the residential school era. In this way, rehumanizing mathematics acts as a tool for reconciliation. Tracy reveals this spirit of reconciliation in the following: "My dad wanted to say '*Miigwech*' for the team coming into his path. My dad is a residential school survivor and for him to be involved academically is an honor. School was a negative experience for him. To see his daughters and granddaughters succeeding in school and to be involved in such research is an honor."

The PD participants also noted that the children engaged enthusiastically with mathematics intellectually, emotionally, and culturally. Over the course of the PD, non-Anishinaabe teachers began to see their students in a new light, became excited about the "incredible" spatial talent that had previously gone unrecognized in their students, and were motivated to "up their game," excitedly planning new activities to meet and match the needs and strengths of their students. Inclusion of Anishinaabe educators and the community within the PD circle provided the new perspectives and engagement that further contributed to the success of the program.

■ Implications/Discussion

While our work was carried out in a very particular context, we feel that our general approach provides important guiding principles for a shift in PD. Our work demonstrates the importance of creating meaningful connections and building relationships with the goal of improving mathematics teaching within a framework of reconciliation and reciprocal learning. Mathematics as a gatekeeper subject inspires teachers to think about issues of equity. One of the biggest strengths of the PD is that it enables teachers to make authentic contributions to mathematics education and to build respectful relationships that are mutually beneficial. One second-grade teacher, Cristol, shared how the PD helped her redefine what mathematics means to her:

> This work has enabled me to move beyond my own negative experiences and frustrations with teaching and learning math, and redefine what math means to me. Math no longer exists as a block of time on my day plan, as it has become second nature for me to view many aspects of my teaching through the lens of spatial reasoning. This new understanding has led me to see connections through art, literacy, science, mapping skills, and much more.

Shifting power structures, creating a level playing field among participants, and removing the hierarchy of typical PD in which "the experts" deliver and teachers receive—all these practices open compassionate spaces for everyone to authentically contribute expertise. In the beginning of the PD, we often heard teachers say, "I'm not good at math," only to watch them excel at a spatial reasoning challenge, validating their spatial talent and strengthening their mathematics identities.

■ Rehumanizing Mathematics as Compassionate, Playful, Rigorous, and Culturally Responsive

We hope that sharing our stories and experiences will prove to be one step in a long and difficult journey of reconciliation. Rehumanizing mathematics as reconciliation privileges Indigenous knowledges in the teaching and learning of mathematics, amplifies voices previously silenced, and demonstrates the importance of respectful and reciprocal partner relationships in advancing student success. In our experience, supporting young children and teachers mathematically provided entry points for building trust and formed a bridge between schools and the First Nation communities they serve.

This chapter highlights what is possible when we embrace a rehumanizing mathematics approach that provides "indigenous peoples with space to create and be indigenous" (Smith 2012, p. 232), a space in which Indigenous and non-Indigenous educators can shape the work together, build relationships, promote healing, and feel empowered to transform an oppressive and colonial educational system into one that is more humane for students.

Rochelle Gutiérrez (2012b) envisions a system that "would allow students to feel 'I'm doing this mathematics in *my* language, using algorithms from *my* home culture, answering questions that are of importance to me, and serving the needs of *my* community'" (p. 31). Our PD emphasizes the vision of mathematics for Indigenous *teachers*, demonstrating respectful and reciprocal partner relationships in the process of reconciliation *and* rehumanizing mathematics.

Jason illustrates this point with the following comment: "Being a part of the math PD helped me to see that reconciliation is happening and that we as Anishinaabe are respected. And our language could help math concepts become more clear to a variety of learners." For Nathalie Sinclair (2017), Canada Research Chair in Tangible Mathematics, learning about the Anishinaabemowin number system from Jason helped her "on the path to understand that it's important to not just focus on translating, but on how the way of thinking about numbers is different, and that this is what we really want to learn about and preserve—a unique and rich way of thinking that the English language doesn't enable."

For too long, Indigenous content was entirely absent from the curriculum. According to Marjolaine: "To include Indigenous knowledge in math and science represents, for me, a movement towards the understanding by the education field that our ways of knowing are valid and as logical and scientific as Western ways. To me, it was a tacit acknowledging that Indigenous math and science knowledge is equal to Western ways, and for that, I remain profoundly grateful."

Tracy describes what it meant to be involved: "When you're always looking in from the outside and not always agreeing with what's being decided on your behalf—you feel like an outsider. This PD changed that." She goes on to describe the long-lasting commitment to this project: "Year after year, my family, we feast this project. We feast everyone who is involved in it. That invites our grandfathers, our grandmothers, and our ancestors who sit with everyone, with all the teachers, the kids, and everyone who is involved."

For non-Anishinaabe educators, the PD created space to develop awareness and understanding of Anishinaabe knowledges, histories, and perspectives; to show solidarity in the struggle for language revitalization; and to connect with communities in meaningful ways. Bev reflects on the project:

> What began as an invitation to support schools in improving student achievement in mathematics became an opportunity to understand identity and power issues. Mathematics formed a bridge that allowed me to develop relationships, to witness firsthand the systemic barriers to participation in school mathematics for Indigenous parents, children, and educators—and the urgency of change needed. My commitment to equity has been given new life. It was a great honor to learn from Elders and Anishinaabe educators who shared knowledge with such generosity of spirit. The personal relationships formed with all members of the PD have been life-changing.

In a speech to an assembled group of educators, Heather Campbell, the director of the school district, shared that, in her view, the project "gives teachers, students and families a great deal of hope." Linda Tuhiwai Smith suggests that the "research stories that need to be told are small stories from local communities across time and space . . . the stories of transformation and hope" (p. 225). Diverse voices gathered for the purpose of teaching and learning mathematics in a good way, creating a synergy that encapsulates rehumanizing mathematics as reconciliation. The Anishinaabe people already have a word for this: *Gaa-maamiwi-asigaginendamowin*. Or as Elder Mike Kabatay says, "We don't call it math, it's just the way of life."

Acknowledgments

We dedicate our chapter to the memory of Dan Jones #language-warrior. The authors also extend heartfelt appreciation to Elders Ogimaawigwanebiik (Nancy) Jones, Mike Kabatay, and Nora Atlookan, and to all of the educators, community members, teachers, educational counselors, and families who contributed greatly to this work. Above all, we thank the children in Treaty #3 territory who continue to inspire and astonish us. We also thank the Dr. Eric Jackman Institute of Child Study Lab School teachers (Ontario Institute for Studies in Education/University of Toronto) Carol Stephenson and Zoe Donoahue for generously sharing their ideas and expertise. We appreciate the leadership of Heather Campbell, Sharla MacKinnon, Elizabeth Morley, Richard Messina, and Chriss Bogert, as well as Seven Generations Education Institute's Brent Tookenay, Angela Mainville, Shelly Jones, Aimee Beazley, and Kim Kirk. We acknowledge the generous support of the N.S. Robertson Foundation and greatly appreciate the work of our team: Zack Hawes, Larisa Lam, Zach Pedersen, Jisoo Seo, and Mischa Berlin. Many thanks to Sarah Higgins for the helpful comments on our final draft. A special thank-you to colleagues Joan Moss and Julie Comay for their inspiration and professional insights in the PD design and the writing of this chapter.

References

Battiste, Marie. *Decolonizing Education. Nourishing the Learning Spirit.* Saskatoon, Saskatchewan, Canada: Purich Press, 2013.

Bruce, Cathy D., Nathalie Sinclair, Joan Moss, Zachary Hawes, and Beverly Caswell. "Spatializing the Mathematics Curricula." In *Spatial Reasoning in the Early Years: Principles, Assertions, and Speculations,* edited by Brent Davis, pp. 85–106. New York: Routledge, 2015.

Donald, Dwayne, Florence Glanfield, and Gladys Sterenberg. "Culturally Relational Education in and with an Indigenous Community." *Education* 17, no. 3 (2011).

Civil, Marta. "STEM Learning Research through a Funds of Knowledge Lens." *Cultural Studies of Science Education* 11, no. 1 (2016): 41–59.

Gutiérrez, Rochelle. "Context Matters: How Should We Conceptualize Equity in Mathematics Education?" In *Equity in Discourse for Mathematics Education: Theories, Practices, and Policies,* edited by Beth Herbel-Eisenmann, Jeffrey Choppin, David Wagner, and David Primm, pp. 17–33. New York: Springer, 2012a.

_____. "Embracing Nepantla: Rethinking 'Knowledge' and Its Use in Mathematics Teaching." *REDIMAT: Journal of Research in Mathematics Education* 1, no. 1 (2012b): 29–56

Hawes, Zachary, Joan Moss, Beverly Caswell, Sarah Naqvi, and Sharla MacKinnon. "Enhancing Children's Spatial and Numerical Skills through a Dynamic Spatial Approach to Early Geometry Instruction: Effects of a 32-Week Intervention." *Cognition and Instruction* (2017): 1–29.

Lunney Borden, Lisa. "The 'Verbification' of Mathematics: Using the Grammatical Structures of Mi'kmaq to Support Student Learning." *For the Learning of Mathematics* 31, no. 3 (2011): 8–13.

_____. "What's the Word for . . . ? Is There a Word for . . . ? How Understanding Mi'kmaw Language Can Help Support Mi'kmaw learners in Mathematics." *Mathematics Education Research Journal* 25, no. 1 (2013): 5–22.

_____. "Mawkinumasultinej! Let's Learn Together! Developing Culturally Based Inquiry Projects in Mi'kmaw Communities." Canadian Mathematics Education Study Group Proceedings 2014 Annual Meeting, pp. 187–94. http://www.cmesg.org/wp-content/uploads/2015/05/CMESG2014.pdf.

Lunney Borden, Lisa, and Elizabeth Munroe. "Speaking English Isn't Thinking English: Exploring Young Aboriginal Children's Mathematical Experiences through Aboriginal Perspectives." In *Language, Culture, and Learning in Early Childhood: Transcultural Home, School, and Community Contexts*, edited by Ann Anderson, Jim Anderson, Jan Hare, and Marianne McTavish, pp. 64–81. New York: Routledge, Taylor & Francis, 2016.

Mix, Kelly S., and Yi-Ling Cheng. "The Relation between Space and Math: Developmental and Educational Implications." *Advances in Child Development and Behavior* 42 (2012): 197–243.

Moss, Joan, Catherine Bruce, Beverly Caswell, Tara Flynn, and Zachary Hawes. *Taking Shape: Activities to Enhance Geometric and Spatial Thinking.* Toronto: Pearson School Canada, 2016.

Moss, Joan, Zachary Hawes, Sarah Naqvi, and Beverly Caswell. "Adapting Japanese Lesson Study to Enhance the Teaching and Learning of Geometry and Spatial Reasoning in Early Years Classrooms: A Case Study." *ZDM: The International Journal on Mathematics Education* 47, no. 3 (2015): 1–14.

National Council of Teachers of Mathematics (NCTM). *Principles and Standards for School Mathematics.* Reston, Va.: NCTM, 2000.

_____. *Curriculum Focal Points for Prekindergarten through Grade 8 Mathematics: A Quest for Coherence.* Reston, Va.: NCTM, 2006.

Ontario Ministry of Education (OME). *Paying Attention to Spatial Thinking K-12: Support Document for Paying Attention to Mathematical Education.* Toronto, Ontario: Queen's Printer for Ontario, 2014.

Sarama, Julie, and Douglas H. Clements. "Building Blocks of Early Childhood Mathematics." *Teaching Children Mathematics* 9, no. 8 (2003): 480–4.

Sinclair, Nathalie. Email message to co-author Bev Caswell, May 2017.

Smith, Linda Tuhiwai. *Decolonising Methodologies: Research and Indigenous Peoples.* 2nd ed. New York: Zed Books, 2012.

The Truth and Reconciliation Commission of Canada (TRC). *Honouring the Truth, Reconciling for the Future: Summary of the Final Report of the Truth and Reconciliation Commission of Canada* (2015). http://www.trc.ca/websites/trcinstitution/File/2015/Findings/Exec_Summary_2015_05_31_web_o.pdf.

Uttal, David, Nathaniel Meadow, Elizabeth Tipton, Linda L. Hand, Alison R. Alden, Christopher Warren, and Nora S. Newcombe. "The Malleability of Spatial Skills: A Meta-Analysis of Training Studies." *Psychological Bulletin* 139, no. 2 (2013): 352–402.

CHAPTER 7

Mathequity Hours:
Fostering Wholeness in a Mathematics Learning Community

Aris Winger, *Georgia Gwinnett College, Lawrenceville*
Michael Young, *Iowa State University, Ames*
Idris Stovall, *University of Pennsylvania and the Mathematical Sciences Institute, Philadelphia*
Sarah Sword, Eden Badertscher, Miriam Gates, Una MacDowell, and Al Cuoco,
Education Development Center, Inc., Waltham, Massachusetts

The authors of this article represent a racially and professionally diverse subset of a community working together on Designing for Equity by Thinking in and about Mathematics (DEbT-M), a National Science Foundation–funded Mathematics Science Partnership aimed at closing the opportunity gap for secondary students who have been systematically marginalized in their mathematics experiences. The name honors Gloria Ladson-Billings's (2006) stance that the United States does not have an achievement gap but owes an "educational debt" to millions of underserved students.

In working to address this educational debt, we provide significant professional development (PD) for secondary teachers in mathematics and equity, as described in the section "Examples from Mathequity" below. But in doing this professional work, we found that we had to create a new space, "Mathequity Hours," in which we work on mathematics and equity *together*.

To situate our work, we open with quotations from three Black professors of mathematics, coauthors of this chapter and leaders in the DEbT-M community:

> When people come and say, "I hate math," they're saying, "I hate my mathematical experience," right? Because math is objectively a beautiful, profound expression of human thought. That is a fact. You cannot expect someone coming from high school math to have a reasonable critique of mathematics. They're saying, "I was devalued in this experience." I hear that. And I say to them, "I'm sorry that's the experience you had, but I'm here to present you with another one. And you have to be open to that. So: Are you willing?" —*Aris Winger*

> I try to make myself visible. —*Michael Young*

> As an African American male, it is a load to carry in terms of just existing and walking in this society of ours. These are things that I have to compartmentalize: the dysfunctions of our society, so that I can be about the mission and vision of

the work: trying to create the next generation of mathematical scientists. But when you're examining your own bias, and engaging others around that, you have to engage that compartmentalization in such a way that you open up. There is a vulnerability that comes along with opening up that was surprising to me [in DEbT-M], because of compartmentalizing for so long. —*Idris Stovall*

Why start with these three statements? We share here a little more about the mathematicians and the basis for those quotations in their lives.

In 1997, a professor sent Aris Winger, then a college student at Howard University, to the American Mathematical Society–Mathematical Association of America Joint Meetings in San Diego. Until then, he had seen mathematics as a solitary endeavor for someone who loved mathematics, which he does and always has. But suddenly he saw a new vision of how mathematics is done and shared as a professional communal activity.

The conference trip is one example of the powerful actions of supportive teachers, professors, and mentors who recognized Aris's potential. As a student from Washington, D.C., he was valedictorian of Paul Laurence Dunbar High School, a rigorous and prestigious public school. His mathematics teachers helped him feel at home in school while holding him to a high standard of academic excellence. He felt valued, seen, and supported at Dunbar, and then again at Howard, where he was an ambitious, dedicated student. When he got to Carnegie Mellon University for his PhD program, he felt well prepared. New mentors there saw his potential as a mathematician, pushed him, and nurtured him. His quotation comes out of this experience of feeling *valued* in mathematics, of knowing how extraordinary that is, and of wanting others to have similar experiences.

Michael Young is also extremely dedicated to mathematics, but he shares a different point of view. His quotation is short, but powerful. He is making a statement about a Black man's experience in mathematics that runs across disciplines, across institutions, across life: the invisibility of Black people in our White culture. Michael, a Black mathematician who has achieved great academic success, still has to fight for visibility in the field. This is a hard thing to talk about—it's easy to dismiss someone's feeling of being "invisible." Often the only Black mathematician in a room, Michael is clearly visible. From a young age, he has been aware that his opinions have not been treated with the same regard as those of others. Throughout his life, he has been surprising people with his mathematical abilities: One of his high school teachers admitted that she hadn't expected him to be as good at math as he was. He was so good that this teacher eventually trusted him to teach the class for her when she was absent. Likewise, college mathematics is a social experience for many students, but for Michael it was not. Many of his college peers—other students who had been in his classes for years and not "seen" him mathematically—were surprised to find out *at graduation* that he was headed to Carnegie Mellon for graduate school. They hadn't talked to him about mathematics during their classes together, and, when applying for graduate schools, they hadn't considered that he might be doing the same and so did not share that experience with him either. Now, at professional conferences, it's easy for colleagues to exclude him from mathematical conversations. He has been extremely successful at every level of his mathematical career, and yet he has to fight to be seen. He, one of a small number of Black mathematicians in this country, has to *try* to make himself visible.

Idris Stovall provides yet a different story. He is collaborating on a mathematics program with the school district that contains many of the schools within the underserved communities in which he grew up. It is quite an experience for him to hear teachers, administrators, and researchers talk about the schools he went to as a child and to hear them talking about the children that he once *was*. In Idris's quotation, we get a glimpse of how much he usually has to compartmentalize in himself—all of those experiences of *being* a black child in those very schools *in* those underserved communities, just for a start —in order to be effective in making the beauty and power of mathematics accessible to another generation of mathematical thinkers.

But . . . if DEbT-M can provide a space in which Idris can be both Dr. Stovall—who won a full ride to Hampton University, who was the first Black student to finish a PhD in mathematics at the University of Massachusetts, Amherst, and who is a Black leader at an Ivy League university—and Idris, the person who once was a child carrying many of the same burdens that the children in this district are and *not* have to compartmentalize, then he is offering a rare gift to the DEbT-M community. This community includes the mathematicians, educators, district leaders, and teachers who participate, as well as the children in the schools in which those teachers and administrators serve. Idris sees the side of himself that is Dr. Stovall, an accomplished mathematician, as "a proof of concept," providing a vision that other young Black learners that mathematics is in their purview.

In general, our culture is not used to holding race and mathematics in our minds at the same time. So, if we want to allow Dr. Idris Stovall, along with Drs. Michael Young and Aris Winger, to bring themselves as both Black men and mathematicians to this work, we have to create spaces for that to happen. In this chapter, we lay out the design of one such space in DEbT-M, Mathequity Hours.

■ Grounding the Work

The following subsections lay out the background and development of the Mathequity Hours project.

What Is DEbT-M?

The authors of this chapter are three Black men (Aris Winger, Michael Young, and Idris Stovall), four White women (Sarah Sword, Eden Badertscher, Miram Gates, and Una MacDowell), and one White man (Al Cuoco). Professionally, we are mathematicians or mathematics educators. We each bring expertise in one or more of the following: race studies, archaeology, sociohistory, critical pedagogy, mathematics, habits of mind, and education research. We represent a subset of the professionals involved in DEbT-M, a partnership between Education Development Center, Inc., Iowa State University, University of Pittsburgh, Duquesne University, a large urban school district, and a smaller suburban school district.

In some sense, we are all research participants in this project because we believe in studying our own work in order to improve. The quotations earlier in this chapter were taken from interviews of the mathematicians undertaken to learn how their own thinking and practice was changing. Although all of the authors and other staff, including district leadership, acted as participants in all PD, we refer to ourselves as "facilitators" in this chapter. "Teacher participants" should be considered the secondary mathematics teachers who self-selected for participation in DEbT-M.

As authors, we have different experiences and come from different disciplines, genders, and races, yet we share a set of beliefs: (1) an explicit focus on race is essential to our work; (2) all students are able and deserve to engage in a community that authentically reflects how mathematicians think about and do mathematics; (3) teachers want to act in their students' best interest; (4) the system of school mathematics has precluded students from engaging in serious mathematics; (5) we have an individual and communal responsibility for reshaping this system to provide each student access to advanced mathematical ideas; and (6) mathematics involves ways of thinking that individuals can learn to use to raise and approach problems and experience the world. These beliefs represent a galvanizing force in our work at the intersection of equity and mathematics, and they drive our approach to research and PD for secondary teachers.

Our shared beliefs led us to create PD consisting of a two-year experience for secondary teacher participants in mathematics, education, and equity. Three weeks of summer PD originally included the following elements:

- A morning **mathematics immersion,** in which we brought together facilitators and teachers. The emphasis was on the critical importance of doing mathematics for oneself in order to experience the effects of struggling with ideas, searching for connections, and clearly articulating ideas. The content connected the mathematics of secondary school and the mathematics used by mathematics professionals—people who use mathematics as part of their work.

- An afternoon **equity** portion in which facilitators and teachers worked together to understand the education system generally—and the system of school mathematics specifically—and how inequity manifests and is perpetuated in these systems. They thought about what constitutes evidence of equity and inequity and how to collect that evidence. Teachers then enacted multiyear efforts to disrupt inequity in their classrooms.

- In the first year of DEbT-M, teacher participants, facilitators, and district administrators participated in a two-day **Courageous Conversations** (Singleton and Linton 2014) training, facilitated by district staff who were official Courageous Conversations affiliates.

When equity issues arose in the mathematics immersion, we wondered how to handle them: interrupt the flow of the mathematics or save those issues for equity PD? Michael suggested that we create a new space, a space we called Mathequity Hours ("Mathequity"), to deal specifically with equity and race issues in mathematics. The joining of the terms was purposeful, to empha-size that this space was about math and equity at once; as such, it was a space to foster wholeness. In this context, "whole" means being a person and a mathematician at the same time, no matter your race, your gender, your discipline, your history with mathematics, or your age. Teachers also considered how to foster that wholeness in the students in their mathematics classes.

In Mathequity sessions, we set up tables of five or six people, composed primarily of teacher participants but also including facilitators. Guided by Courageous Conversations protocols (Singleton and Linton 2014), the rules of Mathequity were that we would speak honestly about the identified topic of the day. Each session was a structured free-for-all, with teachers setting the direction of issues that arose around the topics. Reflecting our belief that teachers want to act in their students' best interests, the Mathequity facilitators trusted that the issues teachers themselves surfaced would be what they needed to address.

What gave Mathequity its power? We developed a trajectory to support teachers—and ourselves—to feel ready and able to change our practice in ways that (1) recognize mathematics as a profoundly human activity and (2) fundamentally reshape the classroom experience in ways that value, engage, and focus on students of color. As Idris shared in his opening quotation, we "engaged . . . in such a way that [we] open up." Mathequity represented a commitment to making sustained changes through conversations in which people allowed themselves to be vulnerable.

Grounding Our Work in Existing Literature

In DEbT-M, literature helps us think about how issues of power and identity are addressed. Gutiérrez (2013) argues that integral to a teacher's work is the explicit attention to supporting students' development of positive personal and learner identities, particularly for students who have traditionally been underserved by the system. Rather than treating "equity" or "social justice" issues as addenda or additional layers, this work on identities is required by the profession whether it is attended to or not (Gutiérrez 2013). In this project, we worked with teachers first to recognize their role in developing the identities of their students and attending to it. In the primary population of students who identify as Black that DEbT-M serves, literature helps with that in specific ways. For example, Berry, Pinter, and McClain (2013), in their critical review of the history of Black children in mathematics education, point to the unfolding of an exclusionary system that has (*a*) been desegregated by law and then resegregated through tracking, (*b*) not attended to the specific needs of Black children, or (*c*) approached Black children from a deficit perspective. This history affects the way that individual Black children experience and learn to navigate schools. Berry (2008) identified factors that supported Black male middle grades students in achieving upper-level mathematics. Educators can act as advocates or fail to recognize the potential of Black students, which is echoed in the work of Stinson (2006). Further, Gholson and Martin (2014) remind us that we must recognize how the intersection of identities, as exemplified by Black girlhood, confer certain opportunities and challenges on students with those identities. Gholson and Martin highlight the importance of social interactions in Black girls' experiences in the discipline of mathematics in school and how teachers can influence those.

Martin (2007) suggests that successful teachers of Black students need the following four capabilities: (*a*) comprehension of Black children's social realities; (*b*) attention to developing mathematical, academic, and racial identities of their Black students; (*c*) recognition of mathematics as a means of empowering their Black students; and (*d*) participation as change agents to work against deficit views of Black students. Gholson (2013) provides three concrete steps to ensure we can do that: (1) identify racial messages children receive, (2) study the local environment at the intersection of issues of race and mathematics, and (3) recognize the sociopolitical history for the community of each child. DEbT-M in general, and Mathequity in particular, works to support teachers who welcome Black children to their mathematics classrooms in a way that values their identity and provides them with a feeling that they belong there.

Collecting Artifacts

Each summer from 2014 through 2017 we video-recorded and transcribed all PD sessions, both to collect evidence of teachers' thinking and to improve our own facilitation skills in this complex environment. These data and participant writings from the PD experiences make up the bulk of the artifacts in what follows. In addition, data including semi-structured interviews between authors about our experiences and an assessment of participating teachers' habits of mind (Sword et al. 2015) are discussed. The artifacts and assessments were collected during the summer PD sessions. Interviews were conducted in the spring of the subsequent school years.

■ Examples from Mathequity

The following examples illustrate how Mathequity works in practice to foster wholeness.

Example 1—Opening mathematical conversations in the context of equity: The case of "the answer" in mathematics

Shared mathematics experiences serve as contexts for conversations in Mathequity. In the summer of 2016, in the mathematics immersion PD, the mathematics team spent significant time de-emphasizing "the answer" as the sole goal of mathematical activity, instead emphasizing the processes and thinking that *led* to answers that teachers gave.

In Mathequity, we stepped back from that mathematical experience that the teachers shared and connected it to the experience of *school* mathematics. We asked teachers, "What does 'the answer' mean to you?" Teachers responded with the following:

- Sense of closure

- Makes me feel like I have a good understanding of the problem

- Sense of accomplishment

We dug into this last response, wondering how the answer and accomplishment are connected. One teacher observed that the answer can provide "a sense of accomplishment that validates your work, and sometimes even your culture." Another suggested that a correct answer can affirm alternative ways of thinking about problems for those who have done something differently. However, partly as a result of the shared mathematical experience, teachers began to consider how a focus on processes instead of answers could affect how children feel *heard* and thus valued in mathematics class.

Emphasizing mathematical processes and what we can learn from our own mistakes offers pedagogical advantages in general and an equity advantage in particular. Adults and children feel valued in their participation in mathematical thinking and discussions when the purpose of the answer shifts from "validation" to tools to learn—to present a starting point for a discussion, or to create opportunities to ask new questions.

The power of this discussion became clear when teacher participants were asked to retake (after fourteen months) a Mathematical Habits of Mind assessment written for high school teachers (Sword et al. 2015). While taking the assessment, a White female middle school mathematics special educator stated that she was no longer "afraid" of this test because she understood that it wasn't the answers that mattered but her thinking. She was now willing to attempt problems she did not know how to solve. Specifically, two of the items she left blank on the Year 0 assessment demonstrated real attempts on Year 1. A Black female teacher noted a parallel experience for her students in emotional support classes, the majority of whom are Black: "My students don't even attempt [the state test] . . . but when they took [it] this year it shocked me; they were really trying! Even if they didn't know it, they were willing to attempt it. They didn't care if they got the answer right or wrong. They just wanted to attempt it. That was really a success for me." Schoenfeld (1988) illustrated mathematical issues that result from focusing on "the answer," and we need to attend to equity issues that arise as well. In unpacking a shared mathematical experience, Mathequity supported humanizing mathematics learning.

Example 2—Connecting our work to student learning: The case of "disrespect"

By opening with "Who gets left out in math class?" one Mathequity session involved a discussion of how "leaving someone out" *happens* in math class. The discussion surfaced the fact that in the normal course of classroom interactions, moments of disrespect occur: student to student, teacher to student, or student to teacher. These moments are often complicated by issues of race and cultural conflict (Milner 2007); in our partner districts it is common for teachers and students to be of different races. This often leads to unintended consequences. For example, Black male youth can invoke a persona through "cool pose": a physical manifestation of aloofness and studied disinterest

(Majors and Billson 1992). This may be misread by teachers, principals, and other adults as defiance and disrespect, while it is often a way to maintain integrity in the face of adversity.

In Mathequity, we discussed "respect" in general, and "cool pose" in particular. Aris asked, "What do we do to students who disrespect us?" Responses included a list of the following punitive actions that we, as educators, had taken in "revenge":

- I don't give them extra time.

- I ignore them.

- I do not give them second-chance grading.

- I lower my expectations.

Each of these actions has implications for students' classroom experience: Through them, we remove opportunities for students to learn and be successful. Mathematics is well known to be a gatekeeper to graduation, college, and future careers. Realizing the cumulative effects of these missed opportunities led to understanding that the resulting disrespect we express in retaliation is far more detrimental than the original perceived disrespect. In that sense, students get "left out."

Discussions began focusing on how to change our responses in these situations so that "disrespect" on the part of the learner, intended or perceived, does not interfere with how we value them or the opportunities for learning to which they are entitled. We came to a consensus that it is not students' responsibility to show respect in order to access learning opportunities. That does not mean we do not address or try to understand disrespect; rather, it means that this must be separated from the learning opportunities we provide.

An essential insight emerged for participating teachers *and* facilitators, many of whom teach in college settings: These moments of "disrespect" are *not about us*. One way we can deal with disrespect is to depersonalize it: Keep the child at the center, remembering that this class is not about how we *teach* math, it's about how children *learn* it. The children will say and do things that seem off base, but we can choose not to mind because we understand it's not personal—"It's not about me." In regards to his role in facilitating this experience, Aris said, "I want to be clear: We did that together. I didn't come up with that answer. We sat in that room and figured it out. We talked. *We* came to that conclusion—'It's not about us.'"

Example 3—Connecting equity conversations to our own mathematics teaching and connecting ourselves to "the system"

The book *Radical Equations* quotes Ella Baker on changing systems; she says, "In order to see where we are going, we must not only remember where we have been, but we must understand where we have been" (Moses and Cobb 2001, p. 3). Toward that end, a powerful set of conversations were driven by "acknowledgement letters." These letters were written by teacher participants and facilitators to acknowledge and forgive actions we may have taken in the past as teachers of mathematics. The facilitators wrote and read their own letters aloud first, and they then asked the teachers to write and share parts of their own letters with the group. One facilitator (Eden) used this example in her letters (all student names are pseudonyms):

> I apologize, Sonia [*a Black female*], for making you feel less than capable when I was trying to encourage others to be as courageous as you in admitting your mistakes. No one followed your example and thus I set you up to appear to be the only person in class who did not know.

Another facilitator (Aris) used "you" in his letter because he is speaking to himself as another person:

> Yes, too often you thought their failure was their fault and had nothing to do with you.

> Yes, you, too, often mistook silence for understanding.

> Yes, you had thoughts of surprise when the Asian kid asked you for math help.

> Yes, you had bad memories of high school when those two black female students were laughing in the back and that made you not want to help them.

> Yes, you have favored the White male, favored the loud, internally derided the shy, demanded that those you have given no voice to speak up and ask questions.

> And NO! I am not being too hard on you. You want to get better, don't you?

By looking honestly and compassionately at ourselves as facilitators, we allowed the teachers to do the same. In sharing these vulnerabilities, we brought visibility to our own imperfection; we modeled our own willingness to be open to learning and to conversations in which we were likely not to get things "perfect." We felt compassion for each other and for the students we have hurt. We talked about race, and we talked about it in the context of our own mathematics teaching practice. This was an individual and *shared* practice. Sharing this practice positioned teacher participants to support each other in pathways to more equitable teaching practices.

The deeply personal nature of the letters meant that teachers sometimes invoked prayers or pointed to times in their personal lives when they had not treated the people around them respectfully. They also described interactions with particular students. In the following excerpts from teachers' letters, with names withheld to preserve privacy, a thread recurs: Teachers recognized that their enculturated perspectives positioned certain students as somehow "less than," and felt resolved to change those perspectives. One White male middle school teacher challenged his perception of the "problem":

> I am too quick to give up on the challenging student. Convenience at times has been my goal, and this makes it easier to let the difficult student go. Misbehaving students are not an interruption to my work, they *are* my work.

A White female middle school teacher discussed how her perceptions of children prompted her to change the nature and rigor of the mathematics she taught:

> Over the course of that year, I began to see students of color as unable to participate in rigorous assignments, especially those in CMP2 [Connected Mathematics Project 2; Lappan et al. 2006]. I believed these students needed mundane math assignments that included multiple opportunities for repetition as well as instruction led and facilitated directly by me. I need to include here that this was the way in which I was taught. I believed that because I taught a class in which every student was identified with either an ESL, Special Ed., or . . . label, they were unable to complete the assignments in the CMP2 book. I rewrote the entire curriculum. I took out anything that I felt was too hard and didn't require true thinking. I did not allow group work because that's when chaos would erupt. I believed a quiet classroom meant I was a good teacher. I led every conversation; I gave assignments that allowed for no student creativity; and I definitely

didn't learn anything about the students that I stood in front of every day. That's how I survived that year. I owe every student that I taught that year an apology.

Another White female high school teacher who taught primarily Black and White students recognized the potential impact of acting in response to her perceptions of students:

> I am sorry for not meeting you where you were—and instead meeting you where I was comfortable, or where I expected you to be. I am sorry for thinking I knew just what your life was like because I grew up in the same neighborhood you did, for downplaying your reality, for not seeing your color, your culture, you. I am sorry for writing that referral—and that other one too—for helping to create a file that would inevitably define your educational career. A file that others would read in order to "get to know you" . . . a you I helped to create. . . . I am sorry for calling on you when I knew you didn't know an answer, just to prove a point. What I am most deeply sorry for though, is remaining silent when coworkers would describe my class as "the bad kids." I am sorry for sitting quiet while peers joked about having job security based on you becoming an adult and starting a family of your own. I am so sorry for never defending you as fiercely as I wanted to, as I could have. I am sorry for not saying simply, "I disagree."

Several teachers identified particular students they had affected. A White female middle school teacher spoke of her own reactions to perceived student disrespect, illustrating the common tendency towards retribution previously discussed, while a White male high school teacher shared a failure and the resulting plea to do better next time.

> You ignored Marcus. He told you that he struggled with math, and you told him that you would be there for him. You lied. You knew he was cutting your class, and you ignored it. You called home and spoke with his parents, but you never followed through. He needed you, and you turned away.

> You mistook Keisha's attitude for disrespect. It was easier to turn away when she was on her phone or talking to her friend then to ask why. You did not take the time to talk to her, ask how she was feeling. Instead you took it personally, like a slap to your face. You said to yourself, "I will show her." You need to be better. You need to be the teacher you promised them you would be.

Another White male middle school teacher wrote:

> Keyshaun, at the beginning of the school year I had great expectations for you. As the semester continued I saw that you weren't interested, you quit trying. I still saw the bright young man that you are. I still saw the potential. I still vowed to persevere to the end. But then I caved, threw my hands up in the air and I quit. I was done pushing. I didn't quit caring, I just didn't have the stamina. I was at my end. I hope that the next Keyshaun I teach that I will have more drive to hang in there a little longer. I want people to see the genius in my Keyshauns.

A Black female high school teacher who taught primarily Black students addressed herself in the second person as she recognized her growth, buoying her hope for progress toward becoming the teacher she wants to be:

> This past year was much better for you than last year. You demonstrated extended patience, stronger consistency, improved questioning, and organization. You kept up with grading in the first semester. There were some great ideas you executed, too. You tell

people that you had a great year and that you're very proud of your accomplishments. You are. I believe you have every reason to be proud of the strides you've made this year. As I acknowledge the beauty in your management of many responsibilities, it's important to acknowledge ways in which your actions had lasting impacts on students.

The process of letter writing is not simply self-flagellation. As suggested by Ella Baker, we are acknowledging how we have been part of a system that maintains inequity. We are not "outside"; we are part of the system. This is imperative. To be able to challenge that systemic machine, we have to understand our own role in it. In understanding that role, we call ourselves to action.

■ Preliminary Evidence of the Impact of Mathequity

Within the space of Mathequity we focus on things we can *do*. We can attend to how we present mathematics. We can choose how to react to students' actions. We can examine our own actions critically but with compassion.

We believe that participating in our research project has changed us as people, teachers, learners, and doers of mathematics. We strive to bring that change into our various other professional roles, including college teaching. Michael reflected:

> [DEbT-M] has changed my practice [in college mathematics teaching], changed my language, and changed my perceptions. This semester I'm teaching calculus. The first exercise is a math identity survey so people can talk about their math experiences and I can come to understand them better.

Teachers also reflected on how participation changes their practice. One teacher wrote, "I look at each student differently now—each student is their own story."

The following reflections, from one Black and then one White female teacher, recognize that their stories are, in fact, intertwined with those of their students:

> If nothing else, it's been a forum where I can talk about being a Black student and a Black teacher, and what those experiences have meant to me—how they have influenced my teaching. Our work has challenged me to examine the defeating ways I think about myself and my students, the limits I have placed on us.

> . . . to me the most important aspect that's come up while teaching is my comfort towards . . . Black students. . . . I talked last summer about my inability to relate to them, which I didn't realize was so hard for them, having a White female teacher and them being Black men, or female students. And I just thought, you know, they're all students, but . . . it's important for me to realize that they are Black students and I need to reach out to them, and not that I'm going to be able to understand what they're going through but being able to show them I'm willing to listen.

We are still in the process of analyzing teacher reflections, but even in this sample, powerful themes emerge. We see recognition of students as individuals, recognition of the importance of race, and recognition of roles in perpetuating inequities. And over and over, we see themes of striving to do better. It's promising. We are also collecting student data, surveys about students' beliefs about mathematics and about themselves as learners, and classroom observation video to understand how this work affects teachers' practice and outcomes for students.

■ Concluding Remarks

Mathequity is about humanizing mathematics spaces. In Mathequity, we discuss what we need to do as mathematics educators to reimagine our current classrooms as spaces in which middle and high school children feel valued as children and mathematicians: valued, visible, and brimming with mathematical potential, as the mathematicians expressed in the opening quotations.

As we think about how to implement Mathequity or aspects of Mathequity in other settings in which we work, there are elements of the work that make it challenging that we want to keep in mind. These include the following:

- We are saying to teachers, who already have almost impossible jobs, "There is much more to do."

- We cannot predict the direction of Mathequity conversations when we introduce the day's topic. We cannot prepare for all that will unfold.

- We, DEbT-M staff and teachers, have to acknowledge our own roles in systemic inequity.

- We have to get to know the teachers and their relationships with each other early in the process. We cannot create a community without acknowledging complex *existing* communities. We wish we had understood that better before we started Mathequity, but we are learning.

- We are unlikely ever to know for *sure* how—or which of—these conversations change teachers' practices.

- The work doesn't end. We have to continually commit ourselves to connecting across racial boundaries. We cannot say, "OK, we've now solved this"—not in ourselves and not in our communities.

But we have supports. We offer each other community. We may feel the problems are unsolvable, but we aren't alone in our efforts to address them. The guidelines provided by Courageous Conversations (Singleton and Linton 2014) help us build trust and space. We offer each other compassion and inspiration. And the teachers keep returning, keep participating in these conversations, keep thinking deeply about their practices. It's worth the effort.

In DEbT-M, we operate out of this belief: As we are transformed, so are the systems in which we operate. We take the stance that there are people who are saying, "I was devalued in this experience." Like Aris, we hear them. We have to be open to that as a field. We have to be willing to build these spaces, to have these conversations. They're risky; they're time consuming. But as a field—a connected set of fields—we have to ask ourselves: Are we willing?

Authors' Note

The material in this paper is based upon work supported by the National Science Foundation under Grant No. DRL-1321216. Any opinions, findings, and conclusions or recommendations expressed in this material are those of the authors and do not necessarily reflect the views of the National Science Foundation.

References

Berry III, Robert Q. "Access to Upper-Level Mathematics: The Stories of Successful African American Middle School Boys." *Journal for Research in Mathematics Education* 39, no. 5 (2008): 464–88. doi:10.2307/40539311.

Berry III, Robert Q., Holly Henderson Pinter, and Oren L. McClain. "A Critical Review of American K–12 Mathematics Education, 1900–Present: Implications for the Experiences and Achievement of Black Children." In *The Brilliance of Black Children in Mathematics: Beyond the Numbers and toward New Discourse*, edited by Jacqueline Leonard and Danny B. Martin, pp. 22–53. Charlotte, N.C.: Information Age Publishing, 2013.

Gholson, Maisie L. "The Mathematical Lives of Black Children: A Sociocultural-Historical Rendering of Black Brilliance." In *The Brilliance of Black Children in Mathematics: Beyond the Numbers and toward New Discourse*, edited by Jacqueline Leonard and Danny B. Martin, pp. 55–76. Charlotte, N.C.: Information Age Publishing, 2013.

Gholson, Maisie L., and Danny Bernard Martin. "Smart Girls, Black Girls, Mean Girls, and Bullies: At the Intersection of Identities and the Mediating Role of Young Girls' Social Network in Mathematical Communities of Practice." *Journal of Education* 19, no. 1 (2014): 19–34.

Gutiérrez, Rochelle. "Why (Urban) Mathematics Teachers Need Political Knowledge." *Journal of Urban Mathematics Education* 6, no. 2 (2013): 7–19.

———. "Embracing the Inherent Tensions in Teaching Mathematics from an Equity Stance." *Democracy & Education* 18, no. 3 (2009): 9–16.

Ladson-Billings, Gloria. "From the Achievement Gap to the Education Debt: Understanding Achievement in U.S. Schools." *Educational Researcher* 35, no. 7 (2006): 3–12.

Lappan, Glenda, James Fey, William Fitzgerald, Susan Friel, and Elizabeth Difanis Phillips. Connected Mathematics Project 2. Boston: Pearson Prentice Hall, 2006

Majors, Richard, and Janet Mancini Billson. *Cool Pose: The Dilemmas of Black Manhood in America.* New York: Simon & Schuster, 1992.

Martin, Danny Bernard. "Beyond Missionaries or Cannibals: Who Should Teach Mathematics to African American Children?" *The High School Journal* 91, no. 1 (2007): 6–28.

Milner, H. Richard. "Race, Culture, and Researcher Positionality: Working through Dangers Seen, Unseen, and Unforeseen." *Educational Researcher* 36, no. 7 (2007): 388–400.

———. *Start Where You Are, but Don't Stay There: Understanding Diversity, Opportunity Gaps, and Teaching in Today's Classrooms.* Cambridge, Mass.: Harvard Education Press, 2010.

Moses, Robert P., and Charles E. Cobb. *Radical Equations: Civil Rights from Mississippi to the Algebra Project.* Boston: Beacon Press, 2001.

Schoenfeld, Alan H. "When Good Teaching Leads to Bad Results: The Disasters of 'Well-Taught' Mathematics Courses." *Educational Psychologist* 23, no. 2 (1988): 145–66.

Singleton, Glenn E., and Curtis Linton. *Courageous Conversations about Race: A Field Guide for Achieving Equity in Schools.* Thousand Oaks, Calif.: Corwin Press, 2014.

Stinson, David W. "African American Male Adolescents, Schooling (and Mathematics): Deficiency, Rejection, and Achievement." *Review of Educational Research* 76, no. 4 (2006): 477–506. doi:10.2307/4124412.

Sword, Sarah, Ryota Matsuura, Miriam Gates, Jane Kang, Albert Cuoco, and Glenn Stevens. "Secondary Teachers' Mathematical Habits of Mind: A Paper-and-Pencil Assessment." In *Annual Perspectives in Mathematics Education 2015: Assessment to Enhance Learning and Teaching*, edited by Christine Suurtamm, pp. 109–18. Reston, Va.: National Council of Teachers of Mathematics, 2015.

PART III

Principles for Teaching
and Teacher Identity

CHAPTER 8

Centering Students' Mathematical Agency at Northwest Indian College

Zachariah Bunton, Cassandra Cook, and Matteo Tamburini,
Northwest Indian College, Bellingham, Washington

This chapter discusses the ongoing transformation in assessment, course content, and pedagogy in the mathematics courses at Northwest Indian College (NWIC), a Tribal College chartered by the Lummi Nation. Its authors are a group of Native and Non-Native educators who have been working at NWIC for over seven years. The transformation began in 2010, when the authors took advantage of a high-quality, research-based professional development opportunity and initiated a process of rehumanizing mathematics in NWIC classrooms. Student tutors, all of whom are Native and some of whom are Lummi Tribal members, continue to shape and improve the implementation of this new pedagogy, while making the faculty more aware of the importance of the students' cultural context. While future improvement is expected, NWIC mathematics classrooms are currently spaces in which students' identities are embraced, all students' mathematical abilities are valued, and there is enough flexibility for students to attend to cultural and familial responsibilities while still being provided with meaningful opportunities to learn mathematics.

■ Place

Northwest Indian College (NWIC) is a Tribal college chartered by the Lummi Nation. The college mission statement is: "Through education, Northwest Indian College promotes Indigenous self-determination and knowledge." The historical context for NWIC's existence is explained below, excerpted from the 2017 NWIC Self-Evaluation Report to the Northwest Commission on Colleges and Universities (Northwest Indian College 2017):

> [The] Tribal college movement has been based on the belief that an effective education for American Indian students was not occurring when they attended exclusively mainstream institutions. The history of Indian education has been forever changed by the acculturation and assimilation of Tribal people through "effective" mainstream education. The intention was to dramatically change—or even eliminate—the language, cultural and religious practices, and social/familial structures that identified Tribes as distinct nations. NWIC is part of [a] resilient movement to reclaim both governance of education and control of its content within . . . Tribal communities.

The origins of NWIC can be traced back to the founding of the Lummi Indian School of Aquaculture in 1973. . . . From its beginning, NWIC grew from the vision of generations of Lummi people who wanted to educate their own children and grandchildren about resources vital to their way of life, such as the salmon, and not abandon traditional ways and Tribal responsibilities. In 1983, the Lummi Nation . . . established [what would later be renamed] Northwest Indian College and welcomed surrounding tribes by expanding its service area to include Tribal communities throughout the Pacific Northwest, while still retaining its identity as a Lummi Nation chartered institution.

NWIC has physical locations in six Native Nations in the Northwest United States. On average, about 80 percent of its students are enrolled in federally recognized tribes, mostly from Washington State, but also from Alaska, the southwestern U.S., and Canada. The main campus, where the authors are based, is located in the Lummi Nation, in northwestern Washington State. Over the course of the past five years, the average number of students enrolled in classes at the Lummi campus each quarter has been around 300. Roughly 70 percent of NWIC students are female.

Over 70 percent of students place into precollege mathematics when they enroll. The mathematical background of many students is similar to that described by Stigler, Givvin, and Thompson (2010), namely that students both "rely on flawed procedural habits," many of which have been developed over the course of years in earlier grades, and that "when students are able to provide conceptual explanations, they . . . produce correct answers." Likewise, students at NWIC share a background with those described by Urbina-Lilback (2016) who "face life responsibilities that reduce their ability to dedicate time to their education."

All our college-level mathematics classes have a prerequisite of Intermediate Algebra to fulfill transfer agreements with other universities, and the majority of students take Elementary and Intermediate Algebra. Most of our experience with changing our curriculum has taken place primarily in those courses, which span linear and quadratic expressions and equations (among other things), with a new emphasis on multiple representations of algebraic objects. Since 2015, we have arranged the schedule so that the classes meet for an average of 350 minutes a week over five days, longer than the standard 250 minutes.

■ People

My name is **Matteo Tamburini**. I was born and raised in Tuscany, Italy. My father's family, going back four generations, has been from the same region. My mother's family was mainly Irish immigrants to the United States. Before working at NWIC, I would have never imagined that sharing this aspect of my identity would become a regular part of what I do in the classroom each quarter.

Both of my parents were college educated. I attended Italian public schools from elementary through high school. After graduation, I moved to the United States and earned a BS in mathematics at the University of Washington. Inspired by naive idealism, I taught through Teach for America in Newark, New Jersey, for three years. After earning an MS in mathematics, I began to work at NWIC in 2009.

Up to that point, I had experienced mostly lecture-based classrooms and had very little experience in collaborative curriculum development. I had no meaningful information about the history of the Lummi or Coast Salish people. As a result, when I started working at NWIC, the best I could do to make the material "culturally relevant" was to alter some of the surface features of exercises taken from mainstream curricula while keeping the broader structures the same. I finally gained insight about teaching and learning mathematics from the Mathematics Education Collaborative (MEC), and I am slowly learning about connecting mathematics to aspects of my students' lived experiences.

My name is **Cassandra Cook**. My father immigrated to the United States from England when I was born. My mother's family migrated to the United States several generations back and has roots in England, Ireland, and Germany. The way I see the world, and the knowledge I do and do not have, comes directly from my ancestors and community, as well as my experience going through the colonial school system. Throughout my life, including college, I thought of mathematics as something universal, and I therefore imagined that everyone would learn mathematics roughly the same way. After graduating with my BS in physics from Western Washington University, I began to teach at NWIC and confronted, for the first time, the unexamined assumptions I had about the teaching and learning of mathematics, as well as my own identity. I learned that the content was not neutral in terms of student access. I was naïve at first, but I now believe that I cannot effectively teach mathematics to any student, especially students from a different culture than my own, simply by explaining the way I understand and interpret a mathematical concept. Although colonialism continues to impact the content and pedagogy of our classrooms, I believe I should strive to challenge the dominant narratives while looking at my own long-held assumptions about mathematics, learning, and teaching.

My name is **Zachariah Bunton**. I am an enrolled member of the Lummi Nation. I was born to Qe'solie, my mother, who descended from an Upper Skagit woman and a Diegueno man; I was also born to T'towinook, my father, who descended from a Musqueam woman and a Lummi man. I've spent my entire life living in the Whatcom County area, and I have experienced both public and tribal schooling. Mathematically, both atmospheres were similar to each other: lectures followed by numerous examples and exercises that highlighted the concepts for the day, and then on to the next topic the next day. While I was able to understand and reproduce the sequences well enough, my peers were not having as much success. They began to seek me out for mathematics help, and I would oblige. This eventually led to the side job of a tutoring position while I was taking classes at NWIC in 2008; I found it a natural capability to "help" others at mathematics. In hindsight, I see that I was not genuinely helping my peers to learn mathematics or even to think about mathematics. In 2011, after working with educators at a MEC workshop, I discovered that I had been undermining their abilities as I was "helping" them when they came to me for tutoring. Providing a series of procedures to follow implies that the learner is incapable of critical thinking and problem solving. I realized there was a definite difference between thinking about mathematics and memorizing mathematics. My work continued as a tutor up until the fall of 2015, when I was asked to fill a role as instructor for an elementary algebra course. This was also the time I began my work as the Site STEM Coordinator for NWIC, where my main role has been to support the mathematics faculty at the NWIC extended sites. While I continue to do this work with faculty, I remain engaged with the students at NWIC both through teaching part-time and working in the tutoring center.

■ Our Journey

Our experience has shown that every educational situation is unique. No single method will work in all possible contexts and, therefore, the story is important. Equally important to the story are these underlying questions that guided the changes we made and that we continue to investigate:

- Who am I?

- What do I know?

- What don't I know?

- How do the relationships among the students and between the students and the instructor impact the classroom environment?

- What does it mean to *learn* mathematics?

- What is the purpose of learning any particular piece of mathematics in supporting specific students' goals?

Previously, all of us, instructors and tutors, had attended predominantly lecture-based mathematics classes. We are now learning to teach differently than the way we were taught ourselves. It is a challenge, and we credit our growth to each other's support and our openness to ongoing discussions, classroom observations, and guidance from the Mathematics Education Collaborative (a nonprofit organization that provided us with high-quality professional development workshops and ongoing support), as well as to the experiences of other faculty grappling with the teaching and learning of mathematics in different contexts. Our small group became a teacher network with similar characteristics to those described by Niesz (2007). She argues that such groups of teachers, and in our case, tutors, "organized for purposes related to teacher learning, inquiry [or] support" are "*poised to be* a powerful source of teacher learning and school improvement." In our case, that potential has become actualized.

In the 2010–2011 school year, an observer of our classrooms would have encountered a very conventional, lecture-based environment. In our Elementary and Intermediate Algebra classes, we still relied heavily on using a typical textbook. Our best attempts at helping the students learn were not dissimilar from the pedagogy used by the Khan Academy (Khan 2011).

In the fall of 2010, we received the Rethinking Pre-College Mathematics (RPM) grant, which first sparked our efforts at faculty collaboration and led us to ask questions about the content, pedagogy, and assessment of our courses. However, our practice has changed primarily because we used the grant funds to attend a two-week professional development course offered by MEC. The authors' experience at the MEC workshop helped to transform our views about the teaching and learning of mathematics, but it did not provide us with mathematical tasks that were particularly connected to the lived experiences of most of our students. The work of our Native student tutors shaped the pedagogy along those lines. For example, one of the tutors soon produced a task about knitting, and, after a long afternoon conversation among faculty and tutors, a disembodied task about geometric shapes morphed into one about decorations on moccasins. The relationships built at that summer workshop became the foundation for the ongoing process of revision of the pedagogy and the content.

The material that we encountered in the MEC workshops was more directly tied to the content of our Elementary and Intermediate Algebra classes. The first attempt at using the MEC materials and process was made in Intermediate Algebra in 2012. Over the course of five years, we gradually expanded to revise our Statistics, Precalculus, and Calculus classes. We made many missteps and learned important lessons along the way.

Our current definition of what it means to rehumanize mathematics emerges from our journey and from our current practice. To rehumanize mathematics means first to make academic mathematics accessible to students from varying mathematical backgrounds. In order to truly do this, it is necessary to foster an environment in which the following principles are followed:

1. Each individual's perspective is respected and brings value to the learning community.

2. Each individual feels welcomed to bring their whole identity—including their cultural background and their personal experiences.

3. All the people involved (teachers, students, and tutors) form genuine relationships that are not limited to the way in which conventional teacher-centric settings dictate classroom interactions.

This definition is consistent with NWIC's mission statement: By making room for individual students to be their whole selves, we are implicitly challenging the process of acculturation and assimilation, thus making room for indigenous self-determination and knowledge. We consider this to be a stepping-stone to a broader rehumanization that includes challenging the meaning of the word *mathematics* itself—for example, by emphasizing the inherent mathematical knowledge and skills that individuals have as a result of their lived experiences and their cultural and historical practices.

■ Content

In NWIC mathematics classes, students work on tasks that revolve around geometric or numerical patterns. The patterns and the tasks chosen have several essential characteristics:

1. Students with various mathematical backgrounds should be able to access the embedded mathematics; in particular, students who are not confident in their academic mathematical skills should still find a point of access.

2. The mathematics itself should lead to deep investigations with many connections for those who are ready.

3. Some tasks should include algebraic patterns embedded with geometrical concepts such as area, perimeter, volume, and measurement to re-establish the essential connections between algebra and geometry that are often neglected in students' previous education.

To rehumanize mathematics, we also include patterns that are relevant to aspects of most students' lives (e.g., beading, number of ancestors, natural resources). This combats the notion that only topics that have emerged from a colonialist society are inherently mathematical or worthy of inclusion in a mathematics classroom. In our Statistics class, we include data about quantities that are more familiar and relevant to our students, such as the yearly size of salmon runs and local weather (including historical trends related to climate change). Most of our classes also include a final project for which students have the option to create or describe their own mathematical patterns. Students have created patterns related to beading, basket weaving, and quilting. With the students' consent, those patterns become part of the permanent curriculum for future quarters.

One example of a student-generated pattern is included below (fig. 8.1). Others are available on this book's page on NCTM's More4U website.

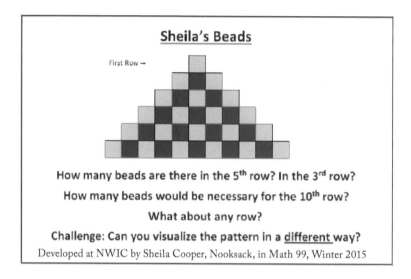

Sheila's Beads

First Row →

How many beads are there in the 5th row? In the 3rd row?

How many beads would be necessary for the 10th row?

What about any row?

Challenge: Can you visualize the pattern in a **different** way?

Developed at NWIC by Sheila Cooper, Nooksack, in Math 99, Winter 2015

Fig. 8.1. A student-generated pattern

We use this pattern in Elementary Algebra, and we expect a student who is proficient to be able to describe the pattern in words, translate their description into an algebraic formula that generalizes the number of beads in the nth row, and construct a graph of the row number vs. the number of beads in that row. Sheila's prompt to visualize the pattern in a different way reflects our common practice of eliciting different ways of seeing from the class. Some of the descriptions that the students have given us include ones such as "The number of gray beads is the same as the row number, and the number of blue beads is one less than the row number" (which might lead a student to the formula $n + (n - 1)$ for the number of beads in the nth row) and "There is one bead in the first row, and two more beads in each row after that" (which might lead to the formula $1 + 2(n - 1)$. We include some sample student work on a different pattern, along with a version of the rubric that we use to give feedback to students, later in this chapter in the section titled "Assessment of Student Learning."

We hope to be able to create more opportunities for students to reflect on the wealth of algebraic structures that are present in their cultures by including tasks drawn from their experiences that they might not have previously associated with mathematics.

■ Method

Our attempts to rehumanize mathematics for the students at NWIC are not as culturally immersive as the examples set out by Dora Andrew-Ihrke (Yup'ik) (Andrew-Ihrke 2013). She draws on her background growing up steeped in the Yup'ik culture and on her extensive work with Yup'ik children in Dillingham, Alaska, weaving the Yup'ik language and specific teachings from elders in her community directly into the mathematics. Our work cannot be as immersive for two main reasons: The students at NWIC come from many different tribal cultures, and the full-time mathematics faculty are not Indigenous to North America and have had very different life experiences than those of NWIC students. In addition, the staff in the Coast Salish Institute (CSI), the college's department that oversees Native Studies programming and is supervised by the Dean of Indigenous Education, has explicitly guided the faculty that we should not teach about what we don't know (e.g., the culture of the many tribes to which NWIC students are affiliated), as suggested by Aveling (2013). Rather, CSI has encouraged the faculty to focus on teaching mathematics.

Aveling discusses what it means for her (a non-Indigenous person) to engage in research with and in Indigenous communities. Her attempts to change her practice relate closely to our own efforts to rehumanize mathematics at NWIC. Aveling conducts research with Indigenous values in mind, endeavoring to establish a human-to-human connection, rather than entering into interactions between researcher and object. In the classroom, we have removed ourselves to a great degree from the conventional role of the mathematics teacher as "keeper" of mathematical knowledge that our students have often encountered in their previous formal mathematics experiences. Instead, we attempt to establish a much more human interpersonal relationship, crucial to the process of rehumanizing mathematics, by focusing classroom time on deepening understanding of mathematical relationships. Students and instructors continuously share an exchange of intimate moments that include genuine inquisitiveness as well as cognitive dissonance from the uncomfortable and confusing state of comparing a new intuition with a previous, contradictory understanding. As teachers we intentionally try to create opportunities for students to reach such a state because this is when they are most challenged to engage in sense making. In our rehumanizing approach, with its emphasis on genuine relationships, it is not the role of the teacher to rescue the student from confusion. We have also learned to seek out cognitive dissonance for ourselves as we genuinely seek to understand what the students are thinking. Questions flow back and forth from student to teacher, teacher to student and, at its best, from student to student; each question is part of a search for a deeper understanding of the mathematical relationship.

Although *Indigenous* is used as a term that groups the majority of our students together, our students remain vastly different in cultural practices and thus have vastly different inherent mathematical knowledge. Our materials and presentation should not give students the impression that we (the teachers) are "experts" in *their* Indigenous knowledge. Avoiding this is necessary not only to honor the identities of our students but also to maintain a human relationship supported by trust and respect. The exception is when a student and an instructor or tutor share a cultural background, in which case the connections are made naturally and propel the discussion of the mathematics. Currently, faculty members have adopted an approach that explores mathematical relationships within contexts familiar to the students without pretending to know their cultural or historical significance. On the other hand, exploring such relationships opens the door for students to be recognized for their knowledge and perspective and to help define what is valuable in a mathematics classroom.

Typically, an eleven-week quarter is divided into three or four units of study. Most class time is spent with students investigating the underlying relationships in a set of visual, geometric patterns described above, referred to as a *menu*. A menu for a two- or three-week period contains roughly five to ten different tasks. Students explore the relationships in whichever order they decide. We demonstrate our rehumanizing approach when we value and respect each student's mathematical perspective by not telling them how to interpret mathematical relationships in any given pattern. Instead, it is our role to encourage students to articulate their own perspective and support them in creating a clear written record of their thinking. Structuring a unit of study in this way, over two or three weeks, allows for the flexibility required to meet most students' needs. For example, if a student has an important family or cultural obligation, or a health-related emergency, they are not unduly penalized because they had to miss a few days of class. The class comes together regularly to process specific tasks. Processing is a time for students to engage with each other, self-selecting to share their work, and to practice articulating *their own* mathematical ideas. The role of the instructor during this time is to sit unobtrusively in the back of the class and to encourage students to share their thinking and ask probing questions, being careful not to share his or her own thinking because the students may interpret it as the "right" way.

In the classroom, we have attempted to make way for our students' own mathematical explorations. Similarly, in our department we have created a space for the leadership of Indigenous instructors who can help both students and other instructors relate class material to contexts that are relevant to students' experiences. It is our aspiration that in the future the people teaching the majority of the classes will be indigenous to the place in which they teach.

■ Environment

Our current pursuit to rehumanize our classrooms is to make academic mathematics genuinely accessible to everyone. Each individual is unique in his or her own history, culture, identity, and learning style. What learners have often experienced in past mathematics classrooms were lectures, multiple-choice quizzes, and memorization of algorithms. This colonial method ignored each learner's identity and unique capabilities. The method acted as a filter: Those who were able to memorize and regurgitate correctly (or "mock-learn," as we refer to it) were those who had the most success. Those who could not mock-learn were left behind. Certain values underpinned the method: To be good at mathematics, you have to be quick at mathematics; you have to get the correct answer; the teacher holds all the knowledge. As Stigler, Givvin, and Thompston (2010) have shown, for many students this method is not beneficial. Our new approach enlists a different set of values that nurture and encourage each learner's identity. Instead of lectures, class discussions emerge from simple, yet deep, prompting questions. Rather than extensive sets of exercises that focus on recipes of steps, learners spend time on a handful of mathematically deep tasks designed so that they can discuss and share their own method with one another and with the instructor. Sometimes the richest conversations emerge when students share vastly different, or even mutually inconsistent, ways of seeing or interpreting a task. These differences typically invoke cognitive dissonance. It is our role, then, to facilitate conversations in which the focus is making mathematically convincing arguments, and everyone's contribution is treated as enriching the group's understanding. This method often contradicts students' assumptions and previous experiences with mathematics.

The environment of the classroom is a key component of this pedagogy. Throughout the quarter, learners repeatedly engage in tasks that invoke cognitive dissonance. In conventional classrooms, when a student is struggling with a specific task, the instructor is the savior who bears answers, and learners quickly move on. By contrast, part of our role as instructors is to state explicitly and demonstrate that we trust students' ability to arrive at a conclusion supported by evidence. This means that the learners' environment must be one in which they feel safe to openly share thoughts and ideas. This also means that instructors are no longer the bearers of answers; they are the guardians of the mathematics environment.

What happens on the first day of the quarter is a good indicator of the overall shift from our previous practice. The seating is arranged so that the students and instructor sit in a circle facing one another so they may introduce themselves at the beginning of class. This arrangement begins to break some students' expectations of what it means to be in a mathematics class. Giving learners time to properly introduce themselves shows everyone the clear intent to respect and value their identity. Some people may speak their native language and provide their lineage from both their parents, a common introduction in Indigenous communities. The instructor's participation in these introductions shows the students that the instructor is an equal member of the learning community.

We then engage the students in a group exercise in which we invite them to share with the class how they count the dots in the pattern in figure 8.2. Dwayne Donald (Papaschase Cree) and colleagues (Donald, Glanfield, and Sterenberg 2011) describe their use of a very similar exercise in their work with the Eagle Flight First Nation. They emphasize that the purpose of this activity is to invite the students into a reciprocal relationship, one in which the teacher is not assessing the correctness of the students' answers but rather is attempting to better understand the students' thinking. We learned of the power of this activity through MEC and the work on number talks of Humphreys and Parker (2015). All of the authors have found that this exercise makes evident each student's mathematical power and the value of a classroom in which the interpersonal relationships allow everyone to participate fully.

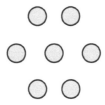

Fig. 8.2. Dot pattern for group exercise

Equally important to the exercise itself is the brief commentary on the activity in which we highlight the following points. First, we emphasize that everyone comes with their own mathematical knowledge. And second, we stress that we can all learn from each other, thus chipping away at the idea that learning is an individual enterprise and re-emphasizing the collective nature of education.

While we do not always make this explicit, we also are challenging the idea that mathematical knowledge is only held by the instructor and more broadly from the colonial institution of school. This is consistent with the remarks made by Daniel Wildcat (Muscogee Nation of Oklahoma) (2014), in which he rejects the idea that there is only one acceptable way to arrive at knowledge, emphasizing the fact that there is natural variability in cultures and customs. He suggests that our classrooms should embrace this variability.

■ Assessment of Student Learning

The process of assessment evolved in tandem with our pedagogy. In 2010, course grades across our mathematics classes were determined with the common technique of attaching point values to assigned work. This practice focuses student attention on the "point-game" of accumulating sufficient points for the desired grade, thereby obfuscating the real goal of taking the course, which is to learn. The point-game challenges the development of genuine relationships between student and instructor, as it sets up an adversarial dynamic between them. A poor score on an exam also unnecessarily penalizes a student for not having learned a concept that they might learn given more time and reinforcement. The point-game was in profound conflict with the instructional methods we used when we began to restructure the environment of our classrooms and our roles in them. We needed a new system. The initial inspiration for change came when a colleague in the RPM project pointed us to the work of Lipnevich and Smith (2009), who found that giving written feedback without a numerical grade produced the best student learning outcomes. However, this shift turned out to be only a small first step in the evolution of our assessment process. We found the following reflective questions to be of great value:

- What specifically do we want students to have learned by the time they leave our courses?

- How do we know they have reached a certain level of proficiency?

- Are there other ways, aside from exams, in which we can know that the students have learned?

We began by collaboratively rewriting the outcomes for each course and creating rubrics with definitions of various levels of proficiency. The rubrics have continued to evolve over time as we learn more about their effectiveness. We look for evidence of students' understanding of the course outcomes in a variety of sources, such as a portfolio of student work containing their exploration of geometric patterns, one-on-one interactions between student and instructor and among students, and conventional exams. All of the tasks that the students complete are scored using rubrics, and we provide only written feedback with no numerical grades. Examples of student work with some representative comments and a rubric are shown in figures 8.3a–c.

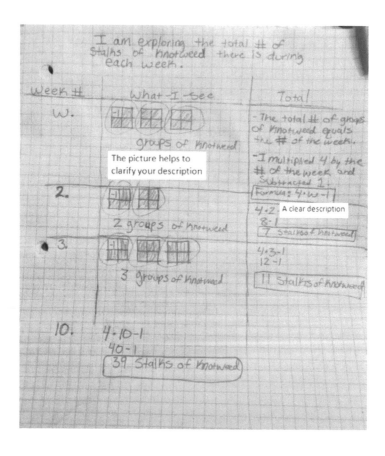

Fig. 8.3a. Typical feedback on the first draft of a student assignment

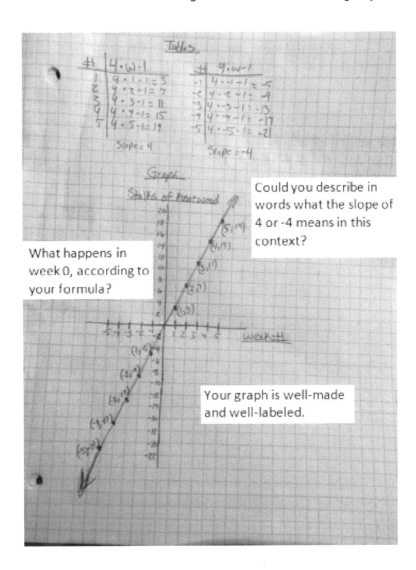

Fig. 8.3b. Typical feedback on the first draft of a student assignment

NWIC Algebra task proficiency rubric	Mathematical Content	Communication	Accuracy (checking and defending)
Fluent	The translation of the task into mathematical concepts is thorough [...]	Graph, pictures, models, diagrams, symbols, and words are used in harmony and presented in a logical way.	The work shows that the some of the conclusions made are supported by more than one argument. [...]
Proficient	The translation of the task into mathematical concepts is completed (contains a graph that shows the slope and extends into negative x-values, a formula, a sentence describing the relationship and a geometric explanation).	Graph, pictures, models, diagrams, symbols, and words are used appropriately. (The graph includes enough points to be able to identify the slope; the axes and variables are labeled)	All conclusions made are supported by the work shown.
Emerging	The translation of the major concepts of the task is partially completed (at a minimum, the work clearly shows a way of seeing).	Graph, pictures, models, diagrams, symbols, and words are inconsistent with each other or unclear.	Some conclusions made are inconsistent with each other and/or with the work shown.
Incomplete			
Comments	*Nice work! What does a slope of 4 mean in this context? explain it in terms of weeks and stalks of knotweed.*	*Your "What-I-See" table is very clear. From your graph, what happens in week #0 is a bit unclear.*	*What does it mean that the slope is both 4 and -4?*

Fig. 8.3c. Rubric for evaluating student assignments

Periodically, students receive updates of their understanding of the course outcomes, and their final grades are determined primarily by their demonstrated understanding by the end of the quarter. Our approach is consistent with the assessment proposals made by Quattromani and Austin-Manygoats (Navajo) (2002). Our current practice and their proposals both include using a portfolio of student work as an assessment tool, measuring proficiency using a rubric that is shared with the students during one-on-one conferences, and emphasizing the growth of students' understanding over time.

■ Student Voices

The comments that we share below reflect the positive engagement and reactions to our work that we have seen from most students. Even so, we do not mean to suggest that all students have evaluated our classroom work in uniformly positive ways:

> [The instructor] made us think in all different ways of getting an answer instead of just the one way in western style schools [and] made us see many ways to get the answer without writing it down on paper in the mindless one way I have learned growing up. (Student evaluation, Introduction to Quantitative Numeracy, Spring 2017)

> I appreciated how [the instructor] provided [materials] that related to Native Americans to help gain my interest in math. (Student evaluation, Survey of Mathematics, Spring 2017)

[The instructor] helped me see that there are multiple ways of seeing things and that you should ask how others see things because it could help broaden your mind. (Student evaluation, Intermediate Algebra, Winter 2017)

When students are allowed to have hands-on activities with their learning they will not only learn but remember. . . . For instance when I was trying to comprehend college algebra, my math instructor related to sewing; by showing me that I could use my sewing ruler in fractions [the instructor] demonstrated through the way I knew. (Student paper on Place-Based Learning, prepared for a Native Environmental Science Course, Spring 2017)

In [Elementary Algebra], patience was emphasized for me. I learned new perspectives from my peers that broadened my understanding of whatever math concepts we were working on at the time. Because it was promoted to integrate culture into math, I felt more engaged in the learning, I soon found myself having fun and getting satisfaction from solving menus and completing final projects. It was the first time I was able to complete a final math project which not only included math, but also, sacred colors, symbols, and even a poem to go along with the patterns that I created. This is when math started to become meaningful for me and I now enjoy it. (Personal communication from student who has now completed the first quarter of Calculus)

■ Conclusion

It is our hope that sharing this portion of our journey toward rehumanizing mathematics for our students may be useful, perhaps even inspirational, to others who may be interested in a similar pursuit. If we were to start back at the beginning, we would tell ourselves to take the pen out of our own hands more often. If we want to see what our students have to contribute and the unique ways in which they each think mathematically, we need to create an environment in which they do not have to leave who they are and what they already know at the door. We need to let go of the idea that there is only one correct way of thinking and embrace diverse approaches to mathematics. We would tell ourselves to model listening and asking questions to better understand each other's perspective, as opposed to imposing a list of steps to be memorized. As part of our practice of rehumanization, we remind ourselves that each person in the classroom, students as well as teachers, are human beings beyond their institutional classroom roles, and true learning can only happen with trust and respect. Our transition continues as we challenge and broaden the definition of what counts as mathematics.

References

Andrew-Ihrke, Dora. "Making a Square." Math in a Cultural Context (2013). https://www.youtube.com/755sBTe5Dcw.

Aveling, Nado. "Don't Talk about What You Don't Know: On (Not) Conducting Research with/in Indigenous Contexts." *Critical Studies in Education* 54 (2013): 203–14.

Donald, Dwayne, Florence Glanfield, and Gladys Sterenberg. "Culturally Relational Education in and with an Indigenous Community." *in education* 17 (2011). http://ineducation.ca/ineducation/article/view/73/286.

Humphreys, Cathy, and Ruth Parker. *Making Number Talks Matter*. Portland, Maine: Stenhouse, 2015.

Khan, Salman. "Adding and Subtracting Rational Expressions." Khan Academy (2011). https://www.youtube.com/watch?v=y_DweTAEYWk.

Lipnevich, Anastasiya A., and Jeffrey K. Smith. "Effects of Differential Feedback on Students' Examination Performance." *Journal of Experimental Psychology: Applied* 15 (2009): 319–33.

Quattromani, Libby, and Joanna Austin-Manygoats. "Culturally Relevant Assessment for the American Indian Student." In *Changing the Faces of Mathematics: Perspectives on Indigenous People of North America*, edited by Walter Secada and Judith Elaine Hankes, pp. 83–98. Reston, Va.: National Council of Teachers of Mathematics, 2002.

Niesz, Tricia. "Why Teacher Networks (Can) Work." *Phi Delta Kappan* 88, no. 8 (2007): 605–10.

Northwest Indian College. *Year Seven Self-Evaluation Report* (2017). http://www.nwic.edu/institutional-research-assessment-and-planning/accreditation.

Stigler, James, Karen B. Givvin, and Belinda J. Thompson. "What Community College Developmental Mathematics Students Understand about Mathematics." *MathAMATYC Educator* 1 (2010): 4–16.

Urbina-Lilback, Ruth N. "Snapshots of Equitable Teaching in a Highly Diverse Classroom." *Mathematics Teacher* 110 (2016): 126–132

Wildcat, Daniel. "Keynote Address at the 5th Annual Teaching and Learning Institute, Sept. 15, 2014." NWIC videos (2015). https://www.youtube.com/watch?v=JH22IkiqwHE.

CHAPTER 9

"I Can Solve All the Problems":
Latinx Students (Re)Write Their Math Stories

Melissa Adams, *The Ohio State University, Columbus*

By fourth grade, Antonio had become the mental math king of my classroom—he could see numbers in ways that no one else in the room did (including me). When I wanted to see a strategy that could surprise me, I knew I could count on him. Antonio was quiet, and when he would think about numbers, his face scrunched up behind the thick frames of his glasses until he suddenly raised a triumphant finger in the air, exclaiming, "I got it!" in victory.

Antonio had been my student for two years at the time. The year he became my student he had been forced to repeat third grade, and he seemed to identify with this sense of failing. Every time I passed out a mathematics problem, he would avoid working on it, sometimes slowly underlining every word, sometimes doodling. When I approached him to discuss his thinking in relation to the problem he would stay quiet. If I persisted, he would burst into tears. How did that child, who had such a sense of despair when it came to mathematics learning, become my triumphant finger waver? The shift I observed in how Antonio viewed himself as a mathematician prompted me to wonder about the mathematics identities of the other students in my classroom. I consider *math identities* in this context to be "the dispositions and deeply held beliefs that students develop about their ability to participate and perform effectively in mathematical contexts and to use mathematics in powerful ways across the contexts of their lives" (Aguirre, Mayfield-Ingram, and Martin 2013, p. 14).

Latinx students are routinely subjected to racialized schooling experiences (del Rosario Zavala 2014; Martin 2006; Valenzuela 1999). Throughout early elementary school, Antonio, like many emergent bilingual Latinx students, was seen through a deficit lens, characterized by what he was perceived as *not* being able to do (Lopez Leiva and Khisty 2014; Solórzano and Yosso 2002; Valencia 1997, 2011). Using a LatCrit framework, we can also see how students face multiple forms of oppression within schools as a result of their (and their families') race, language, gender, immigration status, class, and other dimensions of identity (Solórzano and Bernal 2001). When Antonio started third grade, he was not provided with any Spanish services. His language was seen as a problem to be fixed, rather than a resource that could help him learn mathematics (Civil and Planas 2012; Ruiz 2010). As a result, other people's views of Antonio's capabilities ignored his totality, narrowing his abilities in mathematics.

These schooling practices subtracted skills from Antonio, a violent and painful process common to the Latinx schooling experience (Valenzuela 1999). He was ascribed an identity of failure, and his language was used to mark him as deficient. He was one of many of my students who experienced the marginalization of their language (and, subsequently, their selves) in mathematics classrooms. This marginalization resulted from these students being seen as out of place in mathematics classrooms, but it also affected how they saw themselves in relation to mathematics (Gutiérrez 2002).

While Latinx students are often ascribed identities in much the way Antonio was, I view identity as "something you do, not who you are" (Gutiérrez 2013, p. 9). In other words, while Antonio moved through school, his identity was not fixed; it was shaped as he enacted it. At times, the ways others viewed him became part of what he did (such as crying when asked mathematics questions), while at other times he was rewriting and performing an identity of success (such as declaring "I got it!" for all to see). Antonio, and the way in which his mathematics identity and practices changed, show that this rewriting of identities can challenge narrow, deficit-based views of Latinx students.

Rewriting identities of failure into identities of power and possibility are part of a larger process of rehumanization in which the student's whole self is included and recognized in the classroom and in mathematics. I see rehumanization as requiring reciprocal recognition (Butler 2001), a practice in which all members of a classroom community are seen and see one another as whole, complete selves. Dehumanization occurs when some students are given a "legible and visible face," while others are not (Butler 2001, p. 23) as a result of norms that limit what students can become. Rehumanization, on the other hand, seeks to make all students heard, seen, and capable; it requires an effort to confer agency and power to those typically subordinated. I see this work as adding to stories of how emergent bilingual Latinx students can be empowered in and through mathematics (Domínguez 2011, 2016; Domínguez and Adams 2013; Gutstein 2003; Turner 2003; Turner et al. 2013).

■ Our Classroom

The research that informs this chapter comes from my fourth year of teaching and my second year with this particular group of students, whom I taught for three years, from third through fifth grades. This was a bilingual classroom where the vast majority of students came from homes in which one or both parents are immigrants and very proudly identify as Mexican. In order to fully understand the context of my classroom and my research, I should say that I am a proud Latina. My mother, who immigrated from Honduras, put significant effort into ensuring that I lived in Spanish and knew my culture. It is no coincidence that one of my primary goals as an educator was to help my students feel proud of themselves, their families, their language, and their culture. When directives or common practices became obstructions to that goal, I would resist in order to ensure that my practice stayed in line with my beliefs.

Our mathematics class was very different from these students' previous experiences. I centered my practice around questioning and encouraging student-generated ideas. I valued their thinking, wanted to understand their ideas, and tried to express that to them as part of a rehumanizing goal. My teaching style is influenced by cognitively guided instruction (CGI), which emphasizes the importance of understanding student thinking and using student ideas to drive mathematics learning (Carpenter et al. 2015). Students are expected to participate, listen to one another, and take risks.

At the same time, our mathematics class was not limited to this instructional style. We also utilized CGI strategies within a classroom community deliberately structured to be culturally affirming and one in which mathematics was part of a larger project of teaching for social justice

(Peterson 2005). Social justice teaching requires fostering critical thinking that is focused on "the continuing transformation of reality, on behalf of the continuing humanization of men" (Freire 1970, p. 68). We did not limit mathematics to a specific time or way of talking, nor did we exclude other ideas and learning from playing a role in our mathematics lessons.

Because of this goal, I would launch cross-curricular units around social justice themes in which mathematics was key to the exploration of social and political questions. Students were then co-planners with me, posing problems and asking questions that drove the unit. As an example, earlier in their academic year, we began a study of worker's rights, fair wages, and wealth inequality using the children's book *¡Si, Se Puede! / Yes, We Can!: Janitor Strike in L.A.* (Cohn, Delgado, and Rodríguez 2002). This book tells the story of how, in 2000, janitors in Los Angeles organized a strike in order to raise their wages. We compared that situation with contemporary news videos of fast-food workers organizing for a $15 per hour minimum wage. We discussed who the workers were and how that connected to what we knew about racial and class hierarchies. Students engaged in several related tasks, including calculating wages before and after the workers' strike and comparing their models of fair wealth distribution with the wealth distribution of the United States. They asked questions about how long it would take a worker at a fast-food restaurant to earn as much as a CEO makes for an estimated hour of work.

Many of the problems posed in this unit were posed by students themselves in an effort to utilize mathematics as a vehicle through which they could better describe social inequalities. As Sonia wrote in a culminating essay:

> ¿Los niños también pueden ayudar en esta situacion? Si!! Te explico: porque aprendimos de las huelgas y boicot en la comida fast food y de los trabajadores que se quejan porque no traen suficiente dinero.
>
> *Can kids also help in these situations? Yes!! Let me explain: because we learned about strikes and boycotts in fast food and about workers who complained because they weren't getting enough money.*

Sonia shows how this learning engaged her in problem posing but also in thinking about how to solve problems. Her own mathematics identity also shows how this attitude is reflected in her beliefs about mathematics and about herself as a mathematician.

■ Methodology

Changes like the ones Antonio experienced sparked many questions about how instructional choices could work to rehumanize my students. It was clear that schools had dehumanized them because of their Latinidad and their language (Adair, Colegrove, and McManus 2017; Flores and Rosa 2015), but could that be changed? While this dehumanization was true throughout their schooling experiences, it was particularly true in mathematics, where most of their teachers had been monolingual English speakers and where Spanish was not used in any way. If these students had been particularly excluded from mathematics but now seemed engaged and excited about it, I felt there had to be something in their stories as mathematicians to account for what I was observing. I also believed that their voices and their stories were the best way to counter the educational decisions they felt had hurt them and to bolster those practices they saw as helpful.

My purpose in centering students' stories is in response to Solórzano and Yosso's (2002) call to employ methodologies that focus on the strengths to be found within the experiences of students of color in order to offer "liberatory or transformative solutions to racial, gender and class subordination" (p. 24). There is a sense in which stories are equivalent to identities (Sfard and Prusak 2005). My research also utilizes the LatCrit framework Solórzano and Bernal (2001) shared by using Latinx student counternarratives of their own experiences at school to challenge the stories that were told about them by others. By choosing these methods, I intend to change the story about Latinx students while showing how their Latinidad was a central factor in their experiences of marginalization at school. The clear focus on student narratives is a concerted effort to bring an interdisciplinary perspective to the field of mathematics education and to challenge what it is we count as mathematical knowledge (Solórzano and Bernal 2001; Gutiérrez 2017).

While I wanted to simply ask students what they remembered and how they saw their experiences with mathematics, I worried that simply interviewing them would not reveal enough detail. I worried, in part, that I might push them to mention what I thought were important changes in their instructional experiences. I also felt that if I were interviewing them, they might have a tendency toward being overly positive about our current class. For that reason, I chose to collect written narratives, modifying Drake's (2006) mathematics stories measure for use with this particular age group.

Data were collected from a total of eighteen students, all of whom had been labeled as English language learners by the school district. Stories were collected over the course of four days, with one narrative collected each day. Students were told that they were welcome to write in whichever language they chose, and they did not have a time limit or length requirement. On the first day, they were asked to participate in a "guided remembering" of mathematics classes in each grade level, and they wrote memories, feelings, and ideas in a web around each grade level from first through fourth grades. On days 2 and 3, they were prompted to write stories of a positive and negative memory of mathematics with as much detail as they could remember about how they felt and what made them feel that way. Lastly, they were asked to imagine themselves in their seventh-grade mathematics class and describe what they imagined themselves doing and feeling at that time.

Once collected, I read the narratives in order to find emergent themes in how students talked about themselves in terms of what they could do in mathematics and to see if students named resources that they find useful in their mathematical practices. I did not want to impose my own codes or assumptions on their stories. Rather, I looked for patterns to emerge from several readings of all the stories. As patterns emerged, I would then go back to read the stories again in search of further evidence for those patterns. In that way, I was able to allow the stories themselves to compose my findings.

■ Findings

Powerfulness in Math

Several students' stories followed a similar pattern that suggested a sense of powerfulness in mathematics. By powerfulness, I mean a feeling that you are in control of your own mathematical learning and understanding and a belief that you have the mathematical abilities to solve problems and make sense of new or challenging mathematical concepts. These stories began with a difficulty that ended in success as a result of self-motivation and hard work. The students in these stories view themselves as agents who control their own fate—the hero in their story is not a smiling teacher or a gold star, it is them. If believing you control your own destiny ties into a productive form of hope, then this points to these students' belief in their own possibilities (Duncan-Andrade 2009). These stories define what mathematical power and agency can and should be. When students are able to see mathematics in this way, I believe they can use mathematics to rehumanize themselves.

In many stories, students used the phrase "no te rindes" (*don't give up*) to push themselves. These students enjoy feeling that they know what to do and that their hard work leads to something that they value—knowledge, understanding, and confirmation of their belief in themselves. José, for example, described a mathematics future filled with excitement, saying he liked thinking about his future mathematics classes because he knows he will always keep learning more and more. Sonia says she enjoys that mathematics offers her the opportunity to learn several ways of solving a problem. For her, this is encouraging and offers choices she can look to when a problem is difficult. Her negative memory shows this understanding and her response of continued persistence:

> Algo que me ha hecho sentir cosas negativas es cuando nos ponen trabajos difíciles que no entiendo. Cuando aprendí primero mis multiplicaciones fueron difíciles para mí porque no sabía como multiplicar. Solo me sabía la tabla del 1 y el 0 pero cuando fui más para el medio del año sabía más porque estábamos practicando. Pero lo que me sigue molestando es que no me acuerdo mucho sobre mis divisiones. Trato de acordarme pero no puedo. Pero lo voy a conseguir porque voy a tratar porque no me doy por vencida.

> *Something that has made me feel negative things is when they give us difficult tasks that I don't understand. When I first learned my multiplications they were hard for me because I didn't know how to multiply. I only knew my 1 and my 0 tables but by the middle of the year I knew more because I had been practicing. But what keeps bothering me is that I can't remember much about my divisions. I try to remember but I can't. But I will get it because I will try because I never give up.*

When Sonia imagines her future in mathematics, she sees mathematics as a potential tool for defense and as a source of empowerment:

> 2 niños que molestan. Se ríen de mi porque soy inteligente pero los ignore porque no entienden nada . . . tratan de hacer me bullying pero no pueden porque les pregunto preguntas de matemáticas.

> *2 boys bother me. They laugh at me because I am smart but I ignore them because they don't understand anything . . . they try to bully me but they can't because I ask them math questions.*

Antonio, the student whose remarkable change sparked this study, says that he will be successful in future mathematics classes because he knows "I can solve all the problems. It just might take me longer than the other kids." He knows that his mathematical ability is dependent on his effort, and he does not allow himself to be discouraged by working at a different pace or thinking in different ways. He writes, "Sometimes I confuse multiplication and division, but then I use it to help me." This flexibility—making use of mistakes—comes from a confidence in himself as a mathematician.

Many of these students' guided rememberings show that they had not always viewed mathematics in this way. Estrella wrote of second grade, "I remember math being so hard I almost stayed there." Of third grade she wrote, "It seemed super hard . . . because we had done two-step problems" and that she remembered learning fractions successfully. Finally, of fourth grade she wrote, "I loved the problem of the day." Her trajectory, over several years, provides evidence of how these students' views of mathematics changed over time and of how they could see themselves differently. When she envisions her future, Estrella writes that in her mathematics class "Math is not so hard. My best friend is on my side. I have gotten A's all year. And so far I think I will get in college free." She had gone from almost being retained in second grade to imagining herself earning scholarships through her mathematics skills—a transformation that reflects her mathematical rehumanization.

Collaboration

Regardless of whether they viewed mathematics as something they had the power to understand on their own or not, many students expressed that they valued opportunities for collaboration. Jenny imagined a positive future class as one including all students working "together like a community," a place in which members were all "respectful, empathetic, and smart, having lots of ideas and strategies to share."

Ernesto's positive memory was about a time I had him discuss his answer with Josefina. "Me hizo un poco feliz, porque yo nunca había ayudado a Josefina" (*It made me kind of happy because I had never helped Josefina before*). Josefina was a successful student, and the experience of helping her made him proud. The opportunity to collaborate with Josefina meant that he felt responsible for her understanding as well. Rather than viewing achieving correctness competitively, he viewed it collaboratively.

Leo also had positive memories around working with others. "Estoy haciendo lo mejor que puedo cuando pido ayuda. Cuando hago el trabajo me siento nervioso, pero cuando estoy trabajando con alguien, me siento mejor porque me están ayudando y explicando" (*I am doing the best I can when I ask for help. When I do the work I feel nervous, but when I work with someone else I feel better because they are helping me and explaining*). For Leo, collaboration was key to lessening his nervousness and helping to build confidence. He looked to his peers as sources of knowledge and support.

Manipulatives

Sonia's third-grade memory states, "Me acuerdo que me dejaban usar materiales" (*I remember when they let me use materials*) in mathematics class. Sonia mentions that she likes the ability to use multiple strategies, including manipulatives, even when she has the answer. Samantha also mentioned manipulatives in her positive memory, stating that "hice todas las multiplicaciones con cubos y se me hizo más fácil . . . por que usé cubos" (*I did all the multiplications with cubes and it was easier for me . . . because I used cubes*). Her memory also goes on to detail how her father, who had requested materials to support her learning at home, "estaba ayudandome y . . . el me puso los cubos y yo saqué todo" (*was helping me and he put the cubes and I got everything*). Leo, too, mentions manipulatives when he says, in a strong and positive statement, "pienso que puedo hacerlo . . . hacer buenas estrategias y practicar y también usar materiales y yo pienso que estoy haciendo bien el trabajo" (*I think I can do it . . . use good strategies and practice and also use materials and I think I am doing a good job*).

Language

All students in the study were bilingual to some extent—expressing themselves and reading the world in English and Spanish. Prior to being in our class, their bilingualism in mathematics class was inhibited because our school district required that mathematics be taught only in English.

Many of their prior mathematics classes were taught by monolingual teachers who could not communicate in or understand Spanish. If students wanted to ask questions, share ideas, or seek clarification, they could only do so in English. Consequently, language was a primary reason for some students having repeated a grade. Out of the eighteen students in my class labeled English language learners, six had been forced to repeat a grade. In other words, one-third of the class had been labeled as failures due, in large part, to their being Spanish speakers. Another four had nearly been retained, including Sonia.

Of the eighteen students in the study, twelve chose to write some or all of their narratives in Spanish. This act, alone, showed me that Spanish was a part of how they remembered and processed their mathematics experiences. It was the language in which they told their mathematics stories. In Antonio's story he shared, in Spanish, an idea pointing at some of his rehumanization: "En el cuarto grado . . . ese grado me hizo aprender matemáticas más mejor . . . El matemáticas es cuando estoy en un buen humor" (*In fourth grade . . . that grade made me learn math better. . . . The math is when I am in a good mood*).

Sonia was the only student who explicitly mentioned the shift in language. Her guided remembering shows that what she remembered from second grade was needing help every day in mathematics workbooks. Her main memory from third grade stated, "Me fascinó que habían puesto el problema del día en español en vez de puro inglés" (*I loved that they had put the problem of the day in Spanish instead of just pure English*). For her positive memory, she wrote the following about third and fourth grade:

> Me gustó las matemáticas en español porque antes en puro inglés no le entendía mucho. Me gustó también que hicieron matemáticas en español y enseñan otras maneras de hacer le matemáticas. Se me hizo más fácil sacar una respuesta y me gustó porque me la explico mejor.
>
> *I liked having math in Spanish because before when it was pure English I couldn't understand it much. I also liked having math in Spanish and showing different ways of doing math. It made it easier for me to get an answer and I liked it because I could explain it to myself better.*

While language was not explicitly raised by all students, there are several indications of the extent to which language mattered in their mathematics journeys. Many students expressed negative memories of mathematics in second grade, a grade in which all students received mathematics instruction in English. Linda, who was retained and placed in special education in the second grade, largely because she was not expressive, wrote, "When I was small, I like math, but when I was in second grade, it was hard to do math and I never pass . . . it was two years I was there." In her guided remembering, Linda writes that in first grade, "I never talked because everyone will not understand what I was doing." For second grade, she describes remembering that her teacher was an English-speaking monolingual and that "I was nervous to talk. . . . I had nobody to talk to." In third grade, when she began receiving instruction in both languages, Linda writes that she remembers, "When I was in third grade, I was nervous to do math because I think that I am not doing great. Well, I do math and I think that I was smart . . . I like the math and coming to learn more in school." In her memories from fourth grade, she showed a real shift in how she felt she could use her language in math class, writing "I was talking now because I realize that I have to talk to not give up."

The Role of Family in Mathematics

One finding I had not expected was the extent to which mathematics identities were also written in the home. In other words, students' mathematics stories showed that their experiences in the home have much to do with how they view mathematics and themselves as thinkers and doers of mathematics. For example, Itzel, who was a very successful student, tended to be very nervous in class and focused on grades and correctness. While most students mention learning skills like how to multiply and divide at school, Itzel's mathematics narratives largely took place at home. She writes:

> Una memoria que me hizo muy felíz era cuando aprendí a multiplicar. Yo estaba en mi casa, me recuerdo que eran las 6:30 pm y mi hermana me estaba dando una clase. Cuando me dio un examen vino una pregunta de multiplicación. Todavía me recuerdo de que se trataba . . . cuando se lo entregué a mi hermana, dijo "Mira Itzel, tu hiciste multiplicaciones."

> *One memory that made me very happy was when I learned to multiply. I was in my house, I remember it was 6:30 pm and my sister was giving me a lesson. When she gave me a test there was a multiplication question. I can still remember what it was about . . . when I gave my sister the test she said, "Look Itzel, you did multiplication."*

The opportunity to practice schooling settings in the home with her sister allows Itzel space to feel successful and to take risks. It is good for her that she has these spaces to create a more positive mathematics identity, but it also leads to questions as to how to recreate this environment in the classroom.

Like Itzel, Salvador and Luisita also found support and spaces for learning in the home. Salvador told a negative memory story of not knowing what to do to solve a problem and feeling very angry. He wrote, "When my mom got home, I told her the problem of the day was hard, so she said that doesn't mean you're dumb and she said better luck next day. And the next day, I did get my answer quick." When Salvador is frustrated with himself for not understanding a problem, his mom is there to encourage him. Luisita also uses family to support her when mathematics is difficult. She begins her positive memory by stating:

> El día más felíz de mi vida fue con mi familia. Mi papá, mi mamá, mis hermanos me ayudaron . . . era difícil, pero lo resolví con mi familia. Desde ese momento me sentí con un alivio y tomé las matemáticas. Desde ese día me gustaba cuando me daban tareas de matemáticas.

> *The happiest day in my life was with my family. My dad, my mom, my brothers and sisters helped me . . . it was hard but I solved it with my family. From that moment, I felt a relief and I took the math. From that day, I liked when I had math homework.*

Another story about the ways in which families were connected to students' mathematics identities came from Sonia. Sonia's mother confirmed this story in a parent meeting, explaining how she had learned the division algorithm, but never understood how to divide.

■ Discussion

The resources that students identify in their narratives serve as guideposts for how to achieve rehumanizing classrooms and also show us the importance of students' stories. They are aware of what facilitates their learning and therefore are capable of having agency or a sense of powerfulness in mathematics. Each resource identified serves a rehumanizing purpose.

Collaboration, for one thing, establishes collective mathematics knowledge, granting everyone access to the thinking that students use and creating positive and reciprocal relationships. The process of sharing ideas facilitates a more complete recognition of others because of the extent to which we become aware of how others approach problems and the way in which we can compare that to our own problem-solving practices. Hearing that students valued collaboration was particularly heartening, because I could remember how reluctant students were to speak when they started third grade. Many of them, like Linda, were unaccustomed to speaking in mathematics class (partly because of language alienation and also because discussion was not a learning strategy in previous classrooms) and resisted speaking or listening to one another, thereby reflecting a dehumanized view of one another.

The way in which these students adopted much more positive attitudes toward collaboration and listened to one another as sources of knowledge showed that this had changed as a result of classroom practices. Being listened to and feeling heard clearly serves a rehumanizing purpose and showcases the extent to which the entire classroom community needs to be involved in processes of inclusion and recognition.

The second resource discussed, manipulatives, were also new to my students when they started third grade. Manipulatives offer concrete visualizations of abstract mathematical thinking and, in this context, provided students tangible, confirmable proof of their conjectures. I would argue, based on the students' stories, that access to manipulatives served as a rehumanizing feature of our mathematics class: It allowed students to find certainty in their ideas, gave them access to resources that they felt helped them, served as confirmation of the value in their mathematical risk taking, and inspired greater participation. Manipulatives facilitated inclusiveness and collaboration, and they allowed for more students to be recognized as mathematicians. Students would see how others used manipulatives and intuit numerical concepts or mimic strategies. The manipulatives played a fundamental role in getting students to recognize one another as resources for learning.

Many students cited family support networks and the sharing of learning among family members (even including students teaching parents skills learned at school) as well as the importance of in-class collaboration, which bolsters the argument that rehumanization requires respect and reciprocal recognition. Jenny even used the words "respectful" and "empathetic" to describe an ideal community of learners. Cammarota (2008) tells us that "a school environment that countervails respect and reciprocity between teachers and students removes any foundation on which Latinx youth might form positive educational relationships" (p. 130). Teachers also need to be members of the community of learners, as teachers gain knowledge from students, share opportunities to learn, and recognize students' selves. Teachers also must respect the ideas and identities that students bring with them and must situate themselves in positions where they make clear how much they stand to gain from knowing and valuing their students.

Finally, it is important to address the issue of language. It is obvious that access to their full linguistic repertoires was important for my students. In fact, we can see their bilingual approaches to mathematics reflected in the writing of their mathematics stories. Most students wrote either in Spanish, or in both languages, reflecting that their language is a fundamental part of their mathematics identities. This suggests that any limitation on students' linguistic resources lessens the extent to which they can develop or express positive mathematics identities. If they feel that a part of themselves is not welcome in mathematics class, how can they develop an identity of belonging in mathematics?

We know that language plays a fundamental role in the construction of an identity as a successful mathematician and that it must be considered as fundamental to the process of learning mathematics. Research has shown the extent to which students are more comfortable solving problems, using advanced strategies to solve problems, and addressing questions requiring their reflection on mathematics if they can do so in their native language (Clarkson 2006; Domínguez 2011). In other words, bilingualism can serve as a resource for students as they engage in mathematical tasks or reflect on mathematical experiences (Domínguez 2011; Turner et al. 2013) and facilitates the inclusion of their whole selves. Furthermore, it is key to note that, in the context of emergent bilingual students, the exclusion of language fundamentally limits any rehumanizing efforts. Sonia told us that, for her, Spanish was part of having more strategies to solve problems and engage in mathematics. She provides yet another example of the extent to which Spanish is a mathematical resource that can increase confidence and allow greater access to mathematical content.

Many of the narratives contained signs that students had taken on new ideas about mathematics and about themselves. In fact, the ways in which Estrella, Linda, and Antonio wrote their narratives show dramatic changes that they recognize as part of their experiences of mathematics.

■ Implications

The research in this chapter began with my questions about the changes that I had observed in Antonio. The positive shift in his attitude and in his mathematics work sparked my thinking about how all my students see themselves in relation to mathematics. What I found was that there was so much that I had not yet seen, even in a student-centered classroom where student voices were valued. I was listening to their ideas, but I had not yet fully listened to their stories. In this case, my changed perspective allowed me to consider how I could address the identities that students described with the belief that it was possible to help students develop a sense of powerfulness in mathematics.

After collecting and studying my students' stories, I realized how much I had not known during my early years of teaching. There is a tremendous power in listening to our students, but this should not be limited to their mathematical thinking. We can know their mathematical ideas and preferred strategies but still not see them completely. Students' stories, about their lives in and out of the classroom, are mathematically valid knowledge. They help us to understand how students approach the learning space and what effects other classrooms have had, and they can serve as an impetus for our own pedagogical choices. I spent the following year after this research teaching the same group of students, and I was very careful with my use of praise and assessing of correctness. While collecting the data, I began holding monthly parent meetings to hear more about the parents' views on our classroom and on the content we were learning, including their own ways of approaching the ideas we studied.

There is so much we can do, as educators, to help students see themselves as powerful in the context of mathematics. To begin with, we must truly believe that our students are the owners of the classroom space. Instead of using the phrase "my class" or "Ms. Adams's class," I tried to always use "our class" and even "your class," reminding students that they would be in the classroom regardless of the teacher assigned to their grade level. Additionally, we must ensure that students' whole selves are welcomed, seen, and heard in the mathematics classroom. Often, their experiences navigating the world will inform their mathematical practice.

I also recommend that, in welcoming students' whole selves, we include all their languages. Doing so allows them to collaborate, discuss, and engage in mathematics, but it also can inform the ways in which we approach and understand mathematical topics (Dominguez and Adams 2013). Educators must encourage and facilitate true, productive collaboration. When students are able to collaborate meaningfully, they can feel powerful like Ernesto, or they can begin believing in themselves, like Leo. Collaboration tells students that others care about their ideas and shows that their presence is necessary for the entire class to learn. Giving students the space to collaborate and the power to use all their linguistic resources allows students like Linda to learn that talking is what keeps them from giving up.

All students, especially those typically subjected to racialized, gendered, and/or classed restrictions, need their mathematics teachers to engage fully in the rehumanizing process of ensuring the inclusion, recognition, and valuing of students' whole selves. Teachers can do this by questioning their practice, context, and their classroom environment while listening openly to the voices of their students. Just as they must be centered in our research methodologies, students of color must be centered in our classroom practices. José described our classroom in a way that I think emphasizes the possibilities for collective rehumanization, saying that in our class he learned that "siempre nos tenemos que apoyar y nunca rendirnos y lucha por lo que quieres . . . porque hablando y caminando y apoyando podemos resolverlo todo" (*We always need to support each other and fight for what you want . . . because together, talking and walking and helping, we can solve everything*).

As a summary of what my research has taught me, here are some takeaways for all of us as mathematics educators:

1. Listen to students, and know who they are and what they need from you and from each other.

2. Recognize and value their families, culture, language, and communities.

3. Design units that make mathematics matter and bring mathematics to life.

4. Encourage collaboration and reciprocity—show that we all work together and learn from each other, even teachers.

5. Know and show that all students are mathematically capable.

References

Adair, Jennifer Keys, Kiyomi S.S. Colegrove, and Molly E. McManus. "How the Word Gap Argument Negatively Impacts Young Children of Latinx Immigrants' Conceptualizations of Learning." *Harvard Educational Review* 87, no. 3 (2017): 309–34.

Aguirre, Julia, Karen Mayfield-Ingram, and Danny Martin. *The Impact of Identity in K–8 Mathematics: Rethinking Equity-Based Practices*. Reston, Va.: National Council of Teachers of Mathematics, 2013.

Butler, Judith. "Giving an Account of Oneself." *diacritics* 31, no. 4 (2001): 22–40.

Cammarota, Julio. *Sueños Americanos: Barrio Youth Negotiating Social and Cultural Identities*. Tucson: University of Arizona Press, 2008.

Carpenter, Thomas, Elizabeth Fennema, Megan Loef Franke, Linda Levi, and Susan E. Empson. *Children's Mathematics: Cognitively Guided Instruction*. 2nd ed. London: Heinemann, 2015.

Civil, Marta, and Núria Planas. "Whose Language Is It?" In *Alternative Forms of Knowing (in) Mathematics,* edited by Swapna Mukhopadhyay and Wolff-Richard Roth, pp. 71–89. Boston: Sense Publishers, 2012.

Clarkson, Philip C. "Multicultural Classrooms: Contexts for Much Mathematics Teaching and Learning." In *Ethnomathematics and Mathematics Education,* edited by Franco Favilli, pp. 9–16. Pisa, Italy: Tipografia Editrice Pisana, 2006.

Cohn, Diana, Francisco Delgado, and Luis J. Rodríguez. *¡Sí, Se Puede!/Yes, We Can!: Janitor Strike in L.A.* El Paso, Tex.: Cinco Puntos Press, 2002.

Del Rosario Zavala, Maria. "Latina/o Youth's Perspectives on Race, Language, and Learning Mathematics." *Journal of Urban Math Education* 7, no. 1 (2014): 55–87.

Delgado, Richard. "Storytelling for Oppositionists and Others: A Plea for Narrative." *Michigan Law Review* 87, no. 8 (1989): 2411–41.

Drake, Corey. "Turning Points: Using Teachers' Mathematics Life Stories to Understand the Implementation of Mathematics Education Reform." *Journal of Mathematics Teacher Education* 9, no. 6 (2006): 579–608.

Dominguez, Higinio. "Using What Matters to Students in Bilingual Mathematics Problems." *Educational Studies in Mathematics* 76, no. 3 (2011): 305–28.

_____. "Mirrors and Windows into Student Noticing." *Teaching Children Mathematics* 22, vol. 6 (2016): 358–65.

Dominguez, Higinio, and Melissa Adams. "Más o Menos: Exploring Estimation in a Bilingual Classroom." *Teaching Children Mathematics* 20, vol. 1 (2013): 36–41.

Duncan-Andrade, Jeff M. "Note to Educators: Hope Required When Growing Roses in Concrete." *Harvard Educational Review* 79, no. 2 (2009): 181–94.

Flores, Nelson, and Jonathan Rosa. "Undoing Appropriateness: Raciolinguistic Ideologies and Language Diversity in Education." *Harvard Educational Review* 85, no. 2 (2015): 149–71.

Freire, Paulo. *Pedagogy of the Oppressed* (1996 edition), translated by Myra Bergman Ramof. London and New York: Penguin Books, 1970.

Gutiérrez, Rochelle. "Beyond Essentialism: The Complexity of Language in Teaching Mathematics to Latina/o Students." *American Educational Research Journal* 39, no. 4 (2002): 1047–89.

_____. "The Sociopolitical Turn in Mathematics Education." *Journal for Research in Mathematics Education* 44, no. 1 (2013): 37–68.

_____. "Living Mathematx: Toward a Vision for the Future." *Philosophy of Mathematics Education Journal* 32, no. 1 (2017).

Gutstein, Eric. "Teaching and Learning Mathematics for Social Justice in an Urban, Latino School." *Journal for Research in Mathematics Education* (2003): 37–73.

Leistyna, Pepi. "Preparing for Public Life: Education, Critical Theory, and Social Justice." In *Handbook of Social Justice in Education,* edited by William Ayers, Therese Quinn, and David Stovall, pp. 51–58. New York: Routledge, 2009.

López Leiva, Carlos A., and Lena Licón Khisty. "'Juntos Pero No Revueltos': Microaggressions and Language in the Mathematics Education of Non-Dominant Latinas/os." *Mathematics Education Research Journal* 26, no. 2 (2014): 421–38.

Martin, Danny B. "Mathematics Learning and Participation as Racialized Forms of Experience: African American Parents Speak on the Struggle for Mathematics Literacy." *Mathematical Thinking and Learning* 8, no. 3 (2006): 197–229.

Peterson, Bob. "Teaching Math across the Curriculum." In *Rethinking Mathematics: Teaching Social Justice by the Numbers.* edited by Eric Gutstein and Bob Peterson, pp. 9–15. Milwaukee, Wis.: Rethinking Schools, 2005.

Ruiz, Richard. "Reorienting Language-As-Resource." In *International Perspectives on Bilingual Education: Policy, Practice, and Controversy,* edited by John E. Petrovic, pp. 155–72. Charlotte, N.C.: Information Age Publishing, 2010.

Sfard, Anna, and Anna Prusak. "Telling Identities: In Search of an Analytic Tool for Investigating Learning as a Culturally Shaped Activity." *Educational Researcher* 34, no. 4 (2005): 14–22.

Solórzano, Daniel G., and Dolores Delgado Bernal. "Examining Transformational Resistance through a Critical Race and Latcrit Theory Framework: Chicana and Chicano Students in an Urban Context." *Urban Education* 36, no. 3 (2001): 308–42.

Solórzano, Daniel G., and Tara J. Yosso. "Critical Race Methodology: Counter-Storytelling as an Analytical Framework for Education Research." *Qualitative Inquiry* 8, no. 1 (2002): 23–44.

Turner, Erin Elizabeth. "Critical Mathematical Agency: Urban Middle School Students Engage in Mathematics to Investigate, Critique, and Act upon Their World." PhD diss., University of Texas, 2003.

Turner, Erin, Higinio Dominguez, Luz Maldonado, and Susan Empson. "English Learners' Participation in Mathematical Discussion: Shifting Positionings and Dynamic Identities." *Journal for Research in Mathematics Education* 44, no. 1 (2013): 199–234.

Valencia, Richard R. *The Evolution of Deficit Thinking: Educational Thought and Practice.* London: Falmer Press, 1997.

_____. *Dismantling Contemporary Deficit Thinking: Educational Thought and Practice.* New York: Routledge, 2011.

Valenzuela, Angela. *Subtractive Schooling: U.S.-Mexican Youth and the Politics of Caring.* Albany: State University of New York Press, 1999.

_____, ed. *Leaving Children Behind: How "Texas-Style" Accountability Fails Latino Youth.* Albany: State University of New York Press, 2005.

CHAPTER 10

¿Es lo Mismo?
Bilingual Children Counting and Making Sense of Numbers

Cristina Valencia Mazzanti, *University of Georgia, Athens*

Martha Allexsaht-Snider, *University of Georgia, Athens*

"Las palabras son símbolos para recuerdos compartidos" (*Words are symbols for shared memories*). —*Jorge Luis Borges*

How are mathematics in Spanish different from mathematics in Tswana, English, Farsi, or Quechua? How are mathematics different when we are able to think about them in both English and Spanish and not only in Spanish or English? How is it different to think about "one" or "uno" or "1"? Questions like these, that explore the connections between mathematics and language, have been answered in different ways and from different perspectives (Barwell, Barton, and Setati 2007; Barwell et al. 2016; Edmonds-Wathen, Trinick, and Durand-Guerrier 2016; Phakeng and Moschkovich 2013). The fact that there is not one way to answer these questions speaks to the fundamental and complex relations between mathematics and language. It also speaks to the fact that both language and mathematics are intrinsically human endeavors and consequently, have a history and a context and cannot be thought of as homogeneous. According to Gutiérrez (2012a), "a focus on the context of learning also serves as a humanizing tool in mathematics education research. It moves us away from a kind of objectified way of knowing something (e.g., students or the "one" path to equity). . . . giving voice to the contextual factors that enable or constrain learning in a given situation is equally important" (p. 18).

In this chapter, we explore the relationship between mathematics and language by reflecting on how Latinx children who are five and six years old develop their number sense, drawing on their linguistic resources in Spanish and English to understand quantity, its symbolic representations, and numbers, in the context of a kindergarten classroom. (We will use the term *Latinx* here, fully understanding that no one term can represent the heterogeneous nature of any group, and that those within such a group may employ different terms themselves.) We use these explorations of children's learning to open questions about the ways we think about number sense, language, and mathematics. We wish to understand how mathematics teaching and learning in today's multilingual classrooms can be more centered around children as well as their lived experiences, making it more humanizing.

■ Perspectives on Language and Translanguaging

When doing research at the intersection of language and mathematics there is a need to problematize and ground one's understanding of language (Moschkovich 2010, 2017). We see language as the complex practices of individuals and communities as they communicate and make meaning of the world. Our understandings reflect and build on translanguaging, particularly as conceptualized in Ofelia Garcia's work (e.g., Garcia and Wei 2014). The term "translanguaging" is used to describe the lived language practices of bilingual and multilingual people. Garcia and Wei define it by writing,

> For us translanguaging does not refer to two separate languages nor to a synthesis of different language practices or to a hybrid mixture. Rather translanguaging refers to *new* language practices that make visible the complexity of language exchange among people with different histories, and releases histories and understandings that had been buried within fixed language identities constrained by nation-states. (p. 21).

This nuanced perspective can be complemented by Canagarajah's (2011) definition of translanguaging as "the ability of multilingual speakers to shuttle between languages, treating the diverse languages that form their repertoire as an integrated system" (p. 401).

Essential to the notion of translanguaging is the idea that multilingual people do not use languages as a series of disconnected or interconnected linguistic systems but instead use a linguistic repertoire that incorporates all their knowledge and abilities about languages. Therefore, a translanguaging perspective allows us to focus on the actual practices of bilingual and multilingual people, in their use of language to communicate and make sense of the world. As we worked to understand the children's use of language and developing number sense in this chapter, we found it particularly useful to consider the notion of "languaging," as a process, rather than language, as an entity, as languaging highlights the communicative nature of language that goes beyond the user knowing a code; it allows for a new way of being in the world. Language is seen not just as a symbolic system, but also as what carries interpretation into being. In Garcia's own words, "Language is not a simple system of structures that is independent of human actions with others, of our being with others. The term *languaging* is needed to refer to the simultaneous process of continuous becoming of ourselves and of our language practices, as we interact and make meaning of the world. [. . .] Languaging both shapes and is shaped by context" (Garcia and Wei 2014, p. 8).

Translanguaging offers a view of language that allows us to better understand children and their learning in ways that are more humanizing. It offers a way to understand the world and bilingual children where being monolingual is no longer the standard or the norm. Gutiérrez (2012b) explains that a focus on context can foster a more humane approach to mathematics; this is reflected in the idea that languaging both shapes and is shaped by context. The understandings we will present in this chapter are grounded in the way translanguaging is situated in a humanizing use of language as a way of being. It creates a lens for us to see the ways bilingual children were engaging in dynamic language practices incorporating their knowledge of number, Spanish, and English. We found that focusing on the children's ways of being as they used languages to engage with each other and their experiences with counting helped us to see the ways in which a translanguaging perspective can support humanizing approaches. Such approaches can encourage children to make connections among their experiences in and out of the classroom as they make sense of number.

■ Perspectives on Counting and Number Sense

Krasa and Shunkwiler (2009) identify that it is at around five and six years of age that children are able to connect the mental processes and symbolic representations associated with quantity to think about value abstractly and place it along the mental number line. These and other elements and processes related to quantity and numbers have been identified as a part of children's number sense development (Dowker 2008; Jordan et al. 2009; Lipton and Spelke 2003). Following on Krasa and Shunkwiler (2009), we understand number sense as a confidence with quantities and their mental manipulation that comes from significant and meaningful experiences with quantities, their symbolic representations, and how they connect to each other.

The central role of language in number sense development has been well established (e.g., Jordan and Kaplan 2009). Being able to connect quantities with the symbolic representations provided by languages (such as "two" or "6") is a necessary skill for children's number sense development. Through these connections, children are able to establish relations between the different mental processes associated with quantity and provide necessary symbolic representations (such as words and numerals) to make sense of quantities. Furthermore, the connections between quantities and symbolic representations allow children to think about them abstractly and use quantities more effectively in mathematical contexts (Jordan et al. 2009; Krasa and Shunkwiler 2009) and in mathematical problem solving (Carpenter et al. 1993). More concretely, when thinking of number and number sense development, there are three possible symbolic representations of quantity that can be associated with language: phonological representations (such as the sound of the word "one"); orthographic symbols (such as the written form of the word "one"); and numeric images (such as the numeral "1") (Krasa and Shunkwiler 2009). However, it is important to clarify that although language is key in developing number sense, children can understand and apply their understanding of quantities without having learned symbolic representations for them (Barth et al. 2005). In this chapter, we will explore how children use two languages to represent quantities and the different ways children are able to learn and make sense of numbers and counting.

■ Contexts and Perspectives

The data presented in this study were collected by the first author (Cristina) as a participant observer, taking the role of a volunteer teacher in a kindergarten classroom. As participant observer and volunteer teacher, Cristina worked with the class an average of two times a week, for a complete school year. Regularly, she was with the class from the start of the day until the end of mathematics instruction; participating in morning work, morning meeting, calendar, and mathematics instruction. As a part of her role in the classroom, Cristina observed and supported mathematics instruction; taught the whole group, developing her own lessons as well as teaching lessons developed by the classroom teacher, and worked with small groups and individual students.

The kindergarten classroom had twenty-two children; twelve were Latinx, seven were African American, two were white, and one was a Karen refugee. Ten of the twelve Latinx children were orally fluent in Spanish. We understand that thinking about the education of Latinx people in the U.S. only as the education of Spanish speakers, English speakers, or bilingual speakers is a limited understanding of their actual lived experiences. Many Latinx people in the United States, like the children in this chapter, are bilingual people who are able to use Spanish and English to learn and make sense of the world. As in most public schools in Georgia, the official language of instruction was English and students were expected to receive all academic instruction in

English. The kindergarten class was regularly taught by Ms. Dominguez, the teacher, and Mrs. Barley, the paraprofessional. Ms. Dominguez was fluent in Spanish and often used it to communicate with parents.

Due to Cristina's active role in the classroom, observations were recorded after classroom visits in journal entries and supported by some note taking during her participation in the classroom, adapting the method used by Hankins (2003) in *Teaching Through the Storm: A Journal of Hope*. In this chapter, we present and interpret edited fragments of the journal entries that recreate some of the classroom events that took place bilingually around counting play money. These fragments were selected because they all occurred in the same winter morning and provide insight into one of the aspects we found most significant about the mathematics learning of this group of students, counting bilingually. The journal entry fragments are presented and written in the first person, from Cristina's perspective. They also reveal much about how Cristina was positioned in the classroom from her own perspective and perhaps from the perspectives of the children: as a bilingual speaker interested in mathematics, which also opened spaces to count and think about numbers in English and Spanish for the children within the classroom routine.

In this chapter, it is possible to see that there is a close relation between the research we present, the classroom we discuss, and our own experiences and stances about language. There is a close tie with Cristina's identity as an immigrant, a Latina, and a multilingual person, and the identity of the students in the kindergarten class. In this instance, I [Cristina] have chosen to use the term *Latina* instead of *Latinx* to define my own identity. I see this as something that extends beyond my gender identity, as I can be Latina in all languages that are central to my identity—Italian, Spanish, and English—which seems essential to me when I take into account all the intersectionalities of my own identity. This research was only possible because the students and Cristina shared both English and Spanish with each other, as well as an experience of the world as bilingual. This research also reflects Martha's (the second author's) perspective as a White teacher educator and a bilingual speaker of English and Spanish. The understandings we developed were catalyzed by Martha's enduring commitment to learning with immigrant and multilingual people in Latinx and Mexican-American communities in the United States as well as in multilingual communities in México and Colombia. Significantly, what we learned stems from our commitment as teachers to see the potential in all children, to think deeply about their learning, and to learn together. In our collaborative work, we have continued to open spaces for each other to be insiders and outsiders, broadening our understanding of children, language, and mathematics through our underlying commitment to equity for all.

■ Children Counting Bilingually

Journal Entry 1—Counting Treinta y seis: *As the children went to their desks and started getting chairs down, they found the different amounts of play money Ms. Dominguez had placed on top of their desks (1 to 3 bills). Some of them simply looked at them or moved them to the corner of their desks, but most children showed them to each other, commenting cheerfully in Spanish or English about how many bills they got. The children chose to add their new bills to the stacks of play money they had collected on previous days and then count them before moving on to other morning activities. That morning, Nicholas was the first to show me his stack of play money and we counted it together by ones in Spanish and English. Later in the morning Gabriel asked me to count with him. While we counted his stack of play money in English, Fernando and Abby also counted theirs in different ways, sitting at a table nearby, letting me know every* *so often how many they had. After a while Abby was very excited to report that, "Fernando tiene treinta y seis." When I asked how would she say it in English, she whisper-yelled, "Thirty-six." I then asked, "y ¿es lo mismo?" [Is it the same?]. In response, Abby, Nicholas, Fernando, and Gabriel all yelled "Sí!" [Yes].*

Interpretation of Journal Entry 1: This first journal entry reveals many of the complexities that unfolded around counting in this kindergarten classroom. All the children in this journal entry were comfortable in Spanish and English and had experiences of regularly counting in both languages with each other and with Cristina. This journal entry also shows how the different linguistic resources of the children allowed for a way of thinking about quantity and equality that is only possible in the context of bilingualism or multilingualism. If the children did not speak both languages, the possibility of thinking flexibly about "36" and the question of the quantity being the same when referred to in English or Spanish would not have arisen. Because Fernando and Abby had been counting together in both English and Spanish, they already had experiences with the idea that both numbers represented the same amount. Knowing and using both languages for counting, as well as being able to compare the phonological representations in Spanish and English for "36," allowed the children to think deeply about quantity. Furthermore, they made connections to words, number-word sequences, and the ways they had known such words and quantities before in Spanish and English and tied that knowledge to number-words (phonological representations) they would use again.

Journal Entry 2—Mary and Drew: *I later observed Mary and Drew count Mary's play money. Mary was counting in English, but when I came by she continued counting in Spanish. She arranged her bills in groups of five, making sure all bills were facing the same way and were perfectly organized in straight rows and columns. She counted them in Spanish with comfort, looking at them, and straightening them on occasion, while I quietly observed and sat by her. As she was counting, Drew who sits next to her and speaks only English, started echoing her counting in Spanish. When Mary realized what Drew was doing, she took a motherly tone and started complimenting him and asking him questions in Spanish, saying "Muy bien, y esto ¿cómo se dice en inglés?" [Very good, and how do you say this in English?]. At that Drew seemed completely lost and looked at me. I smiled and explained to him in English that Mary was just asking how he would say that in English. Drew replied to Mary and they kept counting and interacting about their counting; Mary mainly speaking in Spanish, and Drew replying to her question in English and counting in Spanish. When they reached 11, Drew said to Mary that he did not know how to say that number, so Mary repeated "once" [eleven], with Drew echoing her, until he was able to pronounce it with confidence and to Mary's satisfaction. She then praised him by saying, "Yes, muy bien" [very good], and they kept going in the same way, with Mary teaching Drew the numbers in the teens in Spanish.*

Interpretation of Journal Entry 2: Drew's and Mary's counting shows the learning opportunities that frequently arose for the children in the kindergarten classroom because of the richness and multitude of language resources brought by all the children in the class. Mary's knowledge of counting in English and Spanish, and Drew's curiosity about Spanish, as well as the previous experiences the children had counting in both languages in the context of the classroom, created a dynamic space for both children to explore their understanding of quantity. The process of Mary teaching Drew numbers in Spanish, and Drew learning them, made it so that both children were actively bringing awareness to the way number-word sequences were being used and connected to quantities across two languages. As Drew and Mary were interacting and using the play money, they were making connections between the phonological representations of the quantities in each language and the quantities they represented. The fact that Drew expressed to Mary that he did not know how to say the next number, "once," shows that in the way he and Mary were counting he was understanding and connecting the quantities and the phonological representations in both English and Spanish. Mary opened an opportunity for herself to think about the number-word sequences metacognitively, establishing connections and comparisons between English and Spanish, because of the way she was teaching Drew the numbers in Spanish.

Journal Entry 3—Counting by Tens: *I counted play money in English with La Sa Yaw. We started by making groups of ten and counted them (La Sa Yaw's preferred method of counting). We then counted by ones and then counted again alternating both ways of counting. As we counted, Abby, who had finished her morning work and was playing with Legos on the carpet behind us, came to stand by me, peering over my shoulder. After watching us count for a while, Abby started calling the multiples of ten in Spanish, at the same time as La Sa Yaw or I said them in English.*

Interpretation of Journal Entry 3: Both Abby and La Sa Yaw are avid and resourceful mathematics learners. During Cristina's times in the classroom, La Sa Yaw expressed a strong interest in learning to count by tens. From the first weeks in the classroom, La Sa Yaw would use different opportunities to seek Cristina's help in different counting endeavors she had set for herself. As the year progressed and Ms. Dominguez started emphasizing skip counting, particularly by tens and fives, La Sa Yaw showed great interest in learning such skills. By the time the events in this journal entry took place, La Sa Yaw had become one of the most proficient children in the class at grouping and skip counting. In the way La Sa Yaw and Cristina were counting, they were emphasizing multiples of ten and how to count objects grouped in sets of ten. Consequently, Abby was able to use her Spanish and other learning resources to further make sense of quantity, grouping, counting, and the base-ten number system. Abby, who had spent her morning counting in different ways in Spanish and English, was able to use the phonological representations of numbers in Spanish to highlight the counting strategy La Sa Yaw and Cristina had been using when counting in English. Abby's counting by tens in Spanish in this case shows a complex and effective way of thinking about numbers and quantities and their relation to each other that fully relies on her skills as a bilingual user of Spanish and English.

■ Multilingual Children's Number Sense

The journal entries of children's number sense development provided us with a rich way to think about children's bilingual counting and mathematical learning. More specifically, they allowed us to explore how children were able to use their linguistic resources to promote their own metacognitive awareness of the ways counting works and quantities can be represented, further developing their sense of quantities and how they relate to each other, and thus their number sense. (It is important to clarify that there is no evidence of significant advantages for mathematics performance in learning number-words and number-word-sequences in any particular language [Moschkovich 2017]. We are not seeking to establish an advantage between languages or language structures in learning mathematics.) Such learning was possible because children knew and could use more than one language and consequently more than one phonological representation for a quantity and more than one number-word sequence.

Looking back at the understandings of number sense we presented in the introduction, we see a distance between the actual lived experiences of the children portrayed in the journal entries and the current conceptual frameworks used to understand number sense development. The number sense models we outlined do not explain or represent the number sense development of the children in the journal entries; in these models number sense is presented from the point of view of people who speak only one language. Previously, we explained that students may be able to represent a quantity using language through an orthographic image and a phonological representation. In the case of bilingual and multilingual students, quantities have more than one orthographic image and phonological representation. A student who speaks only English can represent the quantity of "1" through the orthographic image "one" and its corresponding phonological representation. A child who speaks both Spanish and English would be able to represent the same quantity through the orthographic images of "one" and "uno" and their correspondent phonological representations.

Drawing on translanguaging, we are able to move away from a perspective of the world, language, and learning in which speaking one language is considered the norm. However, most current models of number sense reflect and represent a conception of the world and of mathematics in which being monolingual is still considered the norm. As we pursue the goal of mathematics that is more humane and reflective of the lived experiences of children, we see a need to reflect the understandings gained through translanguaging into the frameworks we use to understand mathematics learning. Furthermore, we see the need for conceptualizations that allow for and represent the experiences of multilingual people, such as in the learning that is portrayed in this chapter.

This thinking about a model of number sense that accounts for more than one orthographic image and phonological representation seems central if we seek to humanize mathematics. We need frameworks and ways to think about learning that reflect the lived experiences of all people. We see the need for such frameworks as particularly urgent when considering that it is estimated that more than half the world speaks more than one language (Stavans and Hoffman 2015). It also connects to the previously mentioned idea that both language and mathematics are intrinsically human endeavors and consequently have a history and a context. Looking at children's mathematics learning in context and through conceptual models that account for such contexts opens up possibilities for more humane mathematics (Gutiérrez 2012a).

■ Interpretations and Possibilities for Children Counting Multilingually

The accounts in this chapter provide us with a way to reflect on how we may move toward a more humane way of learning and teaching mathematics in today's multilingual classrooms. The journal entries present mathematics learning that was joyful and humane because it centered around children, their knowledge of language, and their understanding of number. When we set up this research project and conducted data analysis, we did it based on the fundamental belief that multilingualism presents many opportunities and advantages for learning. Furthermore, we teach, learn, and do research with an awareness and appreciation of the power of language and the worlds it opens, particularly for learning.

Like others who have worked with young Latinx children to better understand their mathematics learning, we find such beliefs not only to be humanizing but also necessary for a more generative way of understanding children's learning for teachers and researchers. As Turner and

Celedón-Pattichis (2011) have argued, "encouraging students to tap into familiar experiences and practices—ways of talking, solving problems, and making sense of the world" and "grounding mathematics learning in students' language and culture fosters meaningful relationships with students and positions their out-of-school-experiences as resources for learning rather than deficits to overcome" (p. 151).

In the journal entries, it was possible to see that students engaged with and were supported in bringing their own knowledge into their mathematics learning. They were able to use their knowledge of counting in Spanish, something for which they had not received formal instruction in school, to support their mathematics learning. An example of this is the first journal entry, in which the children had the opportunity to think about 36 using both Spanish and English. The journal entries also portray a learning environment in which bilingual children were in a position to show themselves as competent and able to communicate their understandings as they were being supported in building from their intuitive understandings of mathematics through attention to details in their counting (Carpenter et al. 2017). This is in some ways reflective of cognitively guided instruction (Carpenter et al. 1993, 1999), a model of instruction that has been shown to be effective in supporting children's mathematics learning and particularly bilingual kindergarten students' mathematics learning (Celedón-Pattichis and Turner 2012; Turner and Celedón-Pattichis 2011).

Our interpretations of children's counting and new ways of thinking about number sense have implications for the way we may teach multilingual children, and consequently Latinx children. Acknowledging that bilingual and multilingual children have more than one phonological representation and orthographic image to represent quantity allows us to think of ways to create learning opportunities that support children as they explore quantities through their representations in different languages. Such learning will not only support children's number sense development but could also foster metacognitive awareness of the way number-word sequences are used and the way counting works. We see this broader interpretation of number sense and its development as humanizing, since it centers mathematics learning on children's understanding (the human) instead of imposing a model that does not represent the children's diverse language practices and lived experiences.

As we explore these journal entries and the counting of children portrayed in it, we would like to highlight two important factors we believe were determinant in helping create more humane settings in which children were able to use their linguistic resources to support their mathematics learning. First, in the journal entries it was possible to see that children had freedom to make choices about how to use language and ways of counting, which was essential to the learning that took place. The children used this freedom to actually make sense of numbers. This freedom also allowed for the mathematics learning to be centered on the children themselves, making the experiences more humane by reflecting their experiences of the world and their identities.

Second, we would like to reflect on the fact that powerful learning is oftentimes a communal endeavor, not an individual one. The learning experiences of bilingual children in the class were not all the same, and the learning opportunities for the bilingual children who spoke Spanish were shaped by the fact that they had access to peers and teachers who also spoke Spanish. For La Sa Yaw, the one student in the class who was bilingual but spoke another language other than Spanish, the learning opportunities within the classroom were limited because there was no one else in the class who shared her linguistic background.

In the third journal entry, we were only able to see how La Sa Yaw was developing her mathematical understandings in English because that is the language that we shared with her.

Consequently, our ability to know what or how she was making connections to other languages was limited. This brings awareness to the importance of promoting spaces for children who share the same linguistic background to interact and learn together, and for adults with similar linguistic resources to support them. (These ideas reflect and build on the understandings developed in recent work highlighting translanguaging approaches applied in elementary classrooms serving bilingual and multilingual students [e.g., Kleyn and Yau 2016; Woodley and Brown 2016].) It also reminds us of the need to continue to work on highlighting and interpreting classroom events like the ones portrayed in this chapter, to help make visible and accessible the value of using multiple languages for learning mathematics, for all children.

The examples of learning in this chapter highlight children's ability to learn beyond imagined language barriers and the possibilities of teachers to support children. Teachers who do and do not share the same linguistic background as their students may support them by creating learning environments that offer freedom of choice when counting and opportunities to collaborate with peers. They may also intentionally promote the use of different languages by showing interest and encouraging collaboration among students who share the same linguistic background as well as promoting metacognitive awareness by helping students compare the different languages in their classrooms. Such approaches have been found to support children from all linguistic backgrounds in increasing their metalinguistic awareness and overall knowledge of languages (Woodley and Brown 2016). Teachers can encourage more use of students' full linguistic repertoires in the mathematics classroom by modeling and positioning themselves as learners of mathematics and language. Teachers can also support their students by "seek[ing] a deeper understanding of the role of language in relation to students' identities in the mathematics classroom" (Gutiérrez 2012b, pp. 120–21).

Incorporating families or other members of the community who share the language background of the students in their classrooms is a way for teachers to engage bilingual children's mathematical and linguistic identities. In this regard, we would like to highlight that in this study, although space was provided for children to apply their knowledge of number in multiple languages and further develop it within the classroom, all children had an understanding of number that was grounded in their experiences outside of the classroom, particularly when counting in languages other than English. Consequently, as teachers seek to support their students' number sense development, particularly for students who speak more than one language, they should strive to incorporate an array of experiences that allow students to work from their own understandings, making connections to the knowledge of numbers they have previously developed.

In this chapter, we focused on looking at number sense and counting, but from the journal entries we presented we hope the reader is able to see that the resources the children were bringing as mathematics learners and users of language far surpass what we were able to consider in the space of the chapter. We see in the complexities of the children's interactions the ways in which they bring their own rich experiences and cultural ways of understanding the world to mathematics learning. An example of this is the teaching role taken on by Mary in the second journal entry. As Mary was teaching Drew the numbers in Spanish, she was drawing on her knowledge of the language, but also on her experiences as a student and her understanding of learning and the world. Her questions and guidance were clearly successful in the way they supported Drew's learning and showed a deep understanding and appropriation of her own learning experiences around numbers and language acquisition.

When thinking about Mary and Drew, it seems particularly relevant to revisit the understanding of language that we discussed earlier, to expand the idea of language as a way of being in the world by focusing on language as a way of being in the mathematics classroom. As we seek to make mathematics learning more humane, we should consider what children were able to draw on, do, and learn from each other and with each other in these episodes, when supported in using more than one language. The children's ability to use their full linguistic repertoires, to speak in English and Spanish, shaped the experience of mathematics; it allowed them to engage humanely and fully.

From a research and teaching perspective, an emphasis on language as a way of being in the mathematics classroom allows us to reflect on what became visible about the children's learning and their understanding of mathematics and the world. For us, learning numbers with the children in both Spanish and English highlighted the human nature of mathematics, and allowed us to think critically about how children were using language to develop number sense. It also reminded us that mathematics, and particularly mathematics teaching and learning, are not homogeneous universal practices, but instead are profoundly influenced by who we are and who our students are, our previous experiences, and our current contexts. Mathematics is fundamentally a human experience, and as such, reflects our identities and experiences of the world.

References

Barth, Hilary, Kristen La Mont, Jennifer Lipton, and Elizabeth S. Spelke. "Abstract Number and Arithmetic in Preschool Children." *Proceedings of the National Academy of Sciences of the United States of America* 102, no. 39 (2005): 14116–14121. JSTOR Journals, EBSCOhost.

Barwell, Richard, Bill Barton, and Mamokgethi Setati. "Multilingual Issues in Mathematics Education: Introduction." *Educational Studies in Mathematics* 64, no. 2 (2007): 113–19. JSTOR Journals, EBSCOhost.

Barwell, Richard, Philip Clarkson, Anjum Halai, Mercy Kazima, Judit Moschkovich, Núria Planas, Mamokgethi Setati Phakeng, Paola Valero, and Martha Villavicencio Ubillús. "Introduction: An ICMI Study on Language Diversity in Mathematics Education." In *Mathematics Education & Language Diversity*, pp. 1–21. New York: Springer, 2016.

Canagarajah, Athelstan Suresh. "Codemeshing in Academic Writing: Identifying Teachable Strategies of Translanguaging." *Modern Language Journal* 95, no. 3 (2011): 401–17.

Carpenter, Thomas P., Ellen Ansell, Megan L. Franke, Elizabeth Fennema, and Linda Weisbeck. "Models of Problem Solving: A Study of Kindergarten Children's Problem-Solving Processes." *Journal for Research in Mathematics Education* 24, no. 5 (1993): 428–41. doi:10.2307/749152.

Carpenter, Thomas P., Elizabeth Fennema, Megan Loef Franke, Linda Levi, and Susan B. Empson. *Children's Mathematics: Cognitively Guided Instruction.* Reston, Va.: National Council of Teachers of Mathematics. 1999.

Carpenter, Thomas P., Megan Loef Franke, Nicholas C. Johnson, Angela C. Turrou, and Anita A. Wager. *Young Children's Mathematics: Cognitively Guided Instruction in Early Childhood Education.* Portsmouth, N.H.: Heinemann, 2017.

Celedón-Pattichis, Sylvia, and Erin Turner. "Using Storytelling to Pose Word Problems in Kindergarten ESL and Bilingual Classrooms." In *Beyond Good Teaching: Advancing Mathematics Education for ELLs*, edited by Sylvia Celedón-Pattichis and Nora G. Ramirez, pp. 56–62. Reston, Va.: National Council of Teachers of Mathematics, 2012.

Dowker, Ann. "Individual Differences in Numerical Abilities in Preschoolers." *Developmental Science* 11, no. 5 (2008): 650–54.

Edmonds-Wathen, Cris, Tony Trinick, and Viviane Durand-Guerrier. "Impact of Differing Grammatical Structures in Mathematics Teaching and Learning." In *Mathematics Education & Language Diversity*, edited by Richard Barwell et al., pp. 23–46. New York: Springer, 2016.

Franceschini, Rita. "Code-Switching and the Notion of Code in Linguistics: Proposal for a Dual Focus Model." In *Code-Switching in Conversation: Language, Interaction, and Identity*, edited by Peter Auer, pp. 51–72. London: Routledge, 1998.

García, Ofelia, and Wei Li. *Translanguaging: Language, Bilingualism, and Education*. Basingstoke, U.K./ New York: Palgrave Macmillan, 2014.

González, Norma. "The Funds of Knowledge for Teaching Project." *Practicing Anthropology* 17, no. 3 (1995): 3–6.

Gutiérrez, Rochelle. "Context Matters: How Should We Conceptualize Equity in Mathematics Education?" In *Equity in Discourse for Mathematics Education: Theories, Practices, and Policies,* edited by Beth Herbel-Eisenmann, Jeffrey Choppin, David Wagner, and David Pimm, pp. 17–34. Dordrecht, the Netherlands: Springer, 2012a.

———. "Issues of Identity and Power in Teaching Mathematics to Latin@ Students." In *Beyond Good Teaching: Advancing Mathematics Education for ELLs*, edited by Sylvia Celedón-Pattichis and Nora G. Ramirez, pp. 119–26. Reston, Va.: National Council of Teachers of Mathematics, 2012b.

Hankins, Karen Hale. *Teaching Through the Storm: A Journal of Hope*. New York: Teachers College Press, 2003.

Jordan, Nancy C., David Kaplan, Chaitanya Ramineni, and Maria N. Locuniak. "Early Math Matters: Kindergarten Number Competence and Later Mathematics Outcomes." *Developmental Psychology* 45, no. 3 (2009): 850–67.

Kleyn, Tatyana, and Hulda Yau. "The Grupito Flexes Their Listening and Learning Muscles." In *Translanguaging with Multilingual Students: Learning from Classroom Moments*, edited by Ofelia García and Tatyana Kleyn, pp. 100–17. New York: Routledge, 2016.

Krasa, Nancy, and Sara Shunkwiler. *Number Sense and Number Nonsense: Understanding the Challenges of Learning Math*. Baltimore, Md.: Paul H. Brookes Publishing Company, 2009.

Lipton, Jennifer S., and Elizabeth S. Spelke. "Origins of Number Sense: Large Number Discrimination in Human Infants." *Psychological Science* 14, no. 5 (2003): 396–401.

Moschkovich, Judit N. *Language and Mathematics Education: Multiple Perspectives and Directions for Research*. Charlotte, N.C.: Information Age Publishing, 2010.

———. "Revisiting Early Research on Early Language and Number Names." *EURASIA Journal of Mathematics Science and Technology Education* 13, no. 7b (2017): 4143–56.

Phakeng, Mamokgethi Setati, and Judit N. Moschkovich. "Mathematics Education and Language Diversity: A Dialogue across Settings." *Journal for Research in Mathematics Education* 44, no. 1 (2013): 119–28.

Stavans, Anat and Charlotte Hoffman. *Multilingualism*. Cambridge, U.K.: Cambridge University Press, 2015.

Turner, Erin E., and Sylvia Celedón-Pattichis. "Mathematical Problem Solving among Latina/o Kindergartners: An Analysis of Opportunities to Learn." *Journal of Latinos and Education* 10, no. 2 (2011): 146–69.

Woodley, Heather H., and Andrew Brown. "Balancing Windows and Mirrors: Translanguaging in a Linguistically Diverse Classroom." In *Translanguaging with Multilingual Students: Learning from Classroom Moments*, edited by Ofelia García and Tatyana Kleyn, pp. 83–99. New York: Routledge, 2016.

CHAPTER 11

Listening to and Learning with Black Teachers of Mathematics

Toya Jones Frank, *George Mason University, Fairfax, Virginia*
Deena Khalil, *Howard University, Washington, D.C.*
Beyunka Scates, *Prince George's County Public Schools, Maryland*
Symone Odoms, *Howard University, Washington, D.C.*

Engaging in research with Black mathematics teachers is timely, as a small body of research explores the hard-to-measure contributions of Black mathematics teachers vis-à-vis respect to the sociocultural, sociopolitical, and intellectual assets they bring to school and classroom mathematics experiences. This chapter highlights the racialized experiences, contributions, and dispositions for teaching mathematics of over two dozen Black preservice and in-service mathematics teachers who taught in varied school contexts. Given our positionality as mathematics educators of color committed to uplifting and empowering students of color, we center Black mathematics teachers' experiences, beliefs, and practices in our analysis of what racialized mathematics teaching means. Prevalent throughout the data was a commitment to teaching mathematics to Black children, as many expressed that it was their moral and communal responsibility. Further, they expressed how the kinship ties they developed with their Black students built bridges to mathematics learning, and its possible contributions to community wealth. Finally, teachers expressed the need to teach not only for one's own children and community, but for the advancement of all children in an effort to inform the greater social good. This chapter proposes the promise of what mathematics teacher educators, school leaders, and policy makers can learn from Black teachers to inform teacher education and policy.

■ Why Focus on Black Teachers?

This work lies at the intersection of science, technology, engineering, and mathematics (STEM) teacher recruitment and retention and diversifying the teacher workforce. It foregrounds race as salient to the work of Black mathematics teachers. Conversations about increasing the STEM teacher pipeline are important, yet they are rooted in commodification. These conversations typically include points about increasing the numbers of STEM teachers for economic gain or to make the U.S. more globally competitive. In teacher education and policy circles, conversations about diversifying the teaching force often refer to diversity metrics, where teacher demographics are tokenized to meet organizational improvement measures, while simultaneously glossing over the important sociocultural, sociopolitical, and sociomathematical resources that teachers of color bring to their practice. Until stakeholders realize that the field of mathematics education needs people (of color) just as much, if not more, than people (of color) need mathematics (Gutiérrez 2012), the dehumanizing nature of filling pipelines, STEM or otherwise, with Black teachers will persist.

Rehumanizing the experiences of Black teachers is central to this chapter. We use a race-conscious frame to better understand the complexities of the resources Black teachers draw upon while teaching mathematics that are intimately connected to the Black experience in the U.S. Centering Black teachers in this study gives the mathematics education community an opportunity to learn about Black teachers' unique perspectives on teaching and learning mathematics, perspectives that are sorely absent from mathematics education literature. It is through dialoguing with and learning from Black teachers of mathematics that we begin to recognize their contributions (Gutiérrez 2013). In addition to Black teachers' experiences with respect to race, we also address how interrelated identities, both oppressed and marginalized within particular institutions and systems, intersect to inform the teachers' perspectives.

Based on our interactions with the teacher participants, we believe that they also found this process to be rehumanizing. The data collection process became one of not only collecting their stories but also sharing pieces of our own stories and making connections along the way. Several teachers expressed that they were glad they had an opportunity to "have their say," as Karen, a high school teacher who was teaching abroad, described it. While collecting data for this project, Stacy, a middle-grades teacher in the Pacific Northwest, asked, "Are there many Black mathematics teachers? I don't know any," which led to connecting the participating teachers to spaces we knew where communities of Black teachers of mathematics meet for moral, content, and pedagogical support. For others, the interview process provided space to stop and be reflective about race and its impact on teaching. At times, the proposed 45-minute interviews became 2.5-hour conversations. During our conversations, one could often hear the moment when teachers let down their guard and began to share teaching experiences that were deeply personal, promising, hurtful, humorous, and complicated. Several wanted to know when their ideas would be published for other mathematics educators to better understand their issues and concerns, and we promised them it would be soon. This chapter is our interpretation of these teachers' lived experiences, and we hope that through their experiences, we will not only help to rehumanize Black teachers of mathematics but also broaden notions of effective teaching in mathematics education.

■ The Unique Contributions of Black Teachers

Research about Black teachers has recently made its way into news outlets (e.g., Staples 2017). In one highly publicized report, researchers found that students, regardless of race or ethnicity, had more positive perceptions of teachers of color than White teachers across dimensions such as having high expectations, being supportive, organizing content, and providing meaningful feedback (Cherng and Halpin 2016). Further, students across all races and ethnicities cited Black teachers as being particularly caring and empathetic, an observation highlighted in the literature, especially in research regarding Black teachers who teach Black children (e.g., Egalite, Kisada, and Winters 2015; Ware 2006). Cherng and Halpin (2016) inferred that Black teachers are probably perceived as more caring due to their experiences of navigating the world as a person of color. That is, because of the ways they are often marginalized in society, they "may be uniquely positioned to deal with greater levels of uncertainty that are found in teaching," regardless of their students' races or ethnicities (Gutiérrez 2012, p. 47).

Black teachers are also cited as teaching with community uplift in mind (e.g., King 1993), an idea that we detail later in this chapter. They also express a willingness to teach in schools with high concentrations of Black students, high poverty rates, and the combination of the two (Hrabowski and Sanders 2015). Recent research findings from Gershenson and colleagues (2017) noted that Black students who are experiencing poverty have higher chances of graduating from school when they have at least one Black teacher during their K–12 schooling.

The studies noted above address the benefits of Black teachers broadly. Within mathematics education scholarship, a limited body of research points to the importance of acknowledging assets that Black teachers bring to mathematics teaching and what the field can learn from their work. These assets include shared cultural experiences, use of shared vernacular during instruction, and selection of tasks and pedagogical moves that connect students' lives to meaningful mathematical content (Birky, Chazan, and Morris 2013; Clark, Badertscher, and Napp 2013; Davis, Frank, and Clark 2013; Evans and Leonard 2013; Johnson et al. 2013). A small body of research suggests that Black teachers also help to improve Black students' mathematics performance and achievement (Dee 2004; Klopfenstein 2005).

We argue that Black teachers have demonstrated success with all students, both Black and non-Black, as evidenced by research. In this chapter, we focus on the narratives of pre- and in-service teachers "to counter the erasure of Black excellence" and to highlight Black teachers' funds of knowledge, community cultural wealth, and strength-based assets" (Khalil and Kier, 2018, p. 60). This is particularly important in mathematics education, where Black teachers disrupt the faulty perceptions about who can or cannot do mathematics based on racial stereotypes and negative discourses. Additionally, we explain how a rehumanizing perspective of our/their contributions can inform how other faculty, school leaders, and the public at large can benefit from learning from Black teachers.

■ Our Perspective

We are guided by the perspective that social and cultural factors mediate interactions in a mathematics classroom. Learning mathematics is a racialized experience influenced by multilevel external forces (Martin 2000), meaning that students often benefit or are limited by how their mathematics ability, predicated often on standardized achievement, is perceived based on larger societal messages. These messages often place Black students on the lowest rung of mathematics achievement. As a corollary, they are construed as having limited mathematics ability and are positioned for limited opportunities to learn mathematics in ways that diminish their ways of knowing and being.

We assert that teaching mathematics can be conceptualized in a similar fashion. Teachers are developing their identities as they facilitate mathematics instruction. They bring their prior mathematics learning experiences to their teaching. In addition, by drawing upon intersectionality theory (Crenshaw 1991), we posit that social markers such as gender, age, and religion, when intersecting with race, also influence teachers' instructional practice and dispositions, particularly when these social markers exacerbate oppression or privilege within institutional structures like schools. These experiences, coupled with social, historical, political, and cultural forces of schooling, position teachers of color to experience teaching mathematics differently than those from dominant communities (Clark, Johnson, and Chazan 2009).

When we do not center the experiences and resources brought by Black teachers of mathematics and other mathematics teachers of color, we neglect the unique cultural knowledge that informs their instructional practices and dispositions toward teaching mathematics. Achinstein and colleagues (2010) identified two primary needs for increasing teachers of color: *demographic and democratic imperatives*. That is, (*a*) the demographics of the teaching force should mirror the demographics of the U.S. student population (the demographic imperative), and (*b*) teachers of color have a record of success in educating students of similar racial and ethnic backgrounds (the democratic imperative). Beyond Black teachers solely teaching Black students, we assert, along with others, that the need for Black teachers of mathematics has implications for creating a just and democratic community for everyone. Contemporary research reveals that knowing more about the practices and dispositions of Black teachers is crucial to the success of *all* children (Cherng and Halpin 2016).

This work is both professional and personal. As authors, we are all mathematics educators of color at different places along our career trajectories (aspiring teacher, elementary and secondary teachers, postsecondary teachers). We are aware that our identities, including our racial, gendered and mathematical ones, shape how we approach and make sense of this work. While some of us do research about Black mathematics teachers, all of us have experienced, in some form or another, many of the experiences that the teachers so generously shared.

In the following section, we present findings from interviews we conducted with and reflective writings we collected from over two dozen Black preservice and in-service teachers about their racialized experiences while preparing to teach or teaching mathematics. We collected the data for this study during the 2016–2017 school year. Each of the eleven practicing teachers was individually interviewed using a semi-structured interview format (Kvale and Brinkmann 2009). The interviews ranged in length from fifty minutes to 2.5 hours, resulting in a total of over fourteen hours of interviews. The participating teachers were recruited via social media and through professional networks. At the time of data collection, the preservice teachers who participated were in Deena's mathematics methods course. They engaged in a 1.5-hour whole-class discussion and responded to a series of written prompts throughout the course. Some of these prompts were embedded in a mathematics autobiography exercise for the course, while others were collected via discussion board exchanges.

The participants in this study brought diverse perspectives and experiences. The practicing teachers taught middle or high school mathematics in schools serving predominantly Black students, and about a quarter of them were in more racially and ethnically diverse schools. They taught in schools representing the mid-Atlantic, Pacific Northwest, southern, and western regions of the U.S; one of the participants taught students who were U.S. citizens through the U.S. Department of Defense at a school in Asia. These teachers' years of teaching ranged from three to thirteen years. The elementary preservice teachers' years of field experience in schools that served predominantly Black students ranged from 0 to 6 years, depending on whether they were undergraduate or graduate teachers. Many also had teaching experiences outside of their teacher education program at the historically Black university they attended, including working as substitute teachers, paraprofessionals, or afterschool teachers. We use pseudonyms for all teachers to ensure confidentiality and to avoid revealing identifying information related to their K–12 contexts.

Informed by our critical perspectives and commitments to transformative teaching, the data and interpretations we share are rooted in our diverse experiences. We are all committed to using mathematics, mathematics education, and education more broadly as tools for empowerment, advocacy, and activism. Toya and Deena are two mathematics teacher educators of color with experiences in historically Black universities who formerly taught in mathematics departments in predominantly Black and Brown secondary schools; Beyunka is a veteran Black mathematics teacher who now serves as an instructional leader in a school district that serves predominately Black students; and Symone is a Black preservice teacher at a historically Black university. In addition to coauthoring this paper, Beyunka and Symone responded to some of the findings that resonated with them based on their personal and professional experiences.

We have intentionally chosen to highlight the aspects of the data that point to the promise of listening to and learning with Black mathematics teachers as a means of elevating their work and moving the conversation beyond data points on diversity and achievement metrics. We also turn our attention to how we can use this knowledge to inform mathematics teacher education and policy.

■ Demographic and Democratic Imperatives for Black Teachers of Mathematics

Many of the preservice and practicing teachers we spoke to voiced the **demographic imperative** as a rationale for needing to teach mathematics in schools that primarily served students of color. Most indicated that their presence and knowledge of the contributions of people of color in mathematics were paramount to Black students feeling like they had a place in the broader mathematics community. One participant, Stacy, shared how she was able to use her nondominant ways of knowing about mathematics to push her students, especially her students of color, to see mathematics as a discipline that has far more contributions than just the work of "dead White guys," as her students described it. Empowering students with the knowledge that their nondominant cultures are the foundation to many of today's mathematical theories has great potential to develop positive mathematics identities, that is, how they see themselves and how others position them as mathematics learners and doers (Aguirre, Martin, and Mayfield-Ingram 2013). Additionally, exposing students to nondominant ways of knowing and doing mathematics has the potential to increase students' self-efficacy, or the belief in one's own ability to perform well within a specific context (McMahon, Wernsman, and Rose 2009). This belief in oneself is largely contingent upon students seeing themselves and their people as mathematics doers.

Across almost all of the interviews of the practicing teachers, they expressed student-centered philosophies about teaching and learning mathematics. Several noted that they wanted their students to experience the wonder and joy that they felt when doing mathematics. Most emphasized hands-on learning and conceptual understanding, while a small few had more procedural views of how to teach the content. In all, we surmise that the range of our participants' views about the nature of mathematics and teaching were comparable to what one would expect to find across a sample of mathematics teachers. However, we found their perspectives unique, not because of how they conceptualized mathematics, but rather how they viewed its purposes for Black children. Many spoke to their own experiences as students to describe why teaching mathematics to Black students was important to them.

Karen, a calculus teacher and department chair, studied mathematics at a historically Black college and shared the impact this had on her identity as a mathematics learner and teacher. With a sense of reverence, she described her college professors: "When I got to [my college], you had all these Black women who had PhDs in math; some of them were the first women, first Black person, to get a PhD at their institution." She believed she had an obligation to make them proud and to use mathematics to propel her students to success as her professors did for her. Similarly, many of the preservice teachers shared their family ties to historically Black colleges and universities (HBCU), where service is an integral part of these schools' missions. Salient in our conversations was the integral role of Black teachers of mathematics in shaping how Black students come to see themselves as mathematics doers and learners. Tangie, an algebra II and calculus teacher, explained that sharing her journey to earning a degree in mathematics was integral to working with Black students, and in particular, the girls in her classes. She explained, "I've been them (the Black girls in her classes), so I know how to build them up." We interpret "build them up" as Tangie's way of strengthening her students' mathematics identities. By sharing her challenges and successes, which were comparable to many of her students', she hoped that her students could see that they belonged in advanced mathematics despite what larger messages inside and outside of mathematics education may lead them to believe. In fact, much of what the teachers shared seemed reminiscent of what Carter (2005) calls *cultural navigation*, that is, how teachers of color demonstrate to students of color how to possess both dominant and nondominant identities and successfully move through unfamiliar academic settings.

Achinstein and colleagues (2010) also suggested that teachers who share similar racial and ethnic backgrounds as their students can leverage these shared experiences to foster conducive learning environments and to promote achievement. Such a practice is known as the **democratic imperative**. Several of the teachers we interviewed were teaching in schools or communities where they grew up and used their shared sense of community to bridge their students to more in-depth mathematical understanding. For instance, some shared how they used community experiences as contexts for addressing mathematical ideas, like having students make sense of coordinate geometry through redesigning community spaces. Others described how sharing cultural norms and speaking a similar dialect were springboards for mathematical discourse in their classes. Tangie explained how her students felt safe to express themselves in class. She attributed their comfort to her ability to hear and affirm their mathematical thinking in their own words without fear of being shamed for not using appropriate mathematical vocabulary or standard English. She shared, "I have a teenage son, so I get [them] and what they're trying to say." She believed it was her job to help her students use more formalized ways of discussing mathematics, but she also knew that the ways in which they explained mathematics in their own words were just as valuable.

In all, attempting to better align the demographics of the teaching population with the demographics of students is a notable goal, yet as a sole reason for acknowledging the work of Black teachers of mathematics, this is incomplete and reductive. Additionally, having Black teachers of mathematics in schools as a means of improving the academic performance of Black students is also important, yet insufficient as the reason for diversifying mathematics teaching. Next, we turn our attention to other unique contributions that Black teachers of mathematics bring to their teaching—kinship ties and community building.

■ Looking Beyond the Imperatives—Kinship and Community Building

Kinship Ties

Black teachers offer Black students more than role modeling and cultural navigation. Both pre-service and in-service teachers expressed a sense of kinship with their students. In thinking about how race intersects with other social markers like age and gender, many of the in-service teachers expressed ideas of surrogate parenting, i.e., seeing themselves as mother and father figures. Jared, a sixth-year teacher who was teaching middle school mathematics in his hometown, shared the following about his approach to getting the best out of his students in mathematics class, "I'll do things that I've heard my mother or my father do or say, and I think that it helps me compared to other teachers who don't have those same experiences to draw from." Several of the women participants noted that they sometimes went into "mama mode," as Karen called it, to make their expectations for student learning and engagement known. This practice is often referred to as *othermothering*. It is both an act of care and a political act (Dixson 2003) in that cultivating a caring environment for students opens the space for mathematical risk-taking and allows teachers to protect their students from policies and practices that reify the false notion of Black student inferiority in mathematics.

The younger in-service teachers and preservice teachers often spoke of going into "big brother" or "big sister" mode when trying to connect with their students. The majority of the preservice teachers in this study were millennials and had attended school under the policies of No Child Left Behind, so they had firsthand accounts of the potential damage of having one's intellect and capacity for doing mathematics defined solely by standardized test scores.

Kinship ties such as othermothering highlight how race, gender, and age are all at play when teachers juxtapose to their students. These kinship ties looked different depending upon the personal histories of the teachers (Frank, forthcoming, 2018). For instance, some of the teachers who had experienced mathematical success in their careers as a result of having their mathematical talents cultivated in caring spaces described their mother/father roles while teaching mathematics in very nurturing ways. Others described their kinship ties as expressing care through "tough love" and high expectations in their mathematics classes.

Building Community Wealth

Related to kinship ties, all of the teachers, both practicing and prospective, expressed a sense of mission for teaching mathematics that was rooted in giving back to "the community." In some cases, this meant giving back to the specific communities and schools that had nurtured them. In other cases, "the community" meant the broader community of Black students. In particular, many of the preservice teachers, who were taking mathematics methods courses that approached mathematics education with a critical perspective, shared that their purposes for teaching mathematics were rooted in their desire to build up their students using culturally relevant pedagogy (Ladson-Billings 2014). Related to the literature on preservice mathematics teachers, Presmeg (2000) and McGee (2014) also found that this sense of mission and the goal of teaching mathematics for community uplift and social justice drove Black preservice teachers to persist in their studies as they faced challenges in their mathematics course taking. All of the preservice teachers discussed how they leveraged their shared cultural understandings to engage their students with the content. From our interviews, we learned that Black teachers often saw their presence as more important than matching demographics or raising achievement scores. These teachers saw themselves as contributing to the wealth of their communities (Yosso 2005), especially teachers like Melanie, Jared, and Jeremiah, who taught in the middle or high schools that they attended. They each expressed that because they grew up in the communities where they teach, they do not see these low- to lower-middle class, predominately Black communities through deficit lenses. Instead, they see the unrecognized and untapped cultural capital that their students bring from home because they were once those students. In other words, they "acknowledge the multiple strengths of Communities of Color in order to serve a larger purpose of struggle toward social and racial justice" (Yosso 2005, p. 69) both in their classrooms and their neighborhoods.

Related to community uplift, many of the teachers we interviewed saw their communities as places of untapped wealth while also expressing that mathematics held promise for shifting their communities' economic and political conditions, which were often the result of discriminatory policies and institutional barriers. Gholson (2013) noted how numeracy practices related to money were privileged and necessary for survival in Black communities in the early twentieth century. While knowing how to count is more common now, these teachers espoused the similar notion that possessing mathematical knowledge holds power for social uplift of Black communities, as the accumulation of money and wealth is key to economic and political power in the U.S.

Interpreting the Data

When discussing our findings as authors, Beyunka and Symone shared that giving back to their communities and being examples of how to resist faulty stereotypes and persist despite great odds resonated deeply with their positive mathematical identities. Beyunka sees her role as a mathematics educator as a contributor to her local community's wealth. In fact, Beyunka taught and now supports mathematics teachers in a district not far from her hometown, where her friends and family pushed her to capitalize on her mathematical talent. She shared, "I only had Black mathematics teachers during my K–12 schooling," a realization she did not have until majoring in mathematics in college and having professors of diverse backgrounds. Upon reflection, Beyunka noted that this had a positive impact on her mathematics identity, as she always viewed being Black as going hand-in-hand with being a doer of mathematics. As a district-level leader in mathematics education, she also noted the serious need for stakeholders to acknowledge and cultivate talent in predominantly Black communities, communities that are often overlooked in conversations about success in advanced mathematics.

Symone, taking an African-centered approach to teaching, believes that her role as a mathematics educator is to be the person she needed growing up. This includes rooting her mathematical teaching in the very history from which it derived. That is, making it known that the mathematicians that are hailed as mathematical geniuses (e.g., Pythagoras and Euclid), were once students of African civilizations, which is longstanding knowledge within the field of ethnomathematics (Powell and Frankenstein 1997). Aligning Black students' culture with African schools of thought about mathematics gives way for students to see doing mathematics as wholly compatible with who they are as Black people. In her opinion, the current educational structure is extremely lacking in diversity of thought, thus in dire need of radical change. "There is no revolution in stagnant thought," she explained. "In order for progress to be made, not just within ourselves, but in our generational plight, it is our responsibility as teachers to provide students with a holistic education that enables them to produce knowledge, as opposed to simply consuming it." Symone considers her focus on Afrocentric community assets as an act of kinship to counter the deficit narrative of the "achievement gap" she often heard about, having attended schools only post–No Child Left Behind. She also believes it is critical to support Black students to feel empowered by their cultural, linguistic, and geographic difference.

■ Black Teachers of Mathematics for *All* Children

As noted earlier, Black teachers have demonstrated success with Black students, yet non-Black students also reap the benefits of having Black teachers. Of the in-service teachers we interviewed, Karen and Stephanie taught in schools with higher concentrations of non-Black students. Both of them spoke openly about their ability to build relationships with non-Black students through their shared love of mathematics because of their experiences as being one of a few Black students in their respective schools. Similar to the teachers in the study by Cherng and Halpin (2016), Stephanie attributed her ability to connect to students from diverse backgrounds to "always feeling as if I had to make myself a part of the crowd" as a Black student growing up in a majority-White community. She recognized that her newly appointed position as a part-time teacher and part-time district-level mathematics coach offered her an opportunity to be an "ambassador" for Black teachers in predominately White mathematics classrooms. Similarly, the preservice teachers' experiences of racism as students made them determined to serve as advocates for children of color and pose as exemplars for all children.

■ Implications and Conclusion

Centering the experiences of Black teachers of mathematics teachers from a rehumanizing perspective gives insight into teaching and learning environments not often discussed by policy makers or practitioners. Thus, this work has implications for stakeholders in mathematics education. We close by highlighting some of the lessons we have from listening to and learning from Black teachers of mathematics.

Listen and Honor

We assert that giving Black teachers the space to share their experiences moves us toward a more rehumanizing perspective on diversifying the field of mathematics teaching. Neil (2015) found that Black teachers comprise only about 4 percent of the secondary mathematics teaching force. What better way to learn how to diversify the field than to amplify the voices of those that are often excluded? In addition to listening, we also suggest that stakeholders honor the unique perspectives on teaching mathematics that Black teachers bring to their practice. For instance, what can the field learn when we acknowledge the voices of Black teachers who teach from African-centered perspectives on mathematics? What can we learn from Black teachers who teach in the communities where they were raised, communities often cited as "at risk," yet are seen as possessing unacknowledged community wealth, according to the teachers we interviewed?

Mathematics educators are constantly in search of what knowledge is necessary for mathematics teaching. We believe that this question must be contextualized by asking, "Effective for whom?" and "Whose teacher knowledge counts?" (Martin 2007). The interviews and written narratives of the teachers in this study have taught us that there is still much to be learned about teacher knowledge that lies beyond content knowledge and pedagogical content knowledge. As teacher educators, we are reminded that we must remain open to learning with Black mathematics teachers and honoring the unique and needed perspectives that they bring to our methods courses and professional development session. We must leverage how they see their sense of mission, social justice, and meaningful mathematics engagement as integral to one another and essential to mathematics teaching for the greater good of all students in mathematics classrooms.

Avoid Essentializing and Burdening

We posit that practices that are reminiscent of othermothering and being father figures, as well as other kinship roles, are key to creating strong bonds between families and schools, thus building bridges to broader mathematical participation and building the community wealth of local schools.

This should be done with the caveat that focusing on Black teachers as only possessing expertise in relationship building and classroom management is dehumanizing (Pabon 2016). Several teachers shared that respecting the content and pedagogical expertise that Black teachers bring to mathematics classrooms is key to avoiding Black (especially male) teachers' classrooms from becoming "the discipline stop" (Brockenbrough 2015), where other teachers send Black boys for discipline. That is, an overreliance on Black teachers to "manage" Black children neglects their need for professional growth as mathematics teachers and shifts their relationship-building abilities from an asset to a burden. In the words of one of our teachers, Asa, who was experiencing this very phenomenon, "Don't forget, I teach mathematics, too!"

We see promise in continuing this line of research. In the future, we intend to refine our work through watching Black teachers in practice. We believe this holds promise for expanding notions of knowledge for effective mathematics teaching. We also look forward to examining how specific structures within mathematics education limit Black mathematics teachers' participation, which has implications for recruitment and retention. There is much to learn, and we look forward to the journey.

References

Achinstein, Betty, Rodney T. Ogawa, Dena Sexton, and Casa Freitas. "Retaining Teachers of Color: A Pressing Problem and a Potential Strategy for 'Hard-to-Staff' Schools." *Review of Educational Research* 80 (2010): 71–107.

Aguirre, Julia, Karen Mayfield-Ingram, and Danny Martin. *The Impact of Identity in K–8 Mathematics: Rethinking Equity-Based Practices*. Reston, Va.: National Council of Teachers of Mathematics, 2013.

Birky, Geoffrey D., Daniel Chazan, and Kellyn Farlow Morris. "In Search of Coherence and Meaning: Madison Morgan's Experiences and Motivations as an African American Learner and Teacher." *Teachers College Record* 115, no. 2 (2013): 1–42.

Brockenbrough, Edward. "'The Discipline Stop': Black Male Teachers and the Politics of Urban School Discipline." *Education and Urban Society* 47, no. 5 (2015): 499–522.

Carter, Prudence L. *Keepin' It Real: School Success beyond Black and White*. New York: Oxford University Press, 2005.

Cherng, Hua-Yu Sebastian, and Peter F. Halpin. "The Importance of Minority Teachers: Student Perceptions of Minority Versus White Teachers." *Educational Researcher* 45, no. 7 (2016): 1–14.

Clark, Lawrence M., Eden M. Badertscher, and Carolina Napp. "African American Mathematics Teachers as Agents in Their African American Students' Mathematics Identity Formation." *Teachers College Record* 115, no. 2 (2013): 1–36.

Clark, Lawrence M., Whitney Johnson, and Daniel Chazan. "Researching African American Mathematics Teachers of African American Students: Conceptual and Methodological Considerations." In *Mathematics Teaching, Learning, and Liberation in the Lives of Black Children* , edited by Danny Bernard Martin, pp. 39–62. New York: Routledge, 2009.

Crenshaw, Kimberlé. "Mapping the Margins: Intersectionality, Identity Politics, and Violence against Women of Color." *Stanford Law Review* 43, no. 6 (1991): 1241–99.

Davis, Julius, Toya Jones Frank, and Lawrence M. Clark. "The Case of a Black Male Mathematics Teacher Teaching in a Unique Urban Context: Implications for Recruiting Black Male Mathematics Teachers." In *Black Male Teachers: Diversifying the United States' Teacher Workforce*, edited by Chance W. Lewis and Ivory Toldson, pp. 77–92. Bingley, U.K.: Emerald Group Publishing Limited, 2013.

Dee, Thomas S. "Teachers, Race, and Student Achievement in a Randomized Experiment." *Review of Economics and Statistics* 86, no. 1 (2004): 195–210.

Dixson, Adrienne D. "'Let's Do This!' Black Women Teachers' Politics and Pedagogy." *Urban Education* 38, no. 2 (2003): 217–35.

Egalite, Anna J., Brian Kisida, and Marcus A. Winters. "Representation in the Classroom: The Effect of Own-Race Teachers on Student Achievement." *Economics of Education Review* 45 (2015): 44–52.

Evans, Brian R., and Jacqueline Leonard. "Recruiting and Retaining Black Teachers to Work in Urban Schools." *SAGE Open* 3, no. 3 (2013): 1–12.

Frank, Toya Jones. "Unpacking a Black Mathematics Teacher's Understanding of Mathematics Identity." *Journal of Multicultural Education* 12, no. 2 (forthcoming, 2018).

Gershenson, Seth, Cassandra Hart, Constance Lindsay, and Nicholas W. Papageorge. "The Long-Run Impacts of Same-Race Teachers." IZA Institute of Labor Economics Discussion Paper Series (2017).

Gholson, Maisie L. "The Mathematical Lives of Black Children." In *The Brilliance of Black Children in Mathematics*, edited by Jacqueline Leonard and Danny B. Martin, pp. 55–76. Charlotte, N.C.: Information Age Publishing, 2013.

Gutiérrez, Rochelle. "Embracing Nepantla: Rethinking 'Knowledge' and Its Use in Mathematics Teaching." *Journal of Research in Mathematics Education* 1, no. 1 (2012): 29–56.

———. "The Sociopolitical Turn in Mathematics Education." *Journal for Research in Mathematics Education* 44, no. 1 (2013): 37–68.

Hrabowski III, Freeman A., and Mavis G. Sanders. "Increasing Racial Diversity in the Teacher Workforce: One University's Approach." *Thought & Action* (2015): 101–16.

Johnson, Whitney, Farhaana Nyamekye, Daniel Chazan, and Bill Rosenthal. "Teaching with Speeches: A Black Teacher Who Uses the Mathematics Classroom to Prepare Students for Life." *Teachers College Record* 115, no. 2 (2013).

Khalil, Deena, and Meredith Kier. "Critical Race Design: Emerging Principles for Designing Critical and Transformative Learning Spaces." In *Power, Equity, and (Re)Design*, edited by Elizabeth Mendoza, Ben Kirshner, and Kris Gutiérrez, pp. 55–77. Charlotte, N.C.: Information Age Publishing, 2018.

King, Sabrina Hope. (1993). The Limited Presence of African American Teachers." *Review of Educational Research* 63, no. 2 (1993): 115–149.

Klopfenstein, Kristin. "Beyond Test Scores: The Impact of Black Teacher Role Models on Rigorous Math Taking." *Contemporary Economic Policy* 23, no. 3 (2005): 416–28.

Kvale, Steinar, and Svend Brinkmann. *InterViews: Learning the Craft of Qualitative Research Interviewing.* Thousand Oaks, Calif.: SAGE Publications, 2009.

Ladson-Billings, Gloria. "Culturally Relevant Pedagogy 2.0: aka the Remix." *Harvard Educational Review* 84, no. 1 (2014): 74–84.

Martin, Danny Bernard. *Mathematics Success and Failure among African-American Youth: The Roles of Sociohistorical Context, Community Forces, School Influence, and Individual Agency.* Mahwah, N.J.: Lawrence Erlbaum Associates, 2000.

———. "Beyond Missionaries or Cannibals: Who Should Teach Mathematics to African American Children?" *The High School Journal* 91, no. 1 (2007): 6–28.

McGee, Ebony O. "When It Comes to the Mathematics Experiences of Black Pre-Service Teachers . . . Race Matters." *Teachers College Record* 116, no. 6 (2014): 1–50.

McMahon, Susan D., Jamie Wernsman, and Dale S. Rose. "The Relation of Classroom Environment and School Belonging to Academic Self-Efficacy among Urban Fourth- and Fifth-Grade Students." *The Elementary School Journal* 109, no. 3 (2009): 267–81.

Neil, Bisola. "Using the 2011–12 Schools and Staffing Survey, Restricted File Version, to Identify Factors Associated with the Intent for African American Math Teachers to Turnover." PhD diss., City University of New York, 2016.

Pabon, Amber. "Waiting for Black Superman: A Look at a Problematic Assumption." *Urban Education* 51, no. 8 (2016): 915–39.

Powell, Arthur B., and Marilyn Frankenstein, eds. *Ethnomathematics: Challenging Eurocentrism in Mathematics Education.* Albany: State University of New York Press, 1997.

Presmeg, Norma C. "Race, Consciousness, Identity, and Affect in Learning Mathematics: The Case of Four African American Prospective Teachers." In *Changing the Faces of Mathematics: Perspectives on African Americans,* edited by Walter Secada, Marilyn Strutchens, Martin Johnson, and William Tate, pp. 61–69. Reston, Va.: National Council of Teachers of Mathematics, 2000.

Staples, Brent. "Where Did All the Black Teachers Go?" *Washington Post,* April 17, 2017.

Ware, Franita. "Warm Demander Pedagogy: Culturally Responsive Teaching That Supports a Culture of Achievement for African American Students." *Urban Education* 41, no. 4 (2006): 427–56.

Yosso, Tara J. "Whose Culture Has Capital? A Critical Race Theory Discussion of Community Cultural Wealth." *Race Ethnicity and Education* 8, no. 1 (2005): 69–91.

Where Do We Go from Here?
Next Steps in Rehumanizing Mathematics for Black, Indigenous, and Latinx Students

Imani Goffney, *University of Maryland, College Park*

One of our most basic human needs is belonging (Baumeister and Leary 1995). As humans we desire community, affirmation, love, and acceptance. This is especially true for young people in the formative stages of life. Young people yearn to know they are important, that their voices and their ideas are valued, and that they are seen for who they are now and for who they have the potential to be. This is true for all young people, regardless of gender, race, ethnicity, social status, or primary language.

Schools should be places in which children flourish, but this is often not the case for Black, Indigenous, and Latinx students. Many of these students attend schools and sit in classrooms each day where their cultures are not reflected in the curriculum, where their ideas are not taken up in the public space of class discussions, and where they are seen not as individuals with unique identities and cultural perspectives but instead as data points on a measure of underachievement. The ticket for entrance to these classrooms requires Latinx, Indigenous, and Black students to leave their identities at the door and to participate in a learning environment that has been designed around whiteness as a standard. In these spaces, Indigenous, Black, and Latinx students are forced to surrender and assimilate, suffer in silence, or grapple with the consequences of resisting. Thus, many schools and classrooms around the country are dehumanizing spaces for Black, Indigenous, and Latinx students.

■ Why Focus on Teaching Practices?

Many systemic problems create dehumanizing experiences for Indigenous, Latinx, and Black students both inside and outside of classrooms. These include the racist, class-based formulas and structures for funding public schools (Duncan and Murnane 2011; Ladson-Billings 2006; Lewis-McCoy 2014); the ways in which students of color are over-identified for referral to special education (Artiles, Klinger, and Tate 2006; Blanchett 2006) while simultaneously under-identified for referral to advanced or gifted courses or programs; and the disproportionate likelihood that these students will experience excessive disciplinary attention for behaviors that, when White students commit them, are overlooked or lightly reprimanded (Ladson-Billings 2011).

Undoubtedly, dehumanizing classroom spaces have, at times, been created intentionally to reinforce and protect white privilege (Gutiérrez 2017a; Ladson-Billings 2002). They have also been created unintentionally by well-meaning educators who have not had learning opportunities to explore their own cultural identities and develop robust working knowledge of cultures different from their own, and who seek to make classrooms culture-free in a neutral stance designed to guard against bias and racism. Although there are many systemic factors contributing to the dehumanizing experiences that students have in schools (Gutiérrez 2017b, and Introduction, this volume), this concluding chapter focuses on the classroom, paying close attention to the interactions between teachers and students.

To make schools places where Black, Indigenous, and Latinx children thrive as human beings, a focus on rehumanizing teaching practices is necessary. This will not happen by chance. Improving school structures or changing the curriculum alone still leaves open the broad discretionary, interactional space in which bias and dehumanization play out. Although improving school buildings and structures is important, adding multiple cultural perspectives and lenses across the curriculum matters as well. The most powerful lever, however, is teaching practices, which can change the dynamics of dehumanization at their roots. It takes teachers to make schools into places where all Black and Brown children feel like their humanity is seen and valued. Effective teaching does not exist without attention to social justice, students' identities, and deliberate steps to open access to content. Teachers play a vital role in schools, as students' most important resource for academic learning (Nye, Konstantopoulos, and Hedges 2004; Rivkin, Hanushek, and Kain 2005; Rockoff 2004). How teachers speak, listen, see, and interact with young people matters. They shape the environment and interactions that in turn shape students' sense of themselves and their competence. Teachers can reproduce marginalization or disrupt it. As such, they play an essential role in rehumanizing school experiences of Latinx, Black, and Indigenous students.

Mathematics classrooms have been experienced as particularly dehumanizing. Who is treated as smart, whose ideas are valued, and the continuous focus on error, speed, and "correctness" instantiate a deceptive standard of whiteness (Gutiérrez 2015). The emphases on diagnosis and learning gaps leads to a taken-for-grantedness about "gaps" and being "behind" (Gutiérrez 2008; Ladson-Billings 2007). Changing this dynamic requires close attention to the curriculum but also, as argued above, depends fundamentally on changing the relational structures and values embedded in practices of teaching.

■ Consequences of Being Neutral or Color-Blind

For teachers who are aware that schools and classrooms can be dehumanizing spaces but lack the cultural knowledge or pedagogical competence to address these issues, the use of color-blind and neutral teaching practices serves the purpose of helping to guard against overtly racist or biased actions (at least the perception of them). Such teachers use Popsicle sticks to call on students, post charts with students' achievements on timed tests, assign homework and reduce grades for not completing it, and sanction behavior at the expense of hearing and acknowledging intellectual capabilities. These teaching practices focus on treating all students "fairly," using seemingly unbiased measures of achievement for grouping students by "ability" and supporting narrow views of mathematical competence and learning. However, a closer examination of the implementation of color-blind or neutral teaching practices reveals that these practices primarily affect students of color, as the expectation is for Black, Indigenous, and Latinx students to leave their identities at the door of the school (Bonilla-Silva 2003; Gutiérrez 2015; Ladson-Billings 2007). Even after the school desegregation movement of the 1950s and 1960s, when Black and Brown students were legally allowed in previously all-white schools, whiteness remained the expectation for students and the norm (Lewis-McCoy 2014; Siddle Walker 2009) for measuring their success. Schools were designed to be white spaces, as evidenced by the Eurocentric curriculum, the lack of hiring of Black and Brown teachers even for integrated schools, and the common practice of grouping students by their perceived ability and limiting or expanding their learning opportunities based on ability-level placement. A generous interpretation of the intent of using a color-blind or neutral approach is to reduce bias and overt racist teaching practices. However, the effort to include students of color in white spaces stripped them of their ability to acknowledge or leverage their own cultural identity (Goffney 2018; Ladson-Billings 1995, 2002, 2011).

The impact of color-blind approaches reinforces whiteness as the norm, and privileges white students over students of color (Ladson-Billings 1995; Leonard 2008). Neutral teaching practices are dehumanizing because they fail to recognize and use students' identities, cultural knowledge, and resources to support mathematics learning (Bonilla-Silva 2003). Some of these practices are commonly used in thousands of classrooms and even taught in many teacher preparation programs that (both intentionally and unintentionally) preserve instead of interrupt racism. For example, focusing on students' incorrect answers, diagnosing or anticipating weaknesses or errors in students' mathematical productions, valuing speed over reflection or producing mathematical arguments, and using very narrow perspectives about who can do mathematics, who can be smart in mathematics, and what counts as a mathematical contribution are all dehumanizing teaching practices (Gutiérrez, Introduction, this volume). In some classrooms, teachers may provide students with a nickname instead of learning to pronounce their name correctly, or teachers may require that students speak only in English in their classrooms instead of allowing students who speak multiple languages to use their linguistic resources to support their mathematical thinking. Indigenous, Latinx, and Black students often grapple with the challenges of having to speak a language that someone is forcing them to learn to speak and with not having authority figures in their school who look like them, while also grappling with multiple experiences of being marginalized and failing. Although the intent and purpose of these types of teaching practices may not be to create dehumanizing classrooms, the impact of these practices is that mathematics classrooms are places where many Black and Brown students do not feel like they belong.

■ The Power and Potential of Teachers and Teaching

Despite these challenges, there is powerful potential in focusing on teaching practices that seek to rehumanize mathematics for Black, Indigenous and Latinx students. One first step is for teachers to develop an awareness of the systemic barriers and structural racism that exist in their schools and classrooms, to work to identify patterns that consistently privilege whites, and to learn to use teaching practices that will interrupt patterns of persistent inequities in the mathematics participation and performance of Black, Indigenous, and Latinx students. Teachers often create powerful memories and make significant differences in the lives of their students. Some of these powerful memories are negative and have caused harm to students and communities, while others have been positively life changing.

Shifting students' dehumanizing experiences in mathematics classrooms to rehumanizing positive experiences in mathematics classrooms requires work that is both invisible and visible. Some actions may seem small in light of the enormous complexities of issues of social justice in schools and mathematics classrooms, but each small action can serve as a stone on the pathway to real positive change for students traditionally not served well by schools. The invisible aspects of the work involve disrupting racist, gendered, and linguistically biased patterns of academic performance and success by broadening one's own perspective about who can make mathematics, what it means to do math and participate, and what might count as a valuable mathematical contribution produced by students. This involves carefully making decisions about how to read and interpret students' actions and behaviors, using an asset-based lens for students' engagement in mathematics classrooms and trusting students by sharing the authority of the classroom (Aguirre, Mayfield-Ingram, and Martin 2013; Ball 2017). By selecting and using tasks that leverage students' cultural identities as a resource for learning and doing mathematics and by using tasks that have multiple entry points that support different approaches to engaging with the mathematics content, teachers create opportunities for students to feel whole as a person, to draw upon all of their cultural and linguistic resources while participating in school mathematics, and to be seen as a legitimate participant as a "doer" of mathematics (Gutiérrez 2012).

The visible, more public teaching practices that work to rehumanize mathematics include eliciting, encouraging, and supporting students' in sharing their mathematical ideas, seeing and publicly acknowledging students' individual mathematical strengths and contributions to the class, and using student productions and student representations as valuable contributions that deepen the collective understanding of the class.

◾ Reflecting on Contributions from This Book

The three sections of the book each provide examples of rehumanizing mathematics and suggest models, strategies, resources, and practices for moving this work forward. This section highlights the contributions that each chapter makes toward illustrating the themes launched in Rochelle Gutiérrez's introduction, and it provides the implications for teaching practice that are the focus of this concluding chapter.

Principles for teaching and teacher identity: Using knowledge of systemic oppression and structural barriers to create positive counter-narratives for Black, Indigenous, and Latinx students as mathematics learners

Decades of research in mathematics education provide abundant evidence that teacher knowledge matters and is a primary resource for effective mathematics instruction (e.g., Ball, Thames, and Phelps 2008). Much of this work has focused on specifying what mathematics knowledge is needed for effective teaching and studying how mathematics knowledge is used in teaching, but there has been less investment in understanding the intersection of cultural knowledge or use of culturally relevant teaching practices (Ladson-Billings 1995) for teaching mathematics. The chapters discussed in this section show how educators can use mathematical knowledge, teacher identities, and their knowledge of students' identities as resources for rehumanizing mathematics for Indigenous, Latinx, and Black students consistent with the framing in the introduction.

In chapter 8, Tamburini, Cook, and Bunton offer an example of what it means to be aware of the importance of students' cultural context and to embrace students' identities and create a learning environment where all students' experiences are valued. Their chapter illustrates the redesign of the mathematics courses at Northwest Indian College where teachers used their multiple knowledge bases including cultural knowledge, knowledge of students' histories, identities, experiences, and interests to create an intervention that interrupts traditional, oppressive practices.

By replacing oppressive practices with those that use students' identities, cultural knowledge and experiences as resources for learning mathematics, these teachers have rehumanized mathematics for these students.

In chapter 11, Frank, Khalil, Scates, and Odoms begin by unpacking the dehumanizing experiences of both Black students and Black mathematics teachers. Their chapter shares the racialized experiences, contributions, and dispositions of Black teachers as they work in dehumanizing spaces but seek to create rehumanizing experiences for learning math for Black, Latinx, and Indigenous students. The authors critique the traditional positioning of Black teachers where their primary contribution is focused on kinship or management of students (especially with respect to discipline matters) and instead argue that an important resource for rehumanizing mathematics for Black, Indigenous, and Latinx students is to honor and respect the perspectives, wisdom, and contributions of Black teachers as they work to interrupt oppressive mathematics teaching practices. Their work provides an example of rehumanizing mathematics that includes acknowledging the contributions of Black teachers and using their resources and lenses for redefining what counts as mathematics and broadening ways of doing mathematics.

In chapter 10, Mazzanti and Allexsaht-Snider explore how young children use multiple languages creatively to support their development of number sense, and they discuss which teaching practices support rehumanizing learning experiences for emergent bilingual students. Their chapter provides powerful illustrations from students about the cultural and linguistic resources they used to support their mathematics learning. The teachers in this classroom used practices that not only invited students to bring their identities with them into the classroom but also used their experiences, cultural perspectives and values, and linguistic resources as tools to support working on ambitious mathematics tasks. This chapter illustrates what is possible in rehumanizing classrooms where the teacher seeks to learn from and with students instead of being the sole authority of mathematics knowledge for the class Additionally, using these practices allows teachers to broaden the ways in which students can participate, which expands the collective mathematics understanding of the students in the class. Using these rehumanizing teaching practices also allows teachers to deepen their own understanding and use of mathematics by learning from students.

As a classroom teacher, Adams (chapter 9) observes firsthand the consequences for students learning mathematics in dehumanizing learning environments. This inspired her to want to interrupt these patterns of struggling and failure where her emergent bilingual fourth-grade students resisted participating and grappled with academic success before arriving in her classroom. Her chapter provides illustrations of what is possible when teachers learn to listen to students; recognize and value their families, culture, language, and communities; and design units that are connected to their students' interests and experiences. The practices used in this classroom invite students to use their cultural resources, identities, home language, and interests as resources for doing mathematics.

Providing opportunities for students to create powerful counter-narratives is a central component of rehumanizing mathematics. Creating learning environments for Black, Latinx, and Indigenous students that use their identities, interests, and cultural resources to facilitate meaningful mathematics learning contributes to the development of positive mathematics identities for these students, a process which is rehumanizing.

Attending to students' identities through learning: The use of real-world context related to students' identities and learning of mathematics content and practices

Another cluster of chapters focused on the ways teachers attended to students' identities through learning where a main theme across these chapters focused on using a "real-world context" as a tool to facilitate connections among students' identities, culture, histories, and interests with mathematics content. The chapters discussed in this section provide examples of how educators use their knowledge of systemic oppression and structural barriers for Indigenous, Latinx, and Black students with learning mathematics as a guide for deploying teaching practices to help create powerful positive counter-narratives for the students in their programs and classrooms. Though many of these examples are in nontraditional settings (summer programs, after-school programs, etc.), the teaching practices used are applicable to traditional classroom settings and can create more rehumanizing mathematics learning experiences for Latinx, Black, and Indigenous students in traditional classrooms.

Two of the chapters in this cluster (chapters 2 and 4) focused on the experiences of Black girls. In chapter 2, Morton and Smith-Mutegi describe the Girls STEM Institute (GSI) that was designed to simultaneously build the girls' understanding of number and operations and their mathematical confidence to facilitate the development of positive mathematical identity development. They explore common dehumanizing experiences of Black girls because of the commonly held negative perceptions and stereotypes of Black girls as loud, talkative, confrontational, and in need of social correction (among others), instead of focusing on investing in their academic development and providing more sophisticated opportunities to learn and do mathematics. These teachers in this program used both their knowledge of common negative experiences that Black girls have in mathematics classrooms and their ability to ask probing questions and carefully listen to the girls as they describe their experiences as resources for rehumanizing mathematics for girls in the GSI program. They used this information to guide their teaching practices when supporting the girls to solve real-world mathematics problems in the program's curriculum (such as financial literacy, nutrition, and virtual reality) and to inspire the girls' interests in learning mathematics and build their skills and confidence as mathematics learners. As such, the use of these practices worked to create a rehumanizing experience for learning mathematics for these girls.

In chapter 4, Joseph and Alston also focused on the experiences of Black girls in an out-of-school context in the eMode program. Acknowledging the intersections of their identities as Black students and as girls, the creators of this program designed it to nurture the girls' positive identity development as mathematics learners through the use of "emancipatory pedagogies that promote deep meaning-making of mathematics and Black culture" (p. 51). The teaching practices focused on faith, love, and care. In addition to providing voice to the participants of this program as a rehumanizing experience, the authors also gave several suggestions for translating these practices into traditional classrooms; these included using collaborative small groups and inquiry-based learning instead of lecture and direct instruction, engaging in relationship building with students, and providing access to more mathematics and not less, as typically happens in traditional classrooms.

Osibodu and Crosby, in chapter 3, explore multiple versions of Blackness by using the perspectives of African Americans and Sub-Saharan African immigrants to investigate ways that teachers can see the complexities of the identities of their Black students. By examining the complexities of multiple intersections of identities of what it means to be Black in America, the authors illustrate ways in which students experience oppression. They suggest that rehumanizing mathematics for these students includes acknowledging these complexities and intersections, and protecting the erasure of their identities by bringing back what has been lost (i.e., as described in this chapter, the concept of *Sankofa*). Their work suggests using teaching practices where teachers listen carefully and allow students describe their own identities and experiences and then using this information to generate mathematics tasks and lessons in ways that support students in developing a positive mathematics identity (NCTM 2014).

In chapter 1, Barajas-Lopez and Bang explore "indigenous making and sharing" from a summer program where Indigenous youth, families, community artists, and scientists work together in the Native STEAM project to cultivate Indigenous ways of knowing and being. Using their knowledge of the ways in which Indigenous youth have been negatively positioned in traditional schools, the authors sought to explore examples of rehumanizing mathematics for this population. The authors explain that as the contributions and contemporary practices of Indigenous people in mathematics have been forgotten or erased, in part due to the violent treatment of Indigenous people and the systematic positioning of their contributions as deficient to Eurocentric conceptions of math, rehumanizing mathematics necessarily means working to preserve Indigenous-based pedagogies. These pedagogies do more than just teach mathematics. By using an interdisciplinary lens of mathematics as a cultural activity, not a separate discipline, and leveraging real-world contexts for tasks and problems, valuing nature-culture relations, Indigenous students are positioned and empowered as knowledge producers which is rehumanizing.

The context for the final chapter in this cluster (chapter 5, by Suh and colleagues) is a traditional school setting. "Every Penny Counts" uses mathematical modeling for a student-centered learning project as a strategy for rehumanizing mathematics. Using the social issue of childhood hunger as an authentic, relevant, real-world context, the teachers in this school leveraged the students' interests and lived experiences as resources for engaging in the "Coin Harvest Project." Rehumanizing mathematics requires simultaneous attention to the mathematics content and/or practices that are the focus of study and to the identities, experiences, and cultural resources of the students. Instead of foregrounding or backgrounding these dual foci of content and students, this project provided an illustration of the ways in which mathematical modeling bridges real-world scenarios and mathematics where students were expected to use their funds of knowledge (Civil 2007; González, Moll, and Amanti 2005) as a useful resource for understanding and solving the layers of the mathematical problems in the Coin Harvest project. These layers included raising and saving money with a project goal, making choices for meal items, and budgeting money for a service project designed to benefit their local community. The teachers' use of mathematical modeling and the multiple layers of this project supported its use in multiple grades from first grade to fourth grade, allowing the students to participate in an iterative collective process for building mathematical knowledge and engaging in social action, and it thus provided rehumanizing mathematics experiences for these students.

These four chapters provided models of attending to students' identities through the use of real-world contexts and nurturing teaching practices focused on the whole student, not just their mathematics academic performance. In these examples, teachers used their knowledge of systemic oppression and structural racism as a resource for interpreting students' actions and as motivation for providing a more humanizing mathematics learning experience for Latinx, Black, and Indigenous students.

Professional development that embraces community: Two novel approaches for rehumanizing mathematics for teachers who are Latinx, Indigenous, and Black

The previous two themes focused on the identities of students and teachers and on efforts to rehumanize mathematics for Black, Indigenous, and Latinx students. A final cluster of chapters in this volume focuses on professional development (PD) that embraces community.

In chapter 6, Caswell, Jones, LaPointe, and Kabatay provide a novel approach to professional development that is designed to be rehumanizing both for participants in the professional development itself (teachers, Elders, Counsellors, etc.) and for the students they serve. This chapter gives an example of a humanizing mathematics approach that provides "a space in which Indigenous and non-Indigenous educators can shape the work together" (p. 88). Consistent with the rehumanizing practice of using the identities of Black, Latinx, and Indigenous students as a central resource of the mathematics classroom, this project uses the Indigenous identities of teachers, educators, and community leaders to shape the content and collaborations of the professional development. A goal of this PD program was to privilege the Indigenous knowledges in teaching and learning mathematics as a way of using these contributions and preserving them from the dehumanizing erasure that has occurred in many other spaces. The collaborations between Indigenous teachers and leaders and non-Indigenous teachers created a productive platform for listening, learning, and deepening their own knowledge of both Indigenous culture and strategies for rehumanizing mathematics for these teachers. Teachers who participate in this professional development are better positioned to create more humane classrooms and use rehumanizing teaching practices for the students in their classrooms.

In chapter 7, Winger and colleagues provide a different model of professional development that embraces community. They share their work in a professional community of educators, mathematicians, district leaders, and teachers designed to facilitate productive conversations about equity and mathematics teaching practice and equity and student learning through "Mathequity Hours." These Mathequity Hours differed from traditional professional development by using rehumanizing approaches where participants used their own identities and experiences as resources for considering teaching practices that are rehumanizing, promoting the development of positive mathematical identities in students, and discovering which practices are dehumanizing. Instead of listening to learn from a speaker like a traditional professional development setting, participants engage in dialogue during the Mathequity Hours where they work on mathematics and equity together. In this way, the Mathequity Hours created a rehumanizing space, especially for the Black, Latinx, and Indigenous teachers who have had oppressive and dehumanizing experiences during their own education and in their professional setting. These teachers can use their experiences in the Mathequity Hours to create similar experiences for their own students where collaboration, rich discussion, and real-world contexts are used in ways that connect to students' identities and interests.

Both of these novel approaches to conducting professional development in ways that embrace community and rehumanize mathematics for these participants provide models for new ways of designing and implementing professional development. By acknowledging the dehumanizing experiences that many of these teachers faced in schools and by facilitating meaningful work that supports a re-examination of curriculum and teaching practices with a goal of rehumanizing mathematics for Black, Latinx, and Indigenous students, these projects were able to build positive mathematics identities for the participants in the professional development as well.

■ Teaching Practices for Rehumanizing Mathematics for Black, Indigenous and Latinx Students

In the introduction of this volume, Rochelle Gutiérrez provided a framework of eight dimensions that contribute to rehumanizing mathematics for Indigenous, Black, and Latinx students. Authors across these chapters have offered suggestions about the resources needed and teaching practices associated with rehumanizing mathematics. Below is a description of some of the common themes and takeaways from the individual chapters that are connected to Gutiérrez's eight dimensions and to the focus on teaching practices in this concluding chapter.

1. Teachers need to have a working knowledge of the cultures and identities of the students in their classes. One of the goals for rehumanizing mathematics is to provide opportunities and support for students to develop positive mathematics identities. This work is not best approached from a neutral or color-blind approach, but instead when teachers learn more about their students by listening carefully, building on the mathematics they bring with them to class, and providing opportunities for them to make positive contributions to the mathematics class. This is connected to Gutiérrez's second dimension on "cultures/histories" because, in order to acknowledge students' funds of knowledge, teachers must first obtain this knowledge before they can learn how to use it as a resource for teaching; it is also connected to the third dimension, "windows/mirrors," where students see themselves and others in the curriculum.

2. Teachers need to have a working knowledge of the impact of structural barriers and systemic racism for creating common dehumanizing learning experiences for Black, Indigenous, and Latinx students. This includes knowing how these students are typically read, as well as how their behavior and actions are interpreted in ways that limit their access to high-quality mathematics instruction and position them in a negative and deficient manner. It is challenging to use teaching practices that are rehumanizing without a knowledge of the actions and consequences of dehumanizing and oppressive teaching practices, as rehumanizing mathematics is designed to interrupt these persistent oppressive patterns. In using this knowledge, it is important to note that this knowledge is intended to be a resource—a lens for anticipating and interpreting students' reactions. Teachers must be careful to not make assumptions about typical student experiences. Instead, they should use this knowledge as a resource for carefully listening to students as they share their experiences and their ideas, and as teachers work to create more humane learning spaces and opportunities for them.

3. Rehumanizing teaching practices requires a departure from common teaching practices that privilege lecture and direct instruction, focus on diagnostic or evaluative approaches for remediation, and employ a color-blind or neutral approach where Black, Latinx, and Indigenous students "leave their culture at the door," students are grouped based on their perceived ability, and group membership provides expanded or constrained opportunities to learn and do mathematics. In these classrooms, students work collaboratively and engage in rich discussions while working on tasks connected to their culture, experiences, and interests. In such an environment, students respond to each other more rather than seeking validation from the teacher (the first dimension on "participation/ positioning").

4. Rehumanizing mathematics includes making connections between the mathematics content and students' experiences and interests. Real-world, authentic contexts can be connected to the students' community or culture in authentic ways. These contexts can also be used to provide opportunities for students to expand their lens beyond their own lived experiences and imagine their future opportunities. These practices are connected to dimension #4 (living practice), #5 (creation), #6 (broadening mathematics), and #8 (ownership) by recognizing mathematics as living practice, something in motion that isn't fixed that also allows students to see math as creation, thus providing opportunities for students to invent new algorithms or ways of doing mathematics that are consistent with their own values. Taken together, these strategies broaden mathematics so that students can expand their view and see it in qualitative ways, using their voice, vision, and intuition as resources for doing mathematics. These strategies support students in developing a sense of ownership where doing mathematics is not a requirement for school or a service for others but instead provides individuals with an opportunity to express oneself through mathematics.

5. Rehumanizing mathematics uses a variety of teaching practices, many of which focus on co-constructing mathematics knowledge through collaborations where authority is shared between the teacher and students, broadening types of participation, using multiple strategies for supporting students to demonstrate their mathematical competence and smarts in the public space of the classroom, and facilitating productive work on tasks and projects with multiple entry points and multiple layers that promote deep thinking. This is connected to dimension #1 (participation/positioning) and #6 (broadening mathematics), but it is also connected to #7 (body/emotions), because these teaching practices enable students to bring their emotions into the classroom for productive purposes to facilitate comprehensive engagement in doing mathematics.

■ Conclusion

When teachers have a broad understanding of systems of oppression that are historical and that still persist in public schools and classrooms today, and when they are able to identify patterns that reproduce oppression in classrooms, they can make strategic choices to interrupt these patterns and use the space of their mathematics classroom to promote access, participation, and social justice. Teachers should cautiously but deliberately work to disrupt deficit and dehumanizing learning experiences for Black, Indigenous, and Latinx students. Teaching is powerful, so there is enormous potential in focusing on teacher knowledge and teaching practices. Using humane teaching practices requires vigilance, reflection, and an ongoing critique of the instructional practices and learning environment. As Gutiérrez reminds us in her introduction, member checking can be used as evidence to verify that students find these teaching practices humanizing in ways that will support teachers with extending and expanding their current instructional methods and models or making adjustments as needed. In this way, rehumanizing mathematics requires constant adjustments to ensure that the modifications in teaching do not fall back into a pattern of marginalizing Latinx, Indigenous, and Black students.

References

Aguirre, Julia, Karen Mayfield-Ingram, and Danny Bernard Martin. *The Impact of Identity in K–8 Mathematics: Rethinking Equity-Based Practices*. Reston, Va.: National Council of Teachers of Mathematics, 2013.

Artiles, Alfredo J., Janette K. Klinger, and William F. Tate. "Representation of Minority Students in Special Education: Complicating Traditional Explanations." *Educational Researcher* 35, no. 6 (2006): 3–5.

Ball, Deborah Loewenberg. "(How) Can Teaching Be a Force for Justice?" A keynote address given in the Advancing Excellence and Equity in Education Distinguished Lecture Series. Rutgers Graduate School of Education, New Brunswick, New Jersey, November 2, 2017.

Ball, Deborah Loewenberg, Mark Hoover Thames, and Geoffrey Phelps. "Content Knowledge for Teaching: What Makes It Special?" *Journal of Teacher Education* 59, no. 5 (2008): 389–407.

Baumeister, Roy F., and Mark R. Leary. "The Need to Belong: Desire for Interpersonal Attachments as a Fundamental Human Motivation." *Psychological Bulletin* 117, no. 3, (1995): 497–529.

Blanchett, Wanda. "Disproportionate Representation of African American Students in Special Education: Acknowledging the Role of White Privilege and Racism." *Educational Researcher* 35, no. 6 (2006): 24–28.

Bonilla-Silva, Eduardo. *Racism without Racists: Color-Blind Racism and the Persistence of Racial Inequality in America*. Lanham, Md.: Rowman & Littlefield, 2003.

Civil, Marta. "Building on Community Knowledge: An Avenue to Equity in Mathematics Education." In *Improving Access to Mathematics: Diversity and Equity in the Classroom*, edited by Na'ilah Suad Nasir and Paul Cobb, pp. 105–17. New York: Teachers College Press, 2007.

Duncan, Greg J., and Richard J. Murnane, eds. *Whither Opportunity? Rising Inequality, Schools, and Children's Life Chances*. New York: Russell Sage Foundation, 2011.

Goffney, Imani Masters. "From Oakland to Wakanda: Transforming Classrooms to Become Equitable and Empowering Spaces for Students." Talk delivered at the 2018 Leadership Seminar on Mathematics Professional Development, Portland, Oregon, March 9, 2018.

González, Norma, Luis C. Moll, and Cathy Amanti, eds. *Funds of Knowledge: Theorizing Practices in Households, Communities, and Classrooms*. Mahwah, N.J.: Lawrence Erlbaum Associates, 2005.

Gutiérrez, Rochelle. "A 'Gap Gazing' Fetish in Mathematics Education? Problematizing Research on the Achievement Gap." *Journal for Research in Mathematics Education* 39, no. 4 (2008): 357–64.

_____. "Framing Equity: Helping Students 'Play the Game' and 'Change the Game.'" *Teaching for Excellence and Equity in Mathematics* 1, no. 1 (2009): 4–8.

_____. "Embracing 'Nepantla': Rethinking Knowledge and Its Use in Teaching." *REDIMAT: Journal of Research in Mathematics Education* 1, no. 1 (2012): 29–56.

_____. "Nesting in Nepantla: The Importance of Maintaining Tensions in Our Work." In *Interrogating Whiteness and Relinquishing Power: White Faculty's Commitment to Racial Consciousness in STEM Classrooms*, edited by Nicole M. Joseph, Chayla Haynes, and Floyd Cobb, pp. 253–82. New York: Peter Lang, 2015.

_____. "Living Mathematx: Towards a Vision for the Future." *Philosophy of Mathematics Education* 32, no. 1 (2017a).

_____. "Political Conocimiento for Teaching Mathematics: Why Teachers Need It and How to Develop It." In *Building Support for Scholarly Practices in Mathematics Methods*, edited by Signe Kastberg, Andrew M. Tyminski, Alyson E. Lischka, and Wendy B. Sanchez. Charlotte, N.C.: Information Age Publishing, Inc., 2017b.

Ladson-Billings, Gloria. "But That's Just Good Teaching! The Case for Culturally Relevant Pedagogy." *Theory into Practice* 34, no. 3 (1995): 159–65.

_____. "I Ain't Writin' Nuttin': Permission to Fail and Demands to Succeed in Urban Classrooms." In *The Skin That We Speak: Thoughts on Language and Culture in the Classroom*, edited by Lisa Delpit and Joanne Kilgour Dowdy, pp. 107–20. New York: The New Press, 2002

_____. "From the Achievement Gap to the Education Debt: Understanding Achievement in U.S. Schools." *Educational Researcher* 35, no. 7 (2006): 3–12.

_____. "Pushing Past the Achievement Gap: An Essay on the Language of Deficit." *Journal of Negro Education* 76, no. 3 (2007): 316–23.

_____. "Boyz to Men? Teaching to Restore Black Boys' Childhood." *Race, Ethnicity and Education* 14, no. 1 (2011): 7–15.

Leonard, Jacqueline. *Culturally Specific Pedagogy in the Mathematics Classroom: Strategies for Teachers and Students*. New York: Routledge, 2008.

Lewis-McCoy, R. L'Heureux. *Inequality in the Promised Land: Race, Resources, and Suburban Schooling*. Stanford, Calif.: Stanford University Press, 2014.

National Council of Teachers of Mathematics (NCTM). *Principles to Actions: Ensuring Mathematical Success for All*. Reston, Va.: NCTM, 2014.

Nye, Barbara, Spyros Konstantopoulos, and Larry V. Hedges. "How Large Are Teacher Effects?" *Educational Evaluation and Policy Analysis* 26, no. 3 (2004): 237–57.

Rivkin, Steven G., Eric A. Hanushek, and John F. Kain. "Teachers, Schools, and Academic Achievement." *Econometrica* 73, no. 2 (2005): 417–58.

Rockoff, Jonah E. "The Impact of Individual Teachers on Student Achievement: Evidence from Panel Data." *American Economic Review* 94, no. 2 (2004): 247–52.

Siddle Walker, Vanessa. "Second-Class Integration: A Historical Perspective for a Contemporary Agenda." *Harvard Educational Review* 79, no. 2 (2009): 269–84.

Tate, William F. "'Geography of Opportunity': Poverty, Place, and Educational Outcomes." *Educational Researcher* 37, no. 7 (2008): 397–411.